THE CHURCH IN EMERGING CULTURE
FIVE PERSPECTIVES

THE CHURCH IN EMERGING CULTURE
FIVE PERSPECTIVES

Leonard Sweet (general editor), Andy Crouch, Michael Horton,
Frederica Mathewes-Green, Brian D. McLaren, Erwin Raphael McManus

WWW.ZONDERVAN.COM

The Church in Emerging Culture: Five Perspectives

emergentYS Books, 300 South Pierce Street, El Cajon, CA 92020, are published by Zondervan, 5300 Patterson Avenue SE, Grand Rapids, MI 49530

Library of Congress Cataloging-in-Publication Data

The church in emerging culture : five perspectives / Leonard Sweet,
general editor ; Andy Crouch ... [et al.].
   p. cm.
 ISBN 0-310-25487-6
 1. Christianity and culture. 2. Postmodernism--Religious
aspects--Christianity. 3. Church renewal. I. Sweet, Leonard I. II.
Crouch, Andy.
 BR115.C8C495 2003
 261--dc21

2003005325

Edited by Brian Phipps
Cover and interior design by Mark Arnold
Interior photos by jase
Printed in the United States of America

03 04 05 06 07 08 09 / DC / 10 9 8 7 6 5 4 3 2 1

To Jesse Caldwell III, comrade amd companion.
—Leonard Sweet

For Timothy—may you choose to go to the moon, and beyond.
—Andy Crouch

To Lisa, my best friend.
—Michael Horton

To my coauthors, in appreciation of a good discussion. "As iron sharpens iron, so one person sharpens another." (Proverbs 27:17)
—Frederica Mathewes-Green

*I'd like to dedicate my chapter to my colleagues in emergent (www.emergentvillage.com)
who, although they shouldn't be blamed for places where I'm wrong or stupid or inarticulate,
should be credited for helping create a space for rethinking, reimagining,
and renewing in the gospel. This space has helped and will help me and many others,
including many who will read this book,
to grow in faithfulness to God and the mission God has given us.*
—Brian D. McLaren

To my brother, Alex:

*So few are men of dreams,
Fewer still men of passion.
Yet those who change the world it seems,
Are both thus men of action.*

—your fellow explorer, Erwin

CONTENTS

LEONARD
SWEET

Leonard Sweet

Introduction

Garden, Park, Glen, Meadow

IT HAS BEEN MORE THAN FIFTY YEARS since the publication of H. Richard Niebuhr's classic text *Christ and Culture* (1951),[1] which asked the question, What kinds of relationships does the church want with the culture? *Christ and Culture* has been described as "one of the most influential Christian books of the past century." One theologian has suggested that "no other book has dominated an entire theological conversation for so long."[2] Niebuhr's book made a needed clearing in a forest where a great many scholars were lost, and the church has been camping out in Niebuhr's five-fold clearing ever since.[3] Yet Niebuhr's words aren't the last on the subject. Five decades after *Christ and Culture*, we're still asking: Is the "lived culture" of Christian faith shaped by criteria intrinsic to itself or in mutual exchange with the culture?

Of course the problem of how Christians relate to culture is as old as Christianity itself. The New Testament makes it clear that there were sharp differences of opinion in the first century over how to relate to the culture. Yet, the Christ of the Bible is the Christ of a *culture*. The ultimate act of communication in history, the Incarnation, means that Christ became a part of culture and can't be understood apart from culture. In the same way, you can't live in God without living in the world. That's why this conversation is like debating the relative roles of hydrogen and oxygen in the air we breathe.

The book you're now reading—*The Church in Emerging Culture: Five Perspectives*—ventures into the same forest as Niebuhr explored. This is a book about relationships: the symbiotic relationships between space and time, time and eternity, gospel and culture, church and world, meaning and form.[4] It won't be the last word on the subject, but it represents our continuing struggle, as followers of Christ in a changing culture, to live out the meaning of the incarnation. This is the ongoing struggle articulated by Frank Burch Brown: "As a religion develops, it must orient itself both in relation to the culture of its origins and in relation to the contemporary cultures it encounters—each of which presents alternative possibilities that a religion may reject, modify, or eventually adopt."[5]

For us, a half-century after Niebuhr, the "contemporary cultures" we encounter include both modern and postmodern. And to the degree the church has succeeded in linking its identity with the modern Western culture it has both fought and helped form, it now struggles to understand its identity in a postmodern culture characterized by difference, diversity, and divergence from any single norm. (In both-and postmodern fashion, the more we experience global homogenization, the more we value difference and the assertion of identity markers.) So far in this struggle, much of our conversation tends less toward constructing a new postmodern identity than deconstructing an old modern one (see Michel Foucault's "Maybe the target nowadays is not to discover what we are, but to refuse what we are").[6] We find our brainpower drained by issues of boundaries and allegiances during this transitional time: Which culture do we belong to or react against or withdraw from or seek to transform? The dominant-but-fading modern culture or the fledgling, emergent, divergent postmodern ones? To speak of Christian identity and the identity-culture dilemma in the midst of seemingly parallel cultural universes is to press one of the hottest buttons in the church today.[7]

Today Niebuhr's clearing seems less clear than overgrown with untrimmed notions, overhanging facades, and hanging faces.[8] While acknowledging its influence, some theologians have also made *Christ and Culture* their number 1 love-to-hate book: "We have come to believe that few books have been a greater hindrance to an accurate assessment of our situation than *Christ and Culture*."[9] Niebuhr's approach "justifies the self-congratulatory church transforming the world as it is tamed by it. It implicitly denounces alternative approaches as sectarian, and suggests that the church should be willing to suppress its peculiarities in order to participate responsibly in the culture."[10]

Painting on so large a canvas would tax anyone, and Niebuhr's hand slips often. For some, Niebuhr's monolithic treatment of culture lacks subtleties of analysis or standards for discriminating the good and bad in culture, the cultural dynamics of race, gender, or ideology, and various cultural spheres such as science, art, and politics.[11] For others the "solidity" of Niebuhr's typologies is antihistorical and thus nearly unfalsifiable, with uneasy traffic between the micro and the macro, thereby distorting Christian history and making it difficult for Christians of various tribes and theological stripes to find themselves. Still others take offense at Niebuhr's "rigging of his typology" toward a "conversionist" stance that "sells out to a culture it professes to be transforming" while feigning a pluralist approach and respect for all.

To top it off, there is not much Christ in *Christ and Culture*. In the words of sociologist Robert Bellah, "Niebuhr was nervous about any mediation of God, even through Christ, certainly through the Bible or the church."[12] Jesus' own strategy for cultural interaction—"in," "not of," but not "out of" it either, a triangulation that makes the discussion necessarily complex[13]—makes only a cameo appearance in Niebuhr's discussion. According to theologian Kathryn Tanner, for the Christian, "relations with the wider culture are never simply ones of either accommodation, on the one hand, or opposition and radical critical revision, on the other, but always some mixture."[14]

In spite of all the criticism, William Werpehowski makes a compelling case for *Christ and Culture*'s "abiding value" based on "its delineation of a set of theological considerations regarding creation, judgment, redemption, grace, and sin that rightly condition the infinite dialogue among Christians as they seek faithfully to witness to God in Jesus Christ."[15] Yet while Werpehowski is right that we have yet to come fully to terms with Niebuhr, the critics are also correct: We now need to get beyond Niebuhr, if for no other reason than Niebuhr's theoretical and cultural assumptions were all products of the "tunnel" of modernity.[16]

There are three problems with Niebuhr's tunnel vision.

1. First, Christianity began in premodernity, not modernity or post-modernity. St. Paul launched Christianity in the and-also marketplace of Athens (Acts 17:17), not the Mall of America or the IMS (instant messaging) of AOL. Niebuhr's modern, either-or bias led him to weight the five categories—condemnation of culture, toleration of culture, conversion of culture, adoption of culture, and enrichment of culture—so that his favorite (conversion of culture) would win. But what if Christianity needs multiple ecosystems as much as it needs multiple Gospels? What if God can be found throughout history working in each clearing?

2. Second, Niebuhr understood change in incremental, not exponential, terms. Of course the world has always been changing. Too much hokum goes under the intellectual rubric of "change." In the early twentieth century, when cars were first being produced, the top speed of automobiles was 20 m.p.h. The "experts" of the day were obsessed with the world's new "speed mania," even giving that name to a new "medical condition" (shades of ADD/HDD?) of speed addiction. According to William Lee Howard, M.D., in his admonition to parents, "Speed Mania" (1905), "The facts we have to seriously consider are not those dealing with accidents or risks to lives, nor with the effects on the adult of middle life, but the harmful effects on the very young who are being literally whirled through the world at an age when their nervous systems need quiet and normal development."[17]

There is an old Latin expression: *tempora mutantur et nos, mutamur in illis*—"times change and we change with them." But the enormities of contemporary cultural changes are unprecedented, and Niebuhr didn't anticipate them. Many are even calling our time a "paradigm shift." All contexts heretofore will be unfamiliar and unknown. In times of paradigm shift, Thomas Kuhn argued, everything goes back to zero and starts over anew.[18] No wonder Neibuhr's modern grappling with the Christ-and-culture issue is less than fully satisfactory in our emerging postmodern context.

For the Christian, of course, times of shifting paradigms take us back not to zero, but to origins. Our time is overdue for an original look at the relationship of Christ and culture—not "starting from scratch," but "starting from origins." True originality is a homecoming; not overturning doctrines but returning to the origins of the faith and letting the primeval forest reseed.

3. Third, Niebuhr failed to consider what the relationship of Christ and culture might look like from outside Christendom, a world where the church had—at the time of his writing—a much more preferred place at the table. Niebuhr's assumptions were shaped by a world in which it behooved Robert Chambers, the Victorian Scottish publisher and naturalist, to keep pews in two different churches. If he was absent from one, the congregation presumed he was in the other and his reputation remained intact. In the same way, Niebuhr assumed a world in which Christianity knew its place, and its place was enforced by the back of culture's hand.

Today, nobody cares whether you're in church, and the culture is more likely to backslap you if you are there than if you aren't. The winds of history no longer fill Christianity's sails, especially in the West. Distinguished literary critic George Steiner calls postmodern culture the "after-life" of religion, dominated as it is by "the malignant energies released by the decay of natural religious forms."[19] In this "post-religion" era, Richard Roberts argues, "new religious growths sprout fungi-like on the stumps and trunks of the fallen trees of tradition—and humanity dances with its new spiritual masks."[20] Niebuhr never anticipated the emergence of a post-Christendom West, nor a world in which Christianity (especially traditional, mainline

Christianity) is dying in the West[21] while it's the fastest growing religion throughout much of the rest of the world.[22]

BUT WHILE NIEBUHR'S "CLEARING" IS problematic for a postmodern context, the metaphor is an apt one. The word *culture*, which once referred to goo in a petri dish, is actually taken from the word *agriculture*.[23] And agriculture is what's done to raw land to make it better than it was originally—it is ploughed, fertilized, and tilled—without changing its nature.

Those last four words—"without changing its nature"—characterize the bias of all the contributors to this book. All are attempting to be true to the biblical nature of the Christian faith, no matter how different their plantings. The honeysuckle-climbing vine always grows clockwise. The jasmine vine always entwines itself counterclockwise. The world's best gardeners are unable to make the honeysuckle grow to the left or the jasmine grow to the right. In the Chilean mountains, however, the climbing vine *scyphambus elegans* starts its journey in one direction, then, after a few loops, reverses and climbs in the opposite direction. No amount of pruning or tending can change its zigzaggery. Living things have a resilient, substantial, real nature, and the contributors to this book know the Christian faith as a living thing with such a nature.

While the conversation partners selected for this book decidedly differ on the direction of the exchange between the gospel and culture—some climbing clockwise, others climbing counterclockwise, some climbing both ways—each seeks the same thing: the light of Christ. The continental divide is over whether Christianity requires a recapitulation (evolving) or a repetition (preserving) at each juncture of history. The continental shelf where all gather is the desire to pass on "the faith once delivered to the saints" (JUDE 1:3, NRSV).

The contributors also are of one mind regarding the mystery behind all that goes on in the clearing. Agricultural practices don't grow plants; they create conditions for plants to grow. In the same way, we don't grow churches or leaders; we create conditions for churches and leaders to grow.

All we can do is plant. The growth and harvest are out of our hands.

This book was originally conceived as a matrix, admittedly facile and open to critique, but useful for making visible four general conditions in which Christian faith may be lived and practiced. The matrix represents the church's response to cultural change on two axes, change in method/form/style and change in message/content/substance.

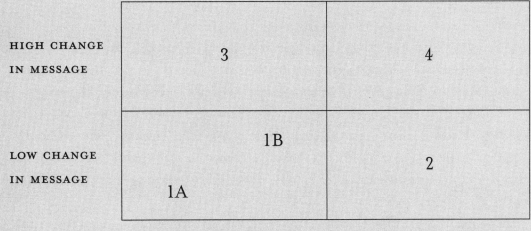

This matrix offers four general categories, which themselves can contain unlimited possibilities. We've chosen conversation partners to represent five possibilities. Two lie in the "low change in method and message" quadrant, one rooted in the Patristic period and the other in the Reformation. The three other conversation partners explore "low change in method, high change in message," "low change in message, high change in method," and "high change in both method and message."

But this introductory essay anatomizes the complex subject of Christ and culture in a different way: by describing four types of clearings (Garden, Park, Glen, Meadow) in which twenty-first century leaders are laboring. The language of "clearing" is another way of talking about "kingdom"—and kingdom is another way of talking about creativity. Each clearing engenders a different ecosystem. Those in the first clearing (Garden) use only tried-and-true seeds that have been inherited. They do everything they can to retain the purity of the seed stock and to pass on the rituals of planting as they've inherited them. We call this the "preserving message/preserving method" clearing.

Like the first, those in the second clearing (Park) use only the seeds that have been passed down from their ancestors, but they exploit new methods of planting the ground. We call this the "preserving message/evolving methods" clearing.

Those in the third clearing (Glen) feel free to fortify the seed stock and to adapt it to meet the challenges of new environments. But like those in the first, they sow this new seed in traditional furrows and with traditional plows. We call this the "evolving message/preserving methods" clearing.

Those in the fourth clearing (Meadow) are open to augmenting the seed stock, even using new techniques of cross-fertilization, hybridization, aquaculture, and the like. Plus they desire to use the latest John Deere tractors, combines, and other equipment. We call this the "evolving message/evolving methods" clearing.

Remember, these four clearings are interpretive categories, ideal typologies meant to stimulate continuing conversation but not to be perfect matches to reality—just as premodernity, modernity, and postmodernity are ideal types. All four clearings exist in dialectic, although each has its own demonology, and devil's spurge can be found in every clearing.

There are many versions and perversions of each clearing, and a cohabitation of views is more the norm than a clean clear-cutting. For example, even though many of the 16 million Southern Baptists live in the Park and are some of the quickest to embrace technology ("One people, one purpose, one click" reads its Web site), the Southern Baptist Convention refuses to permit electronic giving. "God says you bring the offering as an act of worship," argues denominational executive Jack Wilkerson.[24] At the same time, the Garden-based Greek Orthodox Archdiocese of America, with 1.2 million parishioners, became one of the first clients of ParishPay, a Long Island City company that helps churches set up donations by credit card or through automatic bank withdrawals.

In addition, each clearing has its proponents of the three ways of treating social change:

1. **Reactive**—wait until change occurs before you deal with it; assume that while change is always occurring, the future will still be like the past; utilize crisis management.

2. **Responsive**—while change is occurring, get involved to do what you can; anticipate what is probable, and be proactive once you see the direction change is going.

3. **Redemptive**—get ahead of change and try and steer it; no one can escape the reactive and responsive, but learn to read the handwriting on the wall, utilizing futuring and futures research as prophetic professions.

But there are real differences between the four clearings in this transitional time. Unique trigger words set off the differences of tone and touch of each quadrant, and each clearing sees both different problems and the same problems differently.

1. **Intellectual problem**—Are we dealing with the loss of a sense of objective truth or a change in the understanding of what truth is?

2. **Moral problem**—Is it a loss of a sense of biblical authority or a culture of individualism and its morally thin creeds?

3. **Cultural problem**—Is it a loss of a sense of community and roots caused by selling out to culture or an inability to incarnate the gospel in culture? Should the church feed only on its own resources or should it draw from the world's wells?

4. **Spiritual problem**—Is it a crisis of faith (creeds and doctrinal content) or a crisis in the language of faith (words we use to convey doctrine and creeds)?

5. **Ecclesiastical problem**—Is the church itself the problem, with structures not conducive to ministry and mission in this new world, or is the church failing to be the church, less true to itself than true to its time?

6. **Authority problem**—Is tradition to be valued as a tradition, and to what degree do we accord cultural authority to tradition? Do we colonialize culture under Christian authority or is Christianity a colony within culture?

Each clearing is haunted by a dragon with a theological sting in its tail. For clearing 1 (Garden), who gets to decide when and why to stop the historical clock? (Our two authors in this clearing have answered this question differently.) For clearing 2 (Park), when does playing footsies with the culture lead to going to bed with that culture? When does the salt lose its saltiness? For clearing 3 (Glen), how do you know when the separation of content and container has turned into a de facto divorce? For clearing 4 (Meadow), will the real Christianity please stand up? When does Christianity become so morphed that it's no longer Christianity?

The Garden: Preserving Message/Preserving Methods

SOME OF THE FIRST VERSES I memorized as a child enrolled in BMA (Bible Memory Association) are from the Psalms. I've never forgotten them because every time I recite part of them, they wash over my soul like a cleansing flood. Everyone has heard these verses more than once, including these words: "There is a river, the streams whereof shall make glad the city of God."[25]

To this day, I still don't know what those words mean.

So why do they move us so? Do they harken in us some subconscious yearning? Do they beckon us to some path unknown to us? Do they awaken in us baptismal memories of that river? Are they the words that inspired John the Divine to write, "Out of the believer's heart shall flow rivers of living water"?[26]

For those laboring in the Garden, where water is lifeblood and living stream, the answer is obvious. Truth is light revealed, not life reconstructed. Poet W. H. Auden wrote that, "Law, say the gardeners, is the sun." And Law of the sun is "the wisdom of the old,...the senses of the young."[27] Whatever the variety of garden—and the varieties are endless, each one claiming the original seed stock—"Law is Good-morning and Good-night."[28]

The word *garden* comes from an Old English word that means "enclosure." Identity integration is highest in the Garden's fenced enclave of righteousness, where resistance to relaxing the tensions between Christ and culture is highest. With a sense of rootedness in past "Good-mornings" and "Good-nights," the Garden is the culmination of the master plan, a collaboration between the Divine Gardener, master gardeners, horticulturalists (theologians), and the sun's canonical "Good-mornings" and "Good-nights."

Time is measured differently in the self-contained Garden, which takes years, decades, centuries to develop. Some plants take a hundred years to really get blooming. It is hard enough to imagine, in an age of eye-blink gratification, having a five-year plan, much less a 100-year plan. Or a 2,000-year plan. Totally dependent on master gardeners and other "experts" passing on their knowledge to successive generations, the Garden is keenly aware of *kerygma* as a transhistorical identity marked by both permanence of glory and transience of show.

What goes on outside this garden of values is of less concern than in any other clearing. In the Garden, the world of faith is virtually a closed system governed by the immutable laws of God. Beliefs are shaped not by culture but by the church, which can be as much the message as the messenger. Grave by grave, the Garden ground is fertilized and hallowed. The church is not built on layer upon layer of cultural and intellectual plunder. Nor is the church a setter of trends or a seller of fashions. Primrose paths are built on truth that has been disclosed in the blinding sun of revelation and on the humus of ancestral plantings and sacramental blessings. We had better not put our words into their mouths! The church's basic responsibility to society is to be itself, in all its purity and holiness, according to criteria internal to itself.

The Garden demands that one master the art of good soil and good soul. Walk slowly. Prune quickly. Learn the flowers, their preferences for shade and water, and respect the beds in which they prefer to grow. Go with the flow of the seasons and the stimulations of the senses that each season brings. Once again, the only kind of change celebrated in the Garden is intrinsic, not extrinsic.

Of course, you can make the dead so present that the living are largely absent, and in a stroll through many gardens, you are as likely to stumble upon seraphic statuary hidden behind a boscage of evergreen shrubs as upon living flesh. But the Garden is concerned not about a saleable story or a "seeker-sensitive" story or a sell-by-date story but about a sure story, a true story, an authoritatively preserved story in which the mystery of sacramental blessings abounds. The skill that goes into keeping memory alive in the Garden clearing is as immense as the amount of money and time spent on garden tours.

Some gardeners devote energy to removing the snails and slugs, with diminished attention to growing the beautiful; others spend their time planting and nurturing a garden of delights. By God's grace, fruit is produced in each clearing. But in the Garden, lots of energy is expended in controlling the bounty. Its highly manicured, well-managed truths stand tall and proud, let the Barna and Gallup chips fall where they may. The Garden's suspicion of "the world" makes any offense to culture intentional, and the more stylish the cut, the less uncomfortable the clothing. Happiest out of step with the zeitgeist, when the culture zigs in its trimmings and trappings, the Garden's against-the-grain consciousness mostly zags.

The Garden worries not about the weary familiarity of old chestnuts—rituals and rubrics (the tedium of *te deums*) or archaic words and concepts. In fact, if well managed, these rubrics and rituals are what give rich contour and deep form to the Garden, even becoming magnificently manicured giant topiaries that take generations and centuries to produce. What Clifton Fadiman once said about a classic in literature—"When you re-read a classic, you do not see in the book more than you did before; you see more in you than there was before"[29]—the Garden finds true in the faith's original deposits. The more you repeat them, the less rich they become—but the richer you become.

Opposed to opportunities to reinvent the wheel, where the wheel is faith's flywheel, tenders of the Garden defend the clearing root and branch.

The longest memory, the deepest roots, the most consistent turnings get you the best future. Identity means more than identification, whether by self or society. Christian identity means obedience to an authoritative narrative that dictates what methods are holy, honest, and authentic.

The Garden rejects the notion that we can't maintain inherited theological identities and at the same time meet human needs. Walt Whitman wrote about the Civil War, and Emily Dickinson did not. But they both are great poets. Just because rituals and ceremonies were forged for another time and culture does not disqualify them for today. In fact, it makes them road tested and better qualified.

Further, there is no greater irrelevance than the pursuit of relevance. The bugbear of the Garden is a selling out to culture (especially pop culture)— a church so obliging toward the culture, so pleasing and teasing, that the church topples over with truth more relinquished than reclaimed. Bow-wow churches let people feel good about themselves and their world through the endless, senseless discernment for what is new, fading, dated, and dead. The quest for relevance to the "just now," the "modo" (the root word for *modern*), is self-defeating. The new and improved never quite arrives since there is always another new and improved to replace it. When technology is appropriated, as historian Grant Wacker puts it, the Garden seeks out the Garden of Eden equipped with a satellite dish.[30]

The mood in the Garden to alien seeds is not concessive but combative. There is a constant struggle to win back the Garden from the erosions of time and the encroachments of the forest primeval. Depending on the kind of garden (community, public, secret, garth), the walls can be quite high, so high at times that there is a complete withdrawal from the world to preserve the purity of the faith and the church's classic distinctiveness. Anything less would begin the slippery slope into secularity and heresy and death.

The first appearance of Jesus, the Second Adam, after his resurrection? As a gardener. The spirit of the Garden is best conveyed by "Rules for the Icon Painter."[31] Each rule is based on the assumption that it is the icon painter's duty to paint exactly what the ancestors have painted, using the same colors, the same brush strokes, the same lines, and so to blend one's skill into the icon itself that one's own creativity is consumed by the icon.

The Park: Preserving Message/Evolving Methods

PARKS WERE MADE FOR WALKING. In fact, the first public parks in England were known as "public walks," and the wide walkways in parks came to be called "boulevards."

The Park is the favored natural habitat of much of the evangelical world. It is filled with wild variations in themes and expressions, but it is tied together by unifying paths and missions, rocks and rules as ingrained as tree rings.

The Park's use of rocks for demarcations and directions is more than a theological flourish. When Jesus said, "On this rock I will build my church," he didn't mean the church was unchanging. Even rocks change over time, especially when water passes over them, sculpting them into shapes and sizes that fit the climate. The properties of the rock don't change, but the look of it does. Hence Billy Graham's official position, as expressed in his first ministry slogan: "Geared to the Times, Anchored to the Rock."

The fundamental premise of the Park is a truism of life: to stay the same, some things have to change.[32] It's the same English language, but the 1384 Wycliffe translation of the Bible is virtually unreadable today. Is there anyone whose self doesn't change throughout one's lifetime, even while one's sense of self remains the same? Christianity is an organism that changes its clothes as its body matures while its essential selfhood remains the same, like a crustacean that periodically sheds its confining carapace. In fact, one theologian contends that Jesus' distinctive hermeneutical method is one of putting new flesh on dry bones.[33]

In other words, the only way for Jesus to be "the same yesterday, today, and forever" is if church ovens keep baking fresh bread, "fresh every morning."[34] When the Park looks at garden-variety churches, it asks, Can the church be the church without making Jesus possible? The Garden sings, "Dewdrops around us are falling." The Park sings, "But for the showers we plead." If the Garden looks back, the Park looks around.

The Park's rules, often a visitor's first greeting, serve to facilitate exploration and mission. Rather than set up high barriers between the world and itself, the Park relies on rules to regulate the traffic. Unlike locked-gate, invitation-only gardens where preventatives such as control and access are at the highest levels, the Park is open to visitors during appointed hours and under anointed superintendents. The Park's introspective theological entities form extrovertish networks of cooperation and competition on both local and global levels.

The best description of Christ to emerge in the second century is this one from the Epistle to Diognetus: "This is he who was from the beginning, who appeared as new yet proved to be old, and is always young as he is born in the hearts of saints."[35] It is the mission of each generation to help Christ be "born young" in the next generations. It is the mission of each culture to midwife Christ's being "born young" in that indigenous culture. Classics historian E. M. Blaiklock praises Paul for his ability to speak the language of differing cultures: "The rabbi of Jerusalem, the Greek of Tarsus, the citizen of Rome; trilingual, participant in three civilizations, interpreter of East to West; Paul the apostle of Christ, emerges from the record more real than any other personality known to us from his generation."[36]

An advertisement in a *New Yorker* cartoon mocks those who think they can improve on the past: "New!! Improved!! Mom's Old-Fashioned Apple Pie!" While the recipe remains the same, the way it's served and presented constantly changes. The old, old story needs to be told in new ways. In fact, one of the ways Park people know the old, old truths to be true is their ability to assume unbelievable and unfamiliar shapes while remaining themselves and without compromising their integrity.

When words become an obstacle course for seekers in their desperate search for truth, new words need to be found. With varying degrees of fearlessness, people in the Park pick from high culture, pop culture, and folk culture what works and what pleases—whether Mozart or Manilow or Madonna—and use it for the glory and pleasure of God. The question that animates this clearing is, Are we living in our time the incarnation of the gospel? One Christian college (Calvin) had a marketing campaign in the '80s that was based on the Park approach: "We're looking for 1,000 new ways to express a 2,000-year-old tradition."

Technologies have always grown alongside and shaped Christianity. New technologies make possible new forms of thought, new forms of literature, even new forms of faith. How can you have novels before the printing press?

The Park gets historical about belief: people don't believe today like they used to believe, or worship like they used to worship. "The past is a foreign country: they do things differently there."[37] Just as part of Christianity's past as a print culture required new ways of communicating, digital culture requires a new way of communicating.[38] Even Robert Gundry's appeal for a resuscitation of fundamentalism in his "paleofundamentalist manifesto" calls for a "situation-sensitive" strategy for deploying the Bible as guidance in our daily lives.[39]

If leaders in the Garden don't like to drop a net into the culture, leaders in the Park spread their cultural net wide and feel free to experiment with the forms we give to our beliefs, knowing that all forms are fraught with compromise. The Park church views as missional malpractice the church's ferocious debates in the past over methodology, debates which eventually go the way of the slide rule while consuming vast amounts of the church's resources. Before the screen, it was the stereopticon; before rap music, it was quartet singing; before drums in worship, it was the pipe organ; before the Internet, it was the printing press; before the coffee house, it was the table fork, which the twelfth-century Latin church denounced as a "tool of the devil."[40] The church's reaction to Amelia Bloomer's introduction of women's "pants" demonstrates how the idiosyncrasy of today often becomes the good sense of tomorrow.

However, that the church can oppose some forms of its electronification (plugged in, logged on, screens up) while electronifying other features of the church's ministry (electric lights, electric clocks, duplicating machines, electronic pipe organs, central heating, word processors) is as hypocritical in the Park as the handlebar-mustached movie critic Gene Shalit, sitting at his 1940s Remington typewriter, telling twenty-first-century digital kids what movies are worth viewing.

In the Park, leaders do nothing to interrupt the unity and continuity of the tradition. Cultural conformity and Christ don't go together. It's the *uncritical* incorporation of culture that betrays Christ. From the perspective of the Park, the Garden does change—otherwise Christians would be worshiping in Aramaic (or at the very least German!). But the speed of change can seem snail's pace. The Park wonders if the Garden seed doesn't become so coated in tradition and history that it takes forever to break free. Or the church ends up with a seed that can't grow outside the idealized conditions nurtured in the garden. But because the Park is most concerned about speaking the language of the culture, it is most likely to make thoughtless equations of size or power with transcendental or spiritual importance.

Martin Thornton called the story of his life in the church "The Rock and the River."[41] The church stands like a rock for truth that is changeless. But on the other hand, the church stands for the river of life that is ever flowing—making things fresh, cutting new beds, finding new ways.

The Glen: Evolving Message/Preserving Methods

FOR LEADERS IN THE GLEN, biblical spirituality is an unprotected, scant clearing surrounded by encroaching vegetation and forestation. The Glen is a natural depression between hills, a verdant valley that has been shaped in dialogue with its surroundings and somewhat defined by the terrors (and technologies) that encircle. For example, in the Glen, most Christians' contempt for consumer culture is Christianity's mark of sublimity.

The most obvious difference between an open system and a closed system is the closed system's impenetrable boundary. The Glen is an open system that tries to behave as if it were closed. Accustomed to the craggy nooks and jagged crannies of the Glen, which can be as large as the Glen Canyon or as small as Watkins Glen, anything that makes the ongoing search for truth painless or easygoing is suspect.

In the Glen there is a sense that culture has shaped the spiritual responses of people in every time, even that culture can be a foundation for and a font of theological awareness. Historical theologian Jaroslav Pelikan has shown how during the second and third centuries there emerged the notion of sacrifice as a way of speaking about the sacrament—hence of eucharistic ministry as a priesthood.[42] The very fact that the cross wasn't used as a Christian symbol until Constantine challenges the notion of a uniform, single, transhistorical, and transcultural gospel.

Of course, theology cannot be hermetically sealed from its social setting. And if it could, that would sound its death knell since all closed systems will eventually die. Glenners want to know: You mean it's useless to inquire about the wider cultural context in which Christianity emerged and the new understandings that come when seen in that light? You mean that even though Christianity was borne out of Jewish religion, the fact that it was forged in the crucible of ancient classical (Greek and Roman) cultures has no meaning?

Simone Weil said, in the best definition of culture ever uttered, "What is culture? The formation of attention."[43] The attention of the Glen is on faith living dangerously on the brink. If in the Garden and the Park the dangers are underground, in the Glen they are all around. In the watchful defense of the Glen, the destructive forces that threaten are felt deeply. Sheltered only by grace, Glenners are much too cranky for life in the Park. They warn wayfarers that waywardness can lead to death. They warn hikers that not all is a lark. They challenge wanderers from other clearings to open their eyes and read the signs. "See that fog (environmental destruction, political and economic upheaval, rising poverty, consumer capitalism) rolling in? That's the kind of fog that settles in so deeply that you won't be able to see two steps in front of you. Where do you think you're going with that picnic and that Frisbee? This fog doesn't burn off in the morning, followed by a bright and sunny day. Beware!" ("*Why* won't they listen to me?" moan and cry Glenners as a big, happy group of Meadowers tromp off to their own destruction.) No flashy, flashing, perfectly calibrated walking shoe is enough to get you through the awaiting fog and crags. You might be well heeled. You might get farther. You might be more comfortable—for a while. But it's not enough to get you through.

The densest fog in the Glen is technology. When technology enters our consciousness, it alters our view of ourselves and of the world in at least three ways. First, Marshall McLuhan's motto "the medium is the message" reminds us that media is not neutral and that the whole message-method, content-container construct is problematic. Technology carries its own consequences, some unintended and unpredictable. For example, technology facilitated the Holocaust: if no railroads, no telegraph, no poison gas, then perhaps no Holocaust.

Or consider the shrinking of space due to digital technology and its paradoxical effect on our spiritual lives—bringing us together and separating us at the same time. Or take Quentin Schultz's controversial contention that "information technologies foster statistical ways of perceiving and systematic modes of imagining." In fact, he argues that digital technology favors "a closed system that elevates the value of control over moral responsibility."[44]

Or take the reciprocity of media, economics, and religion in a significant section of American religion. I shall never forget a trip to Heritage Village right after the collapse of the PTL Club. The centerpiece of this self-avowed, sacred pilgrimage site? Not the church, but the lovingly detailed mall. Televangelism's sacrilege of consumption in the gospel of prosperity reminds us of the controlling power of the via media.[45] In Jean-François Lyotard's analysis of postmodernity, technology is "a game pertaining not to the true, the just, or the beautiful, etc., but to efficiency: a technical 'move' is 'good' when it does better and/or expends less energy than another."[46] One theologian of the Glen calls the "Alpha Programme" a "marketised evangelism" best described as "the Tupperware Party solution,"[47] not realizing that relationship-based home parties hosted by people you trust and fostering social experiences have been called "the perfect retailing method for the new millennium."[48] Poet-farmer Wendell Berry denounces the industrial-ization of agriculture and advocates farming methods that are biologically sound and economically just. For environmentalist, essayist, and Methodist lay leader Bill McKibben, SUVs are the sum of all villainy and an indictment of a church with a theology about as lasting as a news flash, as probing as a news brief.[49]

From the perspective of the Glen, we are living in a default culture, Web wise and truth foolish, technologically privileged but socially deracinated.

As we have seen, throughout the Glen, fear plays like an obbligato. The Glen's precarious existence, and the dangers of encroachment from the "outside," forces its residents to be acutely aware of the hermeneutics of power *vis a vis* culture, especially technology. Feminist philosopher Donna Haraway's principle that technologies are "instruments for enforcing meanings"[50] is partly what lies behind Marva Dawn's outspokenness in her widely cited warnings about visual technologies in worship. Dawn has caused many leaders to speak up about dumbing down—leaders such as Douglas Webster, who sees the danger of digital technology's "transforming a congregation into an audience, transforming proclamation into performance or transforming worship into entertainment."[51] The fear of liturgy becoming secondary to technology results in the Glen's attacks on the Park's gawky concerns about what's new and trendy.

When liturgy degenerates into dull formalism, leaders in the Glen argue, it's not the liturgy's fault. It's the fault of a spirituality that has gone dry and dull, a church that's being transformed into a humorous parody of St. Paul's injunction to be all things to all people—and a capitulation by Christians who, as philosopher John Locke always protested loudly, "boldly prefix God's most holy name to their inventions."[52] The Glen serves as a rehab center for Christianity, overhauling cliches, healing bedridden dogmas, and pepping up tired phrasings.

There is a vast difference between invention and innovation. Invention comes from the root word *inventus*, which means to start from scratch and discover something new. Innovation's root word is *nova*. Nova means to make new again, to take something that already exists and make it fresh or to put it into practice or to combine it with something else so that something happens. Just as Victorians were great inventors but lousy innovators, so the Glen abounds with theological innovators but lacks inventors. But there is something about going back that makes you go forward. The history of Christianity is filled with "reformers" who sought only to purify what existed, and they ended up propelling Christianity forward at blazing speed.

In John M. Synge's 1904 play *In the Shadow of the Glen*, the Irish playwright describes the Glen as a place that's foggy and where the deep mist can play tricks on one's imagination, such as "a little stick would seem as big as your arm, and a rabbit as big as a bay horse, and a stack of turf as big as a towering church in the city of Dublin."[53] The Garden is suspect of those who live their lives in a foggy place where message and method are hard to distinguish. But why those in the Garden fear the Glen—when the Good Shepherd himself promises to lead us through every valley—is a mystery for Glenners. Glen dwellers revel in the secrets of a seed. They live the mysteries of faith.

As much as some Christians like to come to the Garden alone, Glenners travel in packs with a group consciousness. They are more concerned about cultivating food from the land for the hungry than about the beauty of garden flowers and parklands. The difference between the mentality of the Garden and the Glen is that in the Garden, you are what your parents planted, but in the Glen, you are what your seeds become.

The Meadow: Evolving Message/Evolving Methods

THE MEADOW IS A TRACT OF MOIST, low-lying grassland where wildflowers grow in profusion. In the Meadow, there are lots of boggy places with fragile vegetation and colorful lichens. Mountain meadow vegetation is dominated by wildflowers and thick mats of moss carpeting much of the ground, yet various willows and other many-branched, wiry shrubs may also exist there.

Meadows are nomadic, wandering from space to space depending on the conditions of the surrounding grasslands, wetlands, and woodlands. Meadows mostly just happen. They are not highly managed by humans. They are Mother Nature's navel, some of the most fertile areas in nature. You can almost hear the heart beating underneath the ground.

The Meadow is what happens first after a devastation such as a forest fire. For leaders in the Meadow, the imaginative architecture of the modern world is in ruins, and a new imaginative architecture is emerging. The root metaphors of the modern world have burned out. The emergence of new metaphors on which to build life and prepare for eternity are what some call the "postmodern movement" or "the emerging culture." Claude Levi-Strauss, in his masterpiece *The Raw and the Cooked*, put it like this: "metaphors are based on an intuitive sense of the logical relations between one realm and other realms....Metaphor, far from being a decoration that is added to language, purifies it and restores it to its original nature."[54]

The Meadow is the church's best breeding ground for creativity and innovation. Anything new is partly a cleansing operation,[55] a major function of wetlands and one reason why they are now so esteemed by ecologists and protected by governments who are now undoing (at great expense) their former "fill them in and plug them up" mentality. What used to be seen as the armpits of nature, wetlands are now preserved as nature's womb of fertility and creativity. After all, God chose mud as the material for creation.

The notion that Christians are a new people who form their culture apart from others is anathema to Meadowers. Every culture has a different understanding of the kingdom of God and an Edenic existence. As the song of an elderly southern gentlemen put it, "Ain't but three things in this world worth a solitary dime: / That's old dogs and children, and watermelon wine."[56]

One can affirm distinctions between church and world without affirming a disjunction between church and world. Interaction need not imply interference. The church may oppose the world in its sinfulness, but the church itself is designed for sinners, not for saints. And the fallenness of all cultural forms means that the church identifies with the world in all of its creatureliness.

The Meadow registers the greatest sensitivity to what God is doing in the world, not just in the church. Early Christian theologians spoke of creation itself as a sacrament, and the history of Christianity is filled with those who saw the world as God's "great poem," murmurous with the numinous, emanating, and embodying symbols of the divine purpose.[57] Everything is related to God. There is no atom in which God is not active. The intersections between theology and other discourse communities (science, the arts) are most trodden in the Meadow. For Meadowers, God is often as active in the world as in the church. As any slog through the bogs will reveal, it is needful but hard to differentiate the "wisdom of the world" (1 CORINTHIANS 1:17-31) from the wisdom of the Spirit working in the world.

Meadowers believe people today are starved not for doctrines but for images and relationships and stories. In the last century, Roman Catholic theologian Bernard Lonergan made the case that "the image is necessary for the insight."[58] Whenever someone presents a concept of God that is neat and tidy and well manicured, Meadowers know one thing: that's not God. The Meadow lets a thousand metaphors bloom. In stark contrast to the Garden, where the priority is clearing the ground of weeds, in the Meadow the growing of fresh flowers is paramount. A lot of weeds grow here alongside the wheat (MATTHEW 13:24-30, 36-43). A meadow boasts the highest toleration of weeds. In fact, what farming takes place in the Meadow is no-till farming, in which the seed is planted in the midst of the weeds and the good is trusted to overcome the bad.[59]

The Meadow rewards those species that continually adapt to evolving conditions and permutations. The church's vitality is its versatility, its wild, untamed landscapes (which in the eighteenth century were called "the sublime"). The Meadow church is less concerned with old material to preserve than fresh material to assimilate. Rather than drain swamps and standing water, the Meadow lets the wetlands seed the soil. In fact, meadows were originally wetlands: a meadow is a grown-up pond. That's why the soil of the Meadow is wondrously rich, almost too fecund for many who advise and devise fertility reduction. (Which is why a Meadower in a Garden is frequently known as a heretic.)

The Meadow invites you to run through it with your bare feet and enjoy its fertility and freedom. But the Meadow is filled with chimeras, delusions, and mirages of thought that, like an *ignis fatuus*,[60] entice travelers into danger, plunging them into quagmires, entangling them in theologically fraught thickets, and leading them astray.

The Meadow believes that the story mode of the Gospels, more than the doctrine mode of the Epistles, is the natural habitat for the emerging culture. The Gospels are not written as philosophy or doctrine. The Gospels do not critique or argue. They are written in story, in parable, in poetry. The Gospels tell stories that turn the world upside down. (Is historical continuity as bearer of absolute truth possible to achieve? The Meadow likens such a claim to the man who boasted he had possessed the same axe for 40 years, except for five new hefts and three new blades.)

As with glens, you have to work to get to the Meadow. Meadows are not as easily accessible as parks or gardens. There is no well-trodden path or paved thoroughfare to truth. Every age has to cut its own paths, bypaths, and back roads. In every age, Christianity is constantly being discovered, a notion that claims great names. Historian Ernst Troeltsch, for example, traces the transformation of faith as "charisma" to the institutional embodiment of faith: "In a concrete way the episcopate was substituted for the earlier faith in the Exalted Christ and the Spirit: it is the successor of Christ and of the Apostles, the Bearer of the Spirit, the extension or externalizing of the Incarnation, a visible and tangible proof of the Divine Truth and Power, the concrete presence of the sociological point of reference."[61] The notion that faith's ways of thinking and acting are permanent, God-given fixtures is what Paul would call "law."

All cross-cultural communication, including the crossOcultural communication of the divine with the human, is meiotic. Both parties are active; neither is passive. It is not one way. Everything we do comes laden with cultural baggage. (When we shout, "Hark the Herald Angels Sing," we are taking part in a tune Mendelssohn wrote for the 1840 Gutenberg celebrations at Leipzig that lionized the German Man.) All of our doctrines are at best castles in the air. Fifth-century church historian Socrates Scholasticus thought that "all theological disputes were to be treated as a mere fig leaf for contentions about power and authority."[62]

That's why the Christian community often gets things wrong in a big way. John Calvin considered it a breach of morality not only to play skittles but also to mix sexes at sermons. Martin Luther's take on the Jews does not make easy reading today. For much of church history, the majority of the church has been on the wrong side of social issues such as race, poverty, women, militarism, and the environment. The Vatican was defending slavery just as staunchly as many American Protestants in the 1860s. Christianity has a memory to perish as well as to cherish. Even today, the subtexts of evangelical theology and liberal theology can still feel colonialist and classist respectively.

In a world in which we've gardened everything, the need for more green space magnifies the meadows' presence. Leaders in the Meadow are less interested in a reformational paradigm (where the church has spent the last 500 years) than a missional paradigm. The more Christianity's interest in itself, the more its irrelevance to everything else.

Social anthropologist Claude Levi-Strauss dubbed societies open to trade "hot cultures"—they warm quickly to the new and assimilate change. By contrast "cold cultures" are insular, expending a great deal of energy to maintain central control. A cold culture is the enemy of renewal, holding itself hostage to its history rather than to its heritage. A heritage can be all but lost in the mists of official history and officious memory.

The future gets created by hot cultures. The Meadow is a hot culture with a high sense of intellectual adventure and a high rate of failure. When the church's nerve wilts, it becomes mentally and emotionally sterile and runs the risk of going cold. The Meadow is the canary of ecology. Its residents see round the corner better than the other clearings, and its activities warn us what is coming.

Churches in the Meadow are rich in botanical (theological) diversity.

They are haunted by Christianity's failure to keep pace with developments in the arts and sciences, and especially its deference to early theologians on scientific developments. Why should Cyril or Cyprian be given the last word on stem-cell research? Meadow churches pioneer the use of cutting-edge technology, though more as an art form than as an artifice of evangelism, discovering in the process that "forming and reinforcing relationships with God, the world, and each other is the unexpected fruit of this art-and-technology hybrid."[63]

For churches in the Meadow, Christianity still has not hit its stride. But a word of warning from history: the meadows of today will be the gardens of tomorrow.[64]

1. To mark this fiftieth anniversary, HarperSanFrancisco has reissued *Christ and Culture* with a foreword by Martin Marty, a lengthy preface by ethicist James Gustafson, Niebuhr's student and friend, and a bonus essay, "Types of Christian Ethics" (1942), in which Niebuhr began to work out his analytical framework. See H. Richard Niebuhr, *Christ and Culture* (San Francisco: HarperSanFrancisco, 2001).

2. John G. Stackhouse, "In the World, but...Richard Niebuhr's '*Christ and Culture*'," *Christianity Today* 46 (22 April 2002), 80-81. www.christianitytoday.com/ct/2002/005/8.80.html. Accessed 28 July 2002. Another historian called it, "One of the most influential books of theology of the past two centuries." Frank Burch Brown calls the book "virtually indispensable" in "Christian Theology's Dialogue with Culture," in *Companion Encyclopedia of Theology*, ed. Peter Byrne and Leslie Houlden (New York: Routledge, 1995), 315.

3. Niebuhr's five types are "Christ against culture," "Christ of (or within) culture," "Christ above culture," "Christ transforming culture," and "Christ and culture in paradox." Unfortunately, this fifth option (Niebuhr associated with Martin Luther and Søren Kierkegaard), which I believe (along with his theologian brother, Reinhold) is the most profound one, is also Niebuhr's most confusing one.

4. The author wishes to thank his doctoral fellows at George Fox University for a careful reading and critique of this essay, and is especially grateful for the criticisms and contributions of Donna King, Earl Pierce, and Ray Peacock. The fellows include Duff Gorle, Eric Brown, Marty Williams, Shane Roberson, Warren Schatz, Rob Robinson, Terry O'Casey, Raymond Leach, Chad Johnson, Dwight J. Friesen, Greg Boulton, Craig Henningfield, and Peter Balaban.

5. Brown, "Christian Theology's Dialogue with Culture," 314.

6. Michel Foucault, "The Subject and Power," in *Michel Foucault: Beyond Structuralism and Hermeneutics*, ed. Hubert L. Dreyfus and Paul Rabinow (Chicago: University of Chicago Press, 1982), 216.

7. For German theologian Jürgen Moltmann's discussion of the "identity-involvement dilemma," see chapter 1 ("The Identity and Relevance of Faith") of his *The Crucified God: The Cross of Christ as Foundation and Criticism of Christian Theology* (New York: Harper and Row, 1974), 7-31.

8. For the problems in Niebuhr's typologies, see my *AquaChurch* (Loveland, Colo.: Group Publishing, 2000), 75-81.

9. Stanley Hauerwas and William H. Willimon, *Resident Aliens* (Nashville: Abingdon Press, 1989), 40. Hauerwas and Willimon continue: "Niebuhr rightly saw that our politics determines our theology. He was right that Christians cannot reject 'culture.' But his call to Christians to accept 'culture' (where is this monolithic 'culture' Niebuhr describes?) and politics in the name of the unity of God's creating and redeeming activity had the effect of endorsing a Constantinian social strategy. 'Culture' becomes a blanket term to underwrite Christian involvement with the world without providing any discriminating modes for discerning how Christians should see the good or the bad in 'culture.'" For a similar critique, see John Howard Yoder, "How H. Richard

Niebuhr Reasoned: A Critique of *Christ and Culture*," in *Authentic Transformation: A New Vision of Christ and Culture*, ed. Glen Stassen, D. M. Yeager, and John Howard Yoder (Nashville: Abingdon Press, 1996), 31-89.

10. William Werpehowski, *American Protestant Ethics and the Legacy of H. Richard Niebuhr* (Washington, D.C.: Georgetown University Press, 2002), 107. See also Hauerwas and Willimon's denouncement of *Christ and Culture* for the way it "justified what was already there—a church that had ceased to ask the right questions as it went about congratulating itself for transforming the world, not noticing that in fact the world had tamed the church....The church should be willing to suppress its peculiarities in order to participate responsibly in the culture." *Resident Aliens* (Nashville: Abingdon Press, 1989), 41.

11. Frank Burch Brown makes this point in "Christian Theology's Dialogue with Culture," 320.

12. Robert N. Bellah, "At Home and Not at Home: Religious Pluralism and Religious Truth," *Christian Century* (19 April 1995), 427.

13. As outlined in John 17.

14. Kathryn Tanner, *Theories of Culture* (Minneapolis: Fortress Press, 1997), 119.

15. Werpehowski, *American Protestant Ethics*, 112.

16. According to Huston Smith, the "tunnel" of modernity has four walls: scientism, higher education, the media, and the law. See Ronan Hallowell, "Beyond Modernity's Tunnel—Reclaiming the Primordial Tradition: An Interview with Huston Smith," *California Institute of Integral Studies Lifelong Learning* (spring 2002), www.ciis.edu/lifelong/hustonsmith_interview.html. Accessed 22 January 2002. For a full discussion see Huston Smith, *Why Religion Matters: The Fate of the Human Spirit in an Age of Disbelief* (San Francisco: HarperSanFrancisco, 2001).

17. William Lee Howard, "Speed Mania," *Saturday Evening Post* (30 September 1905), 27.

18. See Thomas S. Kuhn, *The Structure of Scientific Revolutions* (Chicago: University of Chicago Press, 1962).

19. George Steiner, *In Bluebeard's Castle: Some Notes Towards the Redefinition of Culture*, T. S. Eliot Memorial Lectures (New Haven: Yale University Press, 1971), 53.

20. Richard H. Roberts, *Religion, Theology and the Human Sciences* (New York: Cambridge University Press, 2002), 218-19.

21. In the words of Yale Professor Louis Dupré, "The West appears to have said its definitive farewell to a Christian culture....Our secular colleagues are happy to recognize the debt our civilization owes to the Christian faith to the extent that the faith, having been absorbed by culture itself, has become simply another cultural artifact. Christianity has become an historical factor subservient to a secular culture rather than functioning as the creative power it once was." "Seeking Christian Interiority: An Interview with Louis Dupré," *Christian Century* (16 July 1997), 654. Available online: www.religion-online.org/cgi-bin/relsearchd.dll/showarticle?item_id=214. Accessed 23 August 2002.

22. See Philip Jenkins, *The Next Christendom: The Coming of Global Christianity* (New York: Oxford University Press, 2002).

23. Culture is "a simple metaphor from agri-culture," Jacques Barzun reminds us in the prologue to his *From Dawn to Decadence: 500 Years of Western Cultural Life: 1500 to the Present* (New York: HarperCollins, 2000), xv.

24. Sarah Kershaw, "The Collection Plate? Charge It, As Churches Embrace E-Giving," *New York Times International*, 11 August 2002, NYE 23.

25. Psalm 46:4 KJV. The chapter begins, "God is our refuge and strength, an ever present help in time of trouble."

26. John 7:38 NRSV.

27. W. H. Auden writes this in "Law Like Love," in *The Collected Poetry of W. H. Auden* (New York: Random House, 1945), 208.

28. Ibid.

29. Or as he stated elsewhere, "Why should you read Dante? Jane Austin? Lucretius? Voltaire? Because they are great? That is no answer. Their greatness is what we feel after we have read them, often years later." Clifton Fadiman, *The Lifetime Reading Plan* (Cleveland: World Publishing Co., 1960), 26.

30. Grant Wacker, "Searching for Eden with a Satellite Dish: Primitivism, Pragmatism, and the Pentecostal Character," in Richard Hughes, ed., *The Primitive Church in the Modern World* (Champaign, Ill.: University of Illinois Press, 1995), 139-66.

31. The rules are as follows:

1. Before starting work, make the sign of the cross; pray in silence, and pardon your enemies.

2. Work with care on every detail of your icon, as if you were working in front of the Lord Himself.

3. During work, pray in order to strengthen yourself physically and spiritually; avoid, above all, useless words, and keep silence.

4. Pray in particular to the saint whose face you are painting. Keep your mind from distractions and the saint will be close to you.

5. When you have to choose a color, stretch out your hand interiorly to the Lord and ask His counsel.

6. Do not be jealous of your neighbor's work; his success is your success too.

7. When your icon is finished, thank God that His mercy has granted you the grace to paint the holy images.

8. Have your icon blessed by putting it on the altar. Be the first to pray before it, before giving it to others.

9. Never forget: the joy of spreading icons in the world, the joy of the work of icon-painting, the joy of giving the saint the possibility to shine through his icon, the joy of being in union with the saint whose face you are painting.

As reproduced in Jim Forest, *Praying with Icons* (Maryknoll, N.Y.: Orbis, 1997), 24.

32. This was the famous insight of John Henry Newman in *An Essay on the Development of Christian Doctrine*, 2d ed. (London: James Toovey, 1846), 38–39.

33. Or in his exact words, it "emphasizes the possibility for the transformation of a religious tradition by a simultaneous retention of the core-meaning of a familiar term combined with novel treatment of its conventional associations as supported by particularly significant actions." Stephen W. Sykes, *The Identity of Christianity: Theologians and the Essence of Christianity from Schleiermacher to Barth* (London: SPCK, 1984), 19.

34. For more see Leonard Sweet and Karen Elizabeth Rennie, "A Sour Dough Spirituality," in PreachingPlus.com, from *Rev. Magazine* (28 July 2002).

35. Epistle to Diognetus 11:4, *The Apostolic Fathers, Greek Texts and English Translations of Their Writings*, ed. and trans. J. B. Lightfoot and J. R. Harmer, 2d ed., ed. and rev. Michael W. Holmes (Grand Rapids, Mich.: Baker Book House, 1989), 304.

36. E. M. Blaiklock, "The Acts of the Apostles as a Document of First Century History," in *Apostolic History and the Gospel: Biblical and Historical Essays Presented to F. F. Bruce on His 60th Birthday*, ed. W. Ward Gasque and Ralph P Martin (Grand Rapids, Mich: William B. Eerdmans, 1970), 54.

37. These are the opening words of L. P. Hartley's best-known novel, *The Go-Between* (London: Hamish Hamilton, 1953), 9.

38. Mitchell Stephens, *The Rise of the Image, the Fall of the Word* (New York: Oxford University Press, 1998).

39. Robert H. Gundry, *Jesus the Word according to John the Sectarian: A Paleofundamentalist Manifesto for Contemporary Evangelicalism, Especially Its Elites, in North America* (Grand Rapids, Mich.: William B. Eerdmans, 2001).

40. Because of its association with wealth and Byzantine culture. See Michael Bausch, *Silver Screen, Sacred Story: Using Multimedia in Worship* (Bethesda, Md.: Alban Institute, 2002).

41. Martin Thornton, *The Rock and the River: An Encounter between Traditional Spirituality and Modern Thought* (London: Hodder and Stoughton, 1965).

42. Jaroslav Pelikan, The Emergence of the Catholic Tradition (100–600), vol. 1 of *The Christian Tradition: A History of the Development of Doctrine* (Chicago: University of Chicago Press, 1971), 166–71.

43. Simone Weil, *Simone Weil: Writings*, selected with an introduction by Eric O. Springsted (New York: Orbis, 1998), 119.

44. Quentin J. Schultze, *Habits of the High-Tech Heart: Living Virtuously in the Information Age* (Grand Rapids, Mich.: Baker Book House, 2002), 27. Schultze adds, "We imagine cultures not as organic ways of life, but as computer-like networks—closed systems that persons can objectively observe, measure, manipulate, and eventually control" (40).

45. Thomas C. O'Guinn and Russell W. Belk, "Heaven on Earth: Consumption at Heritage Village, USA," *Journal of Consumer Research* 16 (September 1989): 227–38.

46. Jean-François Lyotard, *The Postmodern Condition: A Report on Knowledge*, in *From Modernism to Postmodernism: An Anthology*, ed. Lawrence E. Cahoone (Cambridge, Mass.: Blackwell, 1996), 495.

47. Yet at the same time Richard H. Roberts argues that the "modern/postmodern matrix" presents the church with "immense challenges which, if they are to be met, will require ruthless self-appraisal, a commitment to reflexive socio-cultural analysis and a willingness to venture out in a newly defined enterprise of faith." See Richard H. Roberts, *Religion, Theology and the Human Sciences* (New York: Cambridge University Press, 2002), 187.

48. Pamela N. Danziger, "The Lure of Shopping," *American Demographics* (July/August 2002), 46.

49. Bill McKibben, "Environmental Issues from Hell," *Utne Reader* (September/October 2001), 35.

50. Donna Haraway, "A Cyborg Manifesto: Science, Technology, and Socialist-Feminism in the Late Twentieth Century," in *Simians, Cyborgs and Women: The Reinvention of Nature* (New York: Routledge, 1991), 164 (see passage on pp. 149-81),

www.stanford.edu/dept/HPS/Haraway/CyborgManifesto.html. Accessed 8 August 2002. In the Weberian definition of power, power is "the probability that one actor within a social relationship will be in a position to carry out his own will despite resistance, regardless of the basis upon which this probability rests." See Max Weber, *Economy and Society: An Outline of Interpretive Sociology* (New York: Bedminster Press, 1968), 1:53.

51. Marva Dawn, *Reaching Out without Dumbing Down: The Theology of Worship for the Turn-of-the-Century Church* (Grand Rapids, Mich.: William B. Eerdmans, 1995), 292.

52. "Locke to Philippus van Limborch, 4 August 1704," *The Correspondence of John Locke*, ed. E. S. de Beer (Oxford: Clarendon Press, 1989), 8: 368n.

53. These are the words of the Tramp in John M. Synge, *In the Shadow of the Glen* (Boston: J. W. Luce, 1911), 14.

54. Claude Levi-Strauss, *The Raw and the Cooked: Introduction to a Science of Mythology: I,* trans. John and Doreen Weightman (New York: Harper and Row, 1969), 339.

55. This is what a true reformation does—purifies and restores—as Peter Matheson's wonderful *The Imaginative World of the Reformation* (Edinburgh: T and T Clark, 2000) points out.

56. Tom T. Hall, "Old Dogs, Children, and Watermelon Wine" (1975), *The Best of Tom T. Hall* (Nashville: Mercury, 2000). See also www.allcountry.de/Songbook/Texte_O/Old_Dogs_Children_And_Watermel/body_old_dogs_children_and_watermel.html. Accessed 21 January 2002.

57. The phrase is that of Charles Sanders Peirce, *Collected Papers,* ed. Charles Hartshorne (Cambridge: Harvard University Press, 1938, 1958), 5:119.

58. Bernard J. F. Lonergan, *Insight: A Study of Human Understanding* (New York: Philosophical Library, 1956), 8.

59. Credit for the no-till analogy goes to Steve Ayers of Hillvue Heights Church in Bowling Green Kentucky and author of *Intimacy with God* (Loveland, Colo.: Group Publishing, 2003).

60. *Ignis fatuus:* the light of combustion of marsh gas.

61. Ernst Troeltsch, *Social Teaching of the Christian Churches* (Chicago: University of Chicago Press, 1981), 1:92.

62. "He considered all disputes on dogmatic statements as unnecessary and injurious, due to misunderstanding; and this chiefly because the parties in the dispute did not take pains to understand one another and perhaps did not desire to do so because of personal jealousies or previous and private hatreds." See the introduction to *The Ecclesiastical History of Socrates Scholasticus,* ed. A. C. Zenos, in A Select Library of Nicene and Post-Nicene Fathers of the Christian Church, 2d ser., ed. Philip Schaff and Henry Wace (New York: Christian Literature Co., 1890), 2:xi.

63. Eileen Crowley-Horak, "Testing the Fruits: Liturgical Aesthetics as Applied to Liturgical Media Art" (Ph.D. diss., Union Theological Seminary [New York], 2002).

64. For example, in the Bath National Park in British Columbia, alpine meadows are so fragile that the authorities are posting signs asking people not to walk in the meadow but to walk the paths and stay on the corridors.

INTRODUCTION TO THE CONTRIBUTORS
Leonard Sweet

FOUR YEARS BEFORE HIS DEATH, English essayist and literary critic William Hazlitt wrote an essay titled "Of Persons One Would Wish to Have Seen" (1826). In this essay, he describes a night spent by some friends assembled in Charles Lamb's chambers, playing the game of nominating the great men of the past they would like to engage in conversation and encounter "in their nightgown and slippers." (Lamb teased the company by putting forward Judas Iscariot.)

This book is intended to create a similar experience. Some of the greatest minds of the church today have been asked to face off across the room. We navigate by stars, and the gravitational pull of these five "stars" is steering the church in the twenty-first century.

Conversation is an old word that means "to turn about with." This book is about "turning about" and turning the church toward a right relationship with culture. We invite you to join in the conversation, feel the tension that crackles in the close air, and watch the sparks fly. Note where the conversation gets noisy, where it gets quiet, and whose heart is not in which battles. What tests the temper? What jolts the conversation? What themes resonate below the surface? Depending on your perspective, moments of illumination will alternate with moments of irritation.

Jacques Derrida has said that the "most difficult question" is telling the who apart from the what—separating the author or thinker from the author's work or thought. This introduction is a personal map of the "stars" to reveal who these conversation partners are. A good poem, Nobel laureate Seamus Heaney says, "allows you to have your feet on the ground and your head in the air simultaneously." Likewise, all of these authors are seeking to turn the church back to the "classics" at the same time they are dreaming new dreams for the church.

ANDY CROUCH

Andy Crouch proves the adage wrong that you can't start a fire with young wood. Still in his 30s, Crouch is the young man in our midst who is asking the tough questions (he calls postmodernism "today's academic Rorschach blot on which nervous modernists and others project all their fantasies, both benign and terrifying"), questioning the church, exposing the hullabaloo in the holy, and reminding us that the road from Thebes to Athens, as Aristotle has written, is not the same as the road from Athens to Thebes.

As editor-in-chief of *Re:generation Quarterly* and a featured columnist for *Christianity Today*, Crouch has found receptacles for editorials and essays distinguished by innumerable felicities of thought, unstoppable witticisms, and biting satire, and a home for perspectives on the church that are more than zeitgeist drainage bins. No one exposes the world of placid contradictions, flaccid thinking, or surface clarity more skillfully than Andy Crouch.

An enemy of the offhand, hands-off treatment of subjects and the treatment of people as objects, Andy recommends that when Christians disagree, we "lock ourselves in a room together, for life…Cease the noise of solemn resolutions…The ideal instead is hand-to-hand combat, the kind that not only forces me to wrestle with my opponent's flesh-and-blood humanity but leads us into a dance, a sword fight that could become a conversation" ("Making Enemies for the Sake of the Gospel"). I can testify from experience that Andy practices what he preaches.

A specialist on spirituality and campus life, Crouch bridges the worlds of academe and the church, the life of the cathedral and the life of the chapel. His favorite definition of postmodernism is "advanced consumer capitalism" in which a "sea of options and choices" has "relativized" everything and "rendered everything level." Formerly a staff member with InterVarsity Christian Fellowship at Harvard University, Andy received his theological training at Boston University School of Theology. A lifelong United Methodist, Andy is a worship leader for contemporary services and has edited along with three others a *Worship Team Handbook* (2002).

After an experience at a prayer meeting in the 1860s, Fanny Crosby confessed, "I sprang to my feet shouting 'Hallelujah,' and then for the first time I realized that I had been trying to hold the world in one hand and the Lord in another." Andy hacks his way through theological undergrowth that most dare not enter, able to cross vale and dale because he functions in a gravitational field of divine energy in which "the whole world's in His hands."

MICHAEL HORTON ▷

The great Russian novelist Leo Tolstoy (a vegetarian ascetic) weighed only 126 pounds. The Soviet edition of his collected works, published over a period of 30 years, came to 90 volumes. Tolstoy's words weighed more than his body.

Michael Horton is well on his way, writing faster than most of us can read. Already author or editor of 14 books at a young age, Horton also is editor-in-chief of *Modern Reformation* magazine. From his academic post as associate professor of apologetics and historical theology at Westminster Theological Seminary in California, Michael is bringing back the rallying cries of the Protestant Reformation: *sola scriptura, sola gratia*.

At a time when there is a global rush toward things Orthodox or Catholic (both Roman and Eastern) or Pentecostal, Michael Horton is the pit bull of Protestantism. To those who say Protestantism is a spent force or "deeply unfashionable today," Michael counters that Protestantism can be as seismic a force in the future as it was in the past. For those who see Protestantism's fate so linked with modernity that the end of one (modernity) spells the end of the other (Protestantism), Michael is a fierce polemicist. In tones reminiscent of John Calvin, John Knox, Jonathan Edwards, and J. Gresham Machen combined, Michael decries the way an experience culture has shifted evangelicalism "from a God-centered, Reformation theology to a human-centered, Arminian one."

From his chair as cohost of *The White Horse Inn*, a syndicated radio talk show exploring reformational theology in American Christianity, Michael is championing a second Reformation, shuffling the theological deck of cards to bring together Calvin and Luther, a critical mind and a believing heart. Horton chews up political correctness and spits it out. He speaks a good word for doctrine at the same time as he attacks junk theology and the spiritual atrocities of dispensationalism, the culture of the therapeutic ("God seems more user-friendly, more approachable, more like us, but less worth worshiping or entrusting with our eternal destinies" (*The Face of God*, 1996), church-growth movements, social justice activism, signs and wonders, and personality cults (see his thesis "The Gospel of Power Is an Enemy to the Power of the Gospel" in *Power*

Religion, 1992). To adapt the aphorism about Immanuel Kant, evangelicals can do theology with Horton or against Horton, but certainly never without him.

Michael combines rigorous academics (Ph.D. from Wycliff Hall, Oxford; M.Div. from Westminster Theological Seminary; B.A. from Biola University) with pastoral sensitivity. A minister in the United Reformed Churches, he has served as copastor of two churches in Southern California, where he and his wife, Lisa, reside. Michael is the only one of the contributors to have directly critiqued Niebuhr's *"Christ and Culture"* (chapter 2 of *Where in the World Is the Church?* 1995). He has also written a book on worship (*A Better Way,* 2002) and a primer on the Apostle's Creed (*We Believe,* 1998). He is currently president and chairman of the Council of the Alliance of Confessing Evangelicals.

In every one of his books, Michael challenges evangelicalism's anti-intellectualism, prudish sobriety tests, and humorlessness. He shines his light in the darkness of a church that he believes is in worse shape than the medieval church, cringing in a corner, safely parked in its "Christian subculture," selling out to a meadows mindset that lets the noun Christian become an adjective. Only the true church can fight the "spirits of the flaming night" with Jesus' words from Gethsemane: "Your will be done." Alleluia!

FREDERICA MATHEWES-GREEN ⊕

Don't ask a biologist, "What is life?" Don't ask a philosopher, "What is truth?" Don't ask a physicist, "What is matter?" Don't ask a theologian, "Who is God?" Don't ask, that is, unless you're prepared for a torrent of technical and nit-picking jargon.

Do ask Frederica Mathewes-Green, however, who is not afraid to tackle the basic questions of human existence. Whether in her role as an NPR commentator on *Morning Edition,* as a columnist for *Beliefnet.com,* or as a regular contributor to *National Review Online, Christianity Today, The Christian Reader, Touchstone, First Things* and *Our Sunday Visitor,* Frederica's writings on life and faith are impossible to put down. Often compared to Annie Dillard's, Frederica's writing approaches what George Orwell said he longed for in his prose: the transparent lucidity of a pane of glass.

A Southerner by birth (Charleston, South Carolina) and education (Masters from Virginia Episcopal Theological Seminary), Frederica married in 1974 Gary Mathewes-Green, who would later become Father Gregory, a priest of the Orthodox Church. She and Gary have three children, and Gary is the priest at Holy Cross

Church near Baltimore. Frederica's spiritual pilgrimage from Episcopalianism to Orthodoxy is the subject of her memoir *Facing East* (1997). She draws on a deep knowledge of the ancient and the postmodern in *At the Corner of East and Now: A Modern Life in Ancient Christian Orthodoxy* (1999) and in *The Illumined Heart: The Ancient Christian Path of Transformation* (2001), in which she demonstrates how toughness can be shown as much by a fast as by a fist. In her widely anthologized essays, she throws precisely aimed darts at the most vulnerable places, including our atrophied sense of a life swathed by the divine in mystery and majesty.

Frederica is impressively good at getting debates going on subjects that strike all and scare most (*Gender: Men, Women, Sex, Feminism*, 2002). Her advocacy of early marriages (she got married herself a week after graduating from college) as a creative response to our misbegotten mess shoves culture-centered reasoning off its pedestal as the apex of the universe. And there's a new book just out—*The Open Door: Enter the Sanctuary of Icons and Prayer.*

In a world that is constantly changing, Frederica's writings remind the church that the world is ultimately looking for something stable and unchanging—the Jesus Rock that is more solid and stable than any Jurassic rock.

BRIAN D. McLAREN ⊗

In 1947 young novelist James Kennaway wrote to Bernard Shaw, inviting himself to tea:

I am no fond regarder
Of pompous interview
But I come from Auchterarder
And I'd like to chat with you.

Shaw replied somewhat proudly that "thousands more" would love to do the same. Regrettably, however,

I have not tea enough for you
Nor teacakes in my larder
And so send this rebuff to you
Dear lad from Auchterarder.

Unlike Bernard Shaw, Brian D. McLaren always keeps enough teacakes in his larder and time on his calendar for the "thousands" who seek his advice and counsel on how to do church in a world in which a pastor might ask a new member, "Do you have prior church experience?" and receive the answer, "Well, I was in karate once, and our coach got us doing some meditation." If Thomas Jefferson could write 22,000 letters with a quill pen, imagine what wonders Brian is yielding with a keyboard and a wireless network. A senior fellow with Emergent, Brian is known for a generous and irenic spirit that never posits an "us against them" mentality but finds openings to diverse ways of being Christian.

An English scholar (the unlikely product of a Plymouth Brethren upbringing), Brian left academia in 1986 to become founding pastor of Cedar Ridge Community Church, a nondenominational ministry in the Baltimore-Washington corridor. Widely sought on the lecture circuit, Brian spends a lot of time explaining the meaning of *postmodern*, a word that, depending on who you ask, is charged with meaning, stands for everything wrong with the world today, has lost its momentum (indicating mostly that a lot of time has passed since the 1960s), or does not really mean "anti" or "after" so much as "growing from and moving beyond."

Brian wrote and published music (many of his songs are sung at his church) before he became a published author in 1998. Since then it has been a blitz: *The Church on the Other Side: Doing Ministry in the Postmodern Matrix*, 13 strategies for positioning churches in mission; *Finding Faith: A Self-Discovery Guide for Your Spiritual Quest*, a book that puts to shame the cultivated irreverence of the academic elite; *A New Kind of Christian: A Tale of Two Friends on a Spiritual Journey*, a fictional narrative that has struck a chord across the theological spectrum; and *More Ready Than You Realize*, a theological meditation on the "dance" of evangelism, based on an e-mail exchange between Brian and a dancing partner ("Alice"), that advocates that Christians are more ready to do evangelism than they realize and that postmodern people are more ready to hear the gospel as story (not as argument) than we or even they realize. Brian's most recent writing projects include *The Story We Find Ourselves In*, a sequel to his earlier fictional narrative, as well as collaborations with Leonard Sweet (*"A" is for Abductive: The Language of the Emerging Church*) and Tony Campolo (*Adventures in Missing the Point: How the Culture-Controlled Church Neutered the Gospel*).

Brian is married to Grace, a corporate team-building consultant, with whom he has four children. His hobbies include all things outdoors, especially the breeding of endangered species of turtles, who roam freely in his fenced suburban backyard. In trying to get both the church and academy out of doors, Brian is harking back to the origin of the word *academic*, which derives from the Garden of Academus, where Plato held his classes outdoors. Brian will not be happy until the Make a Wish Foundation can report that the majority of wishes they've helped come true don't involve visits to Disney parks but rather involve visits to places where God does his best work—like meadows.

ERWIN RAPHAEL McMANUS

Those of us who live in seminaries often think that once people have learned spiritual disciplines or a scholarly discipline, they are prepared for ministry in today's world.

Not so. Disciples of Jesus are people who not only have mastered the spiritual disciplines but also are disciplined in the art and science of turning the world upside-down.

Erwin Raphael McManus is turning the world upside-down. A self-proclaimed "cultural revolutionary," he has chosen to engage the one place where the world comes together and the future comes from—Los Angeles. Like Joshua, Erwin's call is to mobilize and lead a tribe of "spiritual warriors" that would bring freedom to the one place that would in turn bring deliverance to all nations. This global tribe of spiritual revolutionaries is known as Mosaic. Mosaic's epicenter is in the heart of L.A., but its reach extends far beyond. From Mosaics in Berkeley, Seattle, and Manhattan to apostolic teams in New Delhi, Istanbul, and Bejing, Mosaic is fulfilling her dream that Los Angeles inhales the world and exhales the gospel. With his wife, Kim, three children, and those who are part of the Mosaic movement, Erwin labors and thrives from the city to the ends of the earth.

The more Erwin particularizes his ministry in a place, the more universal his ministry becomes. For years investing his life and unlocking the neglected potential of the urban poor, Erwin now focuses on unleashing a movement of creativity, entrepreneurialism, innovation, and artistry that will allow the church to do nothing less than astonish the world around her. On his journey he expressed his faith as musician, songwriter, poet, talk-show host, street preacher, crusade evangelist, author, futurist, pastor, professor, church planter, and founder of Awaken. Poet W. H. Auden was right when he wrote that the best an artist can hope for is to be, like cheeses, "local but prized elsewhere."

Erwin serves as cultural architect of one of the most multicultural churches in America. The name of his church—Mosaic—is an incantation of the future. It's also a symbol of his journey. He was born in San Salvador but raised in Miami. His grandfather taught him reincarnation, but his grandmother taught him Jesus. His undergraduate training is in psychology from the University of North Carolina at Chapel Hill where his philosophical quest led him through periods of atheism, agnosticism, and mysticism. But his theological training is from Southwestern Baptist, thanks to Jim Henry of First Baptist Church, Orlando, who led Erwin to faith in Christ. Erwin began his ministry working and planting churches among the poor, but he also has served as a guest professor at numerous universities and seminaries (currently Bethel Seminary).

Partly because of his mosaic past, Erwin is at home in the pluralism of the postmodern setting, although he doesn't like the words *pluralism* and *postmodern* (the latter because of its semantic mobility; the former he redefines as "cultural jazz, a world full of differences, opposites, and contradictions striving to compose a collective melody"). Erwin's Bible is not a big flat prairie. Like any true park, it has pits, peaks, lakes, and valleys.

Erwin's background and church setting enable him to minister to the postmodern and the emerging, the Asian and the Euro, the urban poor and the urban rich, the academic and the aesthetic, the local and the global. Identity can be as much something flowing and fluid as fixed and stable, and the enriching sense of belonging to different cultural terrains is a lasting legacy of Erwin's ministry. Erwin does not write "early to bed with tea" kinds of books. The titles alone (*An Unstoppable Force*, 2001; *Seizing Your Divine Moment: Dare to Live a Life of Adventure*, 2002; *Uprising: A Revolution of the Soul*, 2003) are electric-shock treatments to churches that have dug themselves so deep into a hole that the hole has become a grave. As a futurist, Erwin's globally synoptic analyses show how things change—and not always for the best. But few challenge the church more to take risks and win victories for God. Erwin's radioactive presence is powered by prayer and a recognition that the Holy Spirit moves where he will. We try to move him by our will and way, our gimmicks and gadgets, but he resists all our harnesses. In the poetic mosaic of Christ and culture, parochial and cosmopolitan, urbanscape and countryside, Erwin's writings provide us with "a hole in Heaven's gable."

ANDY
CROUCH

Andy Crouch

Life After Postmodernity

ON A HOT, SUNNY DAY EARLY in the twenty-first century, I took my five-year-old son to see the high-water mark of modernity.

As we drove over the causeway onto Cape Canaveral in central Florida, the third largest building in the world rose on the horizon—the Vehicle Assembly Building, a massive gray box with doors the size of skyscrapers, where the Apollo missions' rockets were prepared for their crawl to the launchpad. Devoid of ornament except for the massive American flag painted on one side, designed along the most utilitarian lines possible (up close, in spite of its scale, it reminds me of the corrugated-aluminum equipment shed on my grandfather's dairy farm), it is an unlikely temple. But it is as much the architectural embodiment of transcendent longings, animated by a compelling master story and focusing the wealth of a civilization, as all the cathedrals of Europe—several of which, come to think of it, could stack very nicely inside.

The moon missions mobilized hundreds of thousands of Americans galvanized into action by the Russian *Sputnik I* satellite and by John F. Kennedy's dramatic call on 12 September 1962 to put a man on the moon within 10 years. Invoking explorer George Mallory (who climbed Everest "because it is there"), Kennedy declared, "Space is there, and we're going to climb it, and the moon and the planets are there, and new hopes for knowledge and peace are there. And, therefore, as we set sail we ask God's blessing on the most hazardous and dangerous and greatest adventure on which man has ever embarked."

{ ✿BRIAN D. McLAREN: *Of course, beneath these noble words hid the chill of the Cold War and the fear of the Russian communists (and the desire to get to the moon before they did for a host of reasons). So even this noble achievement— seemingly of pure science—is intimately connected to the engines of war Andy describes in a few paragraphs.* }

In response to Kennedy's call, NASA and its contractors deployed every tool in the modern arsenal and invented hundreds of new technologies along the way: microscopic control over surfaces and materials, macroscopic systems to harness enormous quantities of force and fuel, mathematical understanding of fluid dynamics and gravitational mechanics, and a global telecommunications system, aided at every step by the recent innovation of computing machines. They not only created the Saturn rockets and lunar landers, machines of dizzying complexity that had to work perfectly the first time; they also created a massive human infrastructure that dwarfed any before it, organized to maximize human talents while eliminating as far as possible every vestige of human error, ambiguity, and risk through intensive and extensive planning, training, rehearsal, and (should all else fail) redundancy.

And they did it.

There are other twentieth-century projects of equally vast scale that were also animated by compelling master stories and focused the energies of an entire nation. But most of them were ultimately failures, horrors, or both—the Holocaust (which was also aided by IBM computer technology), the collectivization of a vast agricultural and industrial economy in the Soviet Union, and of course the Manhattan Project and its mushrooms. The Apollo project, unlike the others, was a sweet success (with the exception of Apollo 1 and the near escape of Apollo 13). Men thundered away from our planet, walked on the moon, came home, and talked about it on the evening news in their taciturn, impossibly confident, sexy astronaut way.

To hear some prophets, and critics, of postmodernism talk, you might think that the Kennedy Space Center and all it represents is now a rusting, nostalgic shadow of its former self. The most overexcited folks will tell you (perhaps throwing in some French) that back in the bad (or good) old modern days, we actually believed we could know something about the world. But the certainties of the modern era are lost. Everything is relative. Scientific certainty is a myth (or a language game or a social construct), and the new generation, who are coming along fast and are about to invade your church (or who are staying away from your church in droves because you are so deucedly modern), don't believe in Truth. They are much more interested in Narrative, or Mystery, or just Nose Rings.

To be sure, these prophets { ⊗ *BRIAN D. McLAREN: I'm not sure which "prophets" Andy is referring to (since my name gets mentioned later on, I was worried I must be among them, but I have been assured otherwise), but his description here shouldn't be seen as an expression of thoughtful postmodern reflection. Rather, Andy's description seems to cobble together the most extreme statements that a motley assortment of people might say either on an off moment or if they don't really know much about what they're discussing. I certainly have never heard any one person regale anybody with this kind of "potted philosophy," but if any has, all I can say is that I join Andy in being turned off. No doubt "moderns," "postmoderns," and "antimoderns" (whatever they are) have created quite a few straw men that they have then attacked with righteous fury.* } probably regale you with this potted philosophy shortly after stepping off an airplane, which is itself a product of the same modern values that made the space program possible—mechanical complexity and precision, redundant systems, coordination, analysis, and control. If the captain's voice had come over the intercom before takeoff and begun to talk dreamily of Narrative or Mystery—"Ladies and gentlemen, it is truly a mystery how we manage to 'fly' to San Diego today. But is 'flight' really a metaphor for something else, and is there really any 'where' which we can truly call a destination?"—the postmodern prophets would have been hustling off the plane along with everyone else. Mystery is fine, but not when it's mission-critical.

And if you happen to visit Kennedy Space Center on the day when my son and I return, as I've promised him we will, you'll see him and every other five-year-old—the supposed heirs of postmodernity, along with most of their parents—dreaming of being an astronaut, gazing in awe at the *Saturn V* rocket that put a man on the moon.

IT'S SIMPLY NOT TRUE that our culture has somehow left modernity behind, even in the way that you can leave downtown Orlando behind but still have miles to go within its limits. { BRIAN D. McLAREN: *Andy is so right: You can't leave modernity behind. But here I think we should be careful not to play into a common and understandable misunderstanding about what many of us mean by the troublesome term* postmodernity*—a term that, although nobody likes it (including Jacques Derrida, who frequently says, "I cannot be held responsible for the use of this term!"), many keep on using because of the failure of a better alternative to appear. Again, postmodernity is not antimodernity. The prefix* post *means "flowing on from or coming after," not "unilaterally rejecting or naively dismissing." The term suggests continuity as well as discontinuity: A postpubescent adolescent, for example, still occupies the same name, lives in the same family, carries on the same story, and is at heart the same person as the prepubescent and pubescent boy. A postgraduate student similarly doesn't become anti-intellectual. If "postmodern prophets" oversimplify and exaggerate the differences sometimes, I hope they can be as mercifully treated as all should be who create ultramodern or antimodern straw men and, having thrashed them, declare to have vanquished postmodernity. In this regard, for Andy to insist that the prefix* post *is completely inappropriate and the prefix* ultra *is appropriate (as he does in the next sentence) strikes me as an either-or way of thinking that is neither necessary nor appropriate. I would never say that modernity is over. Just as the modern world arose in the shadow of the medieval world, and the two overlap and interact even until today (think of the modern West's ongoing dialogue—and too often, warfare—with medieval Islam), I would assume modern and postmodern realities to be both-and, not either-or. When I was in the prime of life in my 30s, I had children: Just because the next generation had been born didn't mean my generation was dead! Postmodernity, in my view, is the infant child of modernity, still small and quite insignificant, that may grow up to learn a little from its parents' mistakes. And of course it will make plenty of its own because we're talking history here, not Heaven!* } We are, if anything, ultramodern—more and more deeply embedded in, and committed to, modernity's fundamental impulses. Anyone opposed to the modern project can say goodbye to the hope of being intelligible, let alone relevant, to the vast numbers of Americans who make their living in medicine, engineering, global finance, and myriad other modern endeavors. The 1990s gave us the postmodern manifesto *The Matrix*, but they also gave us the modern bravado ("Failure is not an option!") of *Apollo 13*.

Yet there is no doubt that modernity has lost some of its swagger. America has never quite recovered from the other adventure into which John F. Kennedy led the country, the Vietnam conflict, whose monument receives one million more visitors per year than the Kennedy Space Center. In the wake of Vietnam (and Watergate, and the oil crisis, and the economic doldrums of the 1970s) America stopped going to the moon, and in the 1980s and 1990s NASA scaled back to projects that, while certainly impressive, were somehow less comprehensive and daring—such as the "smaller, faster, cheaper" interplanetary probes (many of which in turn failed). Americans over 30 today will never forget where they were when the space shuttle *Challenger* exploded, but we will not remember the loss of *Columbia* so vividly. Modernity's limits no longer surprise us.

On their own terms, the moon missions were a success. But somehow they failed at the level of metaphor. The moon and the planets were there, indeed, but we've been there, done that, and "new hopes for knowledge and peace" were not exactly fulfilled. We achieved escape velocity from earth, but not from history.

IN BLOOMINGTON, MINNESOTA, you can visit another enormous building. If current plans for expansion are carried out, it will eventually surpass the Vehicle Assembly Building in size—though it sprawls rather than towers over the landscape. It already encloses 4.2 million square feet of space and receives 10 times as many visitors a day as the Kennedy Space Center. And like the Kennedy Space Center, it is another high-water mark of sorts, the epitome of another facet of modernity. It is here, in fact, that postmodernity really begins.

The similarities between the Mall of America and the Vehicle Assembly Building go further than their size. The Mall of America is a surprisingly utilitarian affair from the outside. All the excitement is within. It too is the architectural expression of a dream, the apotheosis of that magical American combination "retail and entertainment," { ⊕ *FREDERICA MATHEWES-GREEN: My local mall uses the term* shoppertainment *and follows it with an ® so you won't steal their great idea for yourself.* } set free from the constraints of weather and location.

But the differences are also striking. The Vehicle Assembly Building is the expression of one enormous collective effort, a massively coordinated pursuit of an integrated goal. The Mall of America, on the other hand, is a disorienting bricolage of stores, restaurants, indoor theme parks, and even a roller coaster. Even the way it distributes its volume—horizontal and spread out rather than vertical and compact, dozens of entrances rather than a few huge doors—suggests something more haphazard. At the Vehicle Assembly Building, only one thing matters: a safe mission into space. At the Mall of America, you can choose your pleasure. Suits? Sneakers? Lingerie? Legos? Five hundred twenty stores wait to serve you. The Vehicle Assembly Building overwhelms with its one great purpose; the Mall of America overwhelms with its cacophony of options.

And so it is at the Mall of America that the much-heralded features of postmodernity come into view. Take Brian D. McLaren's nice summary of postmodernity in *A New Kind of Christian* (in the voice of his fictional character Neo), constructed by adding *post* to the features of modernity: "postconquest, postmechanistic, postanalytical, postsecular, postobjective, postcritical, postorganizational, postindividualistic, post-Protestant, and postcon-sumerist." Put a few of these into chart form (*p. 69*) and notice how nicely the two buildings seem to line up. { ⊕ *FREDERICA MATHEWES-GREEN: Andy's chart is very helpful. I'd quibble with only the fourth entry, on the grounds that lots of critique goes on behind the scenes. Marketing is a very aggressive science, and all the carefree detachment a mall implies is deliberately achieved. There are multiple, huge, obvious doors in, for example, while the exits are small and concealed. There is a reason for this. The mall experience may be emblematic of postmodernism, but it's achieved by modernist means.* }

So far, so good. But when we get to the last of Neo's points, we start to scratch our heads. Is the Vehicle Assembly Building and all it represents "individualistic," with the Mall of America being "postindividualistic" (whatever that would mean)? { ⊕ *FREDERICA MATHEWES-GREEN: A further complication with individualism is that conformity is being marketed to us under the guise of individualism. We are exhorted to stand out from the crowd by purchasing the mass-produced items that the crowd most approves. Individualism is a profitable illusion. As Andy Warhol said, "Someday everybody will think just what they want to think, and then everybody will probably be thinking alike."* } Not really—as we were tragically reminded in February 2003, even today's mission specialists are still "Spam in a can," quite consciously at the mercy of thousands of other people. Meanwhile, the Mall of America may be a magnet for families on vacation, but its celebration of individual preference and taste is quite simply unparalleled in history. Assuming you

Neo's categories	VEHICLE ASSEMBLY BUILDING	MALL OF AMERICA
Conquest / postconquest	Grand ambitions for the conquest of space, not to mention "peace and knowledge"	Ambitions are small and reachable— something affordable for every budget!
Mechanistic / postmechanistic	Pure machinery, no aesthetics	Machinery hidden; aesthetics, stories primary
Secular / postsecular	Scientific austerity leaves little room for reminders of God	Meditation and prayer room for employees; prominently placed religious information for visitors
Critical / postcritical	Elaborate systems of error-checking, performance review	Only critique comes if you try to walk out of a store without paying
Organizational / postorganizational	Highly regimented bureaucratic structure, the work of a nation-state	Hundreds of autonomous businesses, hundreds of thousands of autonomous shoppers

have a credit card, there are few places you can feel more gloriously autonomous than the Mall of America.

As for the modern moon missions being consumeristic, they actually represented an eagerly embraced national sacrifice that exceeded $25 per year for every man, woman, and child in America. True, they did introduce Americans to Tang and Teflon, but somehow consumerism isn't the word that comes to mind. And the Mall of America postconsumeristic? Not unless I'm missing something. { ❀ *BRIAN D. McLAREN: Andy's line of reasoning assumes that the Mall of America is indeed the icon of postmodernity and that wherever you find consumerism, there you have modernity. No, I would go back to what Andy said before: The Mall of America is a classic example of ultramodernity, not postmodernity. He seems to have pulled a bit of a bait and switch, I fear: told us that postmodernity didn't exist and then told us it did, but located it in an icon that to me is clearly an example of modernity. I'm sure Andy is out to make a worthwhile point or achieve a worthwhile end, but I wish we could get there with him without needing to accept these assumptions.* }

So something is not quite right about Neo's list. Modernity { ❀ *BRIAN D. McLAREN: I think, after this response, that I should avoid redundancy and stop commenting on the huge differences between the way Andy and I use the term postmodernity. It seems clear that for Andy, postmodernity means all that is worst about modernity coalesced into one glob of ultrasuperficial, superdestructive, otherwise negatively prefixed consumerism. With this definition of postmodernity, neither I nor my friends who might be lumped by him in the ignoble club of "postmodern prophets" would agree. When we say Postmodernity, this is not what we mean at all. So here's a proposal. When replying to Andy in the rest of this piece, I'll try to accept (with some pain) his equation: Postmodernity in this chapter equals ultra-modernity. ❀ Having accepted that shift in nomenclature (just as if I were going to say casa instead of house when talking to a Spanish friend, or if I agreed to refer to red as gray for a colorblind friend), speaking Andy-esque, I agree. I agree that the Mall of America, the Kennedy Space Center, Hollywood, Wall Street, and the stainless-steel kitchen sink are shining icons of ultramodernity and that the consumerism that drives them is every bit as profoundly dangerous as Andy says. But I should protest, one last time, that what I and others mean by postmodernity has little to do with this depiction; we're talking about something else. In fact, what we mean by the term is a small, very small (as dwarfed by the size and power of modernity as Martin Luther or Menno Simons were dwarfed by the medieval synthesis of church and political force— so insignificant compared to the Mall of America that Andy can't be blamed for missing it) resistance movement against ultramodernity (which, I realize, Andy believes is postmodernity). How's that for a confusing situation?* } is not particularly individualistic or consumeristic (how could a paradigm favor monolithic organizations and individualism at the same time anyway?). The "modern" 1950s pale in comparison to this "postmodern" era's dissolution of bonds in the family, workplace, and community. By the same token, consumption is woven into every facet of our lives in ways that were unimaginable 50 years ago. Furthermore, modernity—the disciplines of conquest, control, organization, objectivity, and critical thought elevated to a massive scale—is alive and well, continuing to drive our global economy and the aspirations of billions of people. The Mall of America could not exist without the thoroughly modern enterprises that put cash in the wallets of consumers, fly them in from all over the world, and manufacture and distribute goods to the hundreds of stores those consumers visit. And yet we all sense that the Mall of America represents more than modern business as usual. What is going on?

PERHAPS THE BEST WAY to resolve this conundrum is to see that postmodernity is not a departure from modernity but a development within it. And postmodernity—the cultural phenomenon—is most neatly summed up as the outworking (in both philosophy and lifestyle) of the consumer economy that modernity has made possible, just as postmodernism—the intellectual phenomenon—is the intensifying and completion of a modern project that began hundreds of years ago. Postmodernity is, in fact, the product of prosperity. It is the way that modernity, whose still-humming infrastructure is the greatest productivity engine ever created, spends its cash. { ⊕ *FREDERICA MATHEWES-GREEN: See David Brooks'* Bobos in Paradise. *The contemporary ideal is to be both hardworking (bourgeois) and artistically contemptuous of bourgeois ideals (bohemian)—hence "bobos."* } Sitting on history's greatest pile of riches, the surplus of a century of modernity's disciplined efforts to improve the human condition, the postmodern generation is analogous to the heirs of a vast fortune who (in a manner of speaking) no longer have to work for a living. { ♥ *ERWIN RAPHAEL McMANUS: Andy, I couldn't agree with you more. For those of us who play chess, the distinction is between the modern and the hypermodern. Yet the game is on the same board with the same players. What most are describing as a new era is simply the extension of the former. NASA by itself as a metaphor for the modern might be a bit too noble. It's good that you mention Vietnam. Certainly modernity has been fueled by conquest and colonization. At the same time, your metaphor for postmodernity is both illuminating and hilarious. I've been to the Mall of America. (I guess this is a confession.) Your observation that the postmodern is fueled by a consumerism* *borne out of prosperity is so right on target. In some ways, the shift seems to be from mass consumption to niche con-sumption. I think your conclusion that the megachurch is the postmodern church will be a great distress to many "postmodern expressions" that have as their focus their own niche idiosyncrasies.* ▷ MICHAEL HORTON: *While it is certainly true that there has been a backlash against some dominant traits of modernity, it seems pretty obvious that modernity has carried around within itself its own critique (romanticism, for example) and that postmodernism is perhaps just one more "development within" modernity, as Andy suggests. With him I cannot help but think that so much of what we call postmodern is the triumph of global capitalism, as the Mall of America illustrates so well.* }

Who are the heralds of postmodernity? Teenagers and young adults—precisely those who most disproportionately live off the surplus of their parents' toil in the belly of the modern machine. And to whom is post-modernity least relevant? Anyone looking for a job, who quickly discovers that (now that the Internet bubble has burst) employers are not really into postanalytical, postcritical, postobjective workers. Nor (with a wave of cor-porate scandals still breaking as I write) are shareholders enamored of executives who do postmodern things with the books.

But this is not quite the whole story. Postmodernity is certainly the result of prosperity, but it is also the product of modernity's disappoint-ment with its grandest promises. This is the sense in which the postmodern prophets are quite right. The space program and other modern endeavors did not deliver the "knowledge and peace" that Kennedy could speak of with so little irony. Far from it. But they did deliver prosperity, and the things money can buy rushed in to fill the void. Postmodernity channels the exaggerated hopes and promises of modernity, along with those promises' disappointments, into the one thing we can still reasonably hope for: a great sale.

It's not hard, by the way, to fit the two major church movements of twentieth-century America into this grid. Denominational Protestantism is the Vehicle Assembly Building—a massive, integrated, command and control structure whose grandest promises now seem vaguely embarrassing but which even today controls the lion's share of resources and production capacity. That movement attracted the loyalties of a huge percentage of America's population in the 1950s and 1960s, and along the way it infused their culture with certain basic Christian language and principles that circulate widely even now. Don't write it off—especially in its more vital forms, like the Southern Baptist Convention—too quickly.

The megachurch movement, meanwhile, is the Mall of America—a horizontal, preference-driven, bricolage in which consumer choice is carefully cultivated and satisfied through myriad carefully tailored stores (small groups, specialized worship services, and other offerings). Inasmuch as the vast majority of its members are one generation or less removed from the denominations, the megachurch is also dependent on the denominations in much the same way that postmodernity depends on modernity: It taps the denominations' latent surplus of religious instruction and culture while also capitalizing on a widespread sense of disillusionment with those institutions. Like the Mall of America or any postmodern environment of retail and entertainment, the megachurch generates economies of scale by doing many small things well under the same roof. { ⊛ *BRIAN D. McLAREN: I think Andy's comparisons here are very insightful, but again, those of us whose names are (increasingly unhappily!) associated with the despised word* postmodern *(in this chapter, where it doesn't really exist except as a wholly owned subsidiary of modernity) are generally not associated with megachurches. The kinds of churches we seek to plant, lead, and encourage are themselves seeking to find a way beyond the modern megachurch, and I think Andy would be sympathetic to our search because he knows how hard it is to buck "monolithic" modern systems, whether economic or ecclesiastical.* ▷ *MICHAEL HORTON: Once more all I can do here is echo Andy. In an article on the socioethnic narrowness of the megachurch movement, I argued that it is difficult to imagine a successful inner-city megachurch movement. Instead of generating the diversity that we find in the apostolic churches in the inner cities of the Roman Empire, the dominant church-growth models seem to be driven by the same demographics as the suburban mall. Is it even possible to foster anything like the community in Acts 2 on the basis of market research?* }

It is common in some circles to describe the megachurch as modern. But I would argue that the megachurch is the postmodern church, exactly analogous to the Mall of America, except perhaps with more parking. We forget this because we forget what the pioneers of the megachurch were fleeing—the Vehicle Assembly Buildings of the denominations. Some decry the mall-like atmospheres of megachurches, but the Mall of America—postorganizational, postcritical, and all the rest—is the postmodern environment

par excellence. True, the megachurch is not postindividualistic or post-consumeristic, but then again, neither is postmodernity. { ▷ *MICHAEL HORTON: As David Brooks and others have argued, the boomer is typically someone who wants autonomous individualism and warm community simultaneously, without realizing that she cannot have one without seriously qualifying the other. However different their children may be, we dare not lose sight of the subtle ironies and celebrated contradictions of modernity and postmodernity. That postmoderns want more community, for instance, does not entail that they are willing to surrender their protean drives for self-creation. Many of the "postmodern" worship models I have witnessed have simply substituted transcendence-oriented whims ("I really like candles") for their parents' immanence-oriented ones ("I really like the cool technology"). But the real question is whether we are able to take seriously again the principle that God alone gets to prescribe how he is to be worshiped, insofar as that is revealed in Scripture.* }

THIS HAS IMPLICATIONS that have not been fully taken on board among those who want to plant self-consciously postmodern churches. Usually what such a desire comes down to is a sense that a certain market niche—defined by age, lifestyle, or philosophy—is being ignored by the denominational churches and megachurches in a given area. But this is akin to a small store seeking to serve customers that the national chains overlook. If the store succeeds, it (or one of its franchisees) will likely end up in the mall eventually—with no more friction than currently exists between Brooks Brothers and the tattoo parlor a few doors down. Even if the store should for some reason stay independent of the mall, it will be participating in the same consumer economy. (Most likely, of course, it has identified a very small niche with little growth potential and will eke out an existence whose only real reward is the smug satisfaction of not being "mainstream.") { ✸ *BRIAN D. McLAREN: Contrary to what Andy implies, the desire of many of us whom Andy seems to be targeting (rhetorically) is not to target (demographically) an age, lifestyle, or philosophy niche! (My church, for all its flaws, has a full age component, from birth through age one hundred, with GEDs and Ph.Ds, white-collar and blue-collar and no-collar, naturally and artificially bald, pierced and unpierced, but it has taken 20 years of "labors of love" to help our community reach this broad of an age spectrum.) And our desire is not to be postmodern churches either. Speaking for myself (but everyone I am associated with would say the same thing), my desire is to serve God by making disciples of Jesus in authentic community, for the good of the world—the world God loves (I believe!), today's world, and tomorrow's, with all of our massive problems. If I believe Andy's paragraph, where the modern church in all its forms is captive to a banal modernity and where attempts to break free from* *some of the destructive features of modernity are even worse, what can I do but get depressed and give up? Critiquing the status quo is a lot easier than trying to plant and pastor a different kind of church and change the status quo. Andy knows this because he has spent his own blood, sweat, and tears trying to build a magazine (a magazine being a slick product of modernity if there ever was one) that escapes the gravity of modern (or ultramodern) consumerism too. }*

Meanwhile, like any large and successful postmodern enterprise, the megachurches are fast developing their capacity to license and franchise new ministry concepts. Just as Starbucks has readily expanded from coffee into chai, megachurches will continue to acquire the best talent from the current crop of experimental churches (perhaps nearly burned-out young pastors who suddenly have a few more mouths to feed), give them a steady salary, and help them reach many more customers. And just as independent coffee retailers get a free ride on Starbucks' massive efforts at making expensive coffee cool, even those "postmodern" churches that stay independent will be participating in the same cultural phenomenon that the megachurches spearhead.

There are few apologists left for the modern church, even within the modern churches. For modernity is disappointing. Not only is the Vehicle Assembly Building somewhere between plain and ugly, it also echoes uneasily with unkept promises. For every line of John F. Kennedy's speech that still rings in our ears—"We choose to do these things, not because they are easy, but because they are hard"—another line haunts us with its foolish (and ungrammatical) hubris—"This country…was not built by those…who wished to look behind them. This country was conquered by those who moved forward—and so will space." Has space been conquered? Should it ever be? What are the costs of modernity's drive to conquest? Why did we choose to go to the moon but not choose to conquer malaria?

But is postmodernity, as it actually is unfolding, so much better? At least modernity sent a man to the moon—postmodernity can only build a mall. Even supposing we can improve on the Mall of America, would we really want a world that was, for example, purely postorganizational? Do we want a postorganizational military? Postorganizational firefighting forces? Do we want a postcritical world in which careful, reasoned speech carries less weight than image and rhetoric? Will more Down's Syndrome babies and frail elders be killed in a world that is objective or postobjective? {▷ *MICHAEL HORTON: Amen! Despite its talk of epistemic humility, much of postmodern thought is just as prone to violence against the other. Think of the way certain varieties of deconstruction (especially that form associated with Stanley Fish) privilege the reader over the author to such an extent that the former is pronounced dead. If we cannot listen to authors (a practice that is dependent on an ultimate, divine author) and substitute all critical reflection for rhetoric, we will hardly be on guard against egoism. We will become sophists at best and at worst ripe for demagoguery.* } The pleasures of postmodernity, like the pleasures of consumption, are best enjoyed in small quantities. I would guess that the two features Neo ascribes to postmodernity that are most appealing to readers of this book are postindividualistic and postconsumeristic—the two features that postmodernity in actual practice clearly does not have. If we are waiting on the culture to evolve in those two directions, we may wait a long time.

But what if churches were not marching in step with either modernity or its wholly owned subsidiary, postmodernity? What if churches were genuinely living an alternative to both modernity's pretensions of control and postmodernity's fantasy of irresponsibility? What if, to borrow Vernard Eller's image, churches were not "commissaries" dishing up religious services like one more store in the postmodern food court but "caravans" traveling through the culture en route to another, better destination, equipped with the resources needed to make human life livable and joyful in the midst of a difficult journey?

IT IS ONE OF THE GREAT TRAGEDIES of Christian history that the two signs that most distinguished the church as a community—two practices rooted at each end of the axis of its history—had by the modern era been sent packing in different directions and have never truly been reunited. The first was the practice of baptism; the second was the practice of Eucharist—what much of the church has called the sacraments, the two practices of his own that Jesus explicitly commanded his church to continue. {▷ *MICHAEL HORTON: Our bearings have been so deeply set in terms of the poles of conservative and liberal (understandable up to a point, given our history) that we often fail to see that many of the key compromises with worldliness have to do with failures that cut across that divide.*

Conservatives and liberals alike, in my estimation, have dropped the ball on the sacraments. One of the most liberating aspects of Reformed theology for me, having come from a very low-church background, was its covenantal rather than conversionistic paradigm and the importance of Word and sacrament together, under the blessing of the Spirit. Aside from Andy's reticence to accept infant baptism (!), I could not agree more with the significance he gives to baptism and communion in these remarks. One of the reasons we are looking for drama in all the wrong places is because the real drama—the one that brings us into the action and rescripts us as new characters in Christ's body—is blunted in a variety of different ways. It is remarkable the extent to which conservatives and liberals alike are willing to substitute their traditions for the means of grace prescribed in Scripture. God's grace reaches us not just in any old way we see fit but through those means to which he has attached his promise. }

Paul's letter to the Romans gives an example of how deeply baptism had shaped the self-understanding of the early church. Writing to a congregation who were converts and thus presumably had a vivid memory of their own baptisms, in all likelihood by immersion, he could say,

Do you not know that all of us who have been baptized into Christ Jesus were baptized into his death? Therefore we have been buried with him by baptism into death, so that, just as Christ was raised from the dead by the glory of the Father, so we too might walk in newness of life. For if we have been united with him in a death like his, we will certainly be united with him in a resurrection like his. We know that our old self was crucified with him so that the body of sin might be destroyed, and we might no longer be enslaved to sin...So you also must consider yourselves dead to sin and alive to God in Christ Jesus. (ROMANS 6:3-6, 11 NRSV)

It is difficult for modern readers to grasp how concretely Paul is speaking here. The connection he makes between baptism and death is not a strange or innovative idea for the Roman church. They have had the experience of being physically plunged underwater, metaphorically buried and placed in the grave, then raised up from that watery grave by another's hand. Their bodies carry the memory of that death and resurrection, an imitation of both Jesus' own baptism and his final self-renunciation and rescue. { ⊕ *FREDERICA MATHEWES-GREEN: I found this confusing—Andy, are you saying that Jesus only renounced himself "finally," rather than at the original moment of the Incarnation ("he emptied himself, taking on the form of a servant," Philippians 2:7)? I'm not sure that self-renunciation is an accurate term for anything Jesus did—everything he did was fully*

an expression of his human-divine self, but the Incarnation was certainly kenotic, self-emptying. Likewise, the word rescue—
do you mean that he rescues us by his resurrection? That Jesus was rescued by God? "God raised him up," certainly, but the
Resurrection was an expression of the power of God within Jesus rather than something he passively received. }
Baptized persons, Paul insists, have quite concretely died and been raised
with a new identity, setting them free from their old bodies' enslavement to
death and enabling them to "present [their] members to God as instruments
of righteousness" (ROMANS 6:13, NRSV).

Furthermore, when in Romans 12 Paul picks up again on this language
of "presenting" our bodies to God just as candidates present themselves for
baptism, it is to drive home the point that what is raised from the water of
baptism is not individual bodies but a single Body: "I appeal to you therefore, brothers and sisters, by the mercies of God, to present your bodies
[plural] as a living sacrifice [singular], holy and acceptable to God, which is
your spiritual worship...For as in one body we have many members, and not
all the members have the same function, so we, who are many, are one body in
Christ, and individually we are members one of another" (ROMANS 12:1, 4-5, NRSV).
We go under the water as our (old) selves; we rise a new person whose identity
is "hidden with Christ in God" (COLOSSIANS 3:3, NRSV).

All this would have been intuitively clear for Paul's first readers. But
for many contemporary Christians, it is an abstraction that requires explanation and even then has none of the visceral, embodied force that it did
for its first hearers. The decision of most of the church, very early in its
history, to routinely baptize infants and the attendant reframing of that
practice into something closer to circumcision than crucifixion mean that
only Baptist and Anabaptist preachers can now read Paul's words in Romans
(and his other letters, almost all of which are suffused with baptismal
death-and-life imagery) and assume that the congregation has a bodily
memory to correspond with the images in the text. { ▷ *MICHAEL HORTON: My friends*
will not be surprised that I couldn't pass this one up! First, Andy is correct to note that the church began this practice of
including the children in the covenant of grace very early on: with the circumcision of Isaac, to be exact. Doubtless, in both
old and new administrations of that covenant, complacency is always a danger, but the answer is not to restrict the
application of baptism but to call our covenant children to repeatedly renew their baptism. We speak of "remembering your

baptism" not in terms of mental recall but in terms of remembering God's objective claim on us. We remember first and fore-
most the work that God did for us, to us, and within us through our baptism, but we also remember the responsibilities that
this placed on us as his liberated people. That this is not done very well today is an argument against not infant baptism but
the current state of preaching and discipleship, a condition that is no doubt due in large part to the very tendency to reduce
the significance of the sacraments that Andy rightly deplores. } And sadly, even in many churches that
refrain from infant baptism, the powerful connection between baptism
and death and the visceral resurrection implied in the lifting up of the
newly baptized person from the water has been lost, with baptism becoming
more an opportunity for the person to "witness" to his or her commitment
to Christ—as if baptism were about our commitment to Christ rather than
Christ's commitment to us.

And yet baptism could be the church's most powerful response—perhaps
its only response—to individualism. We who are baptized are no longer our
own—we belong to God (ROMANS 14:7-8, NRSV), and in belonging to God we belong
to the other members of the body. To the extent that we continue to grasp for
an individualistic identity, it is a sign of our failure to understand and live
into our baptism; to the extent that we are still distinct persons (which we
are), it is because we are distinct members, with particular gifts, histories,
and callings, filled with the identity and character of the one who "fills all
in all" (EPHESIANS 1:23, NRSV).

Baptism is our birth into a new order, a new community, something
different and distinct from the world in which our prebaptized bodies eked
out an existence. It is also an ongoing testimony to the evangelistic work of
the church, which is not content with self-replication (something that is so
easily presumed in communities that baptize infants) but is always seeking
the lost and offering them the opportunity to truly lose themselves and then
be found, by dying and rising with Christ. The only postindividualistic
community is the fellowship of the baptized. { ▷ *MICHAEL HORTON: Here, at the baptismal*
font (or baptistery!), Proteus is captured, chained, and forced to acknowledge his identity as the "nowhere man," receiving
a new name by belonging to a new people. The new creation is not simply regenerated individuals but the renewal of all
things, in which believers participate by new birth. Think of the New Testament metaphors: vine and branches, body, living
stones built into a temple, the church collectively as Christ's bride, a chosen race, and on we could go. Baptism and

communion both are explained in direct connection with these metaphors. Andy's point is so thoroughly and repeatedly explored in the New Testament that only a culture that is anything but postindividualist could mute its significance for us. }

And so baptism is the first practice that holds out the promise of taking us beyond both modernity and postmodernity, with their equally inhuman agendas of assimilation and fragmentation. The church that baptizes together, stays together—if indeed its leaders teach and live in such a way, like Paul, that the community is constantly reminded of baptism's meaning.

IF BAPTISM OFFERS THE ONLY WAY into true postindividualism, the Eucharist offers the only way into true postconsumerism. If baptism addresses our distorted sense of selfhood, communion offers us a truer way to consume. For in communion we quite literally consume the most basic of goods, food and drink, and that consumption is taken up into Christ.

In a remarkable article titled "The Economy of Mass," Fr. Mark Broski points out how subversive the Eucharist really is to human economies. In most religious systems, including the Hebrew sacrificial system, the more important a sacrifice is, the more important it is that it be costly. The Hebrews sacrificed their firstfruits and their firstborn animals as a sign that relationship with God was of principal importance. Lurking behind this system was the implication that—just as our consumer economy tells us—bigger, expensive, more costly is better.

But the Christian Eucharist turns this system on its head. What we "offer" at the table is the simplest food and drink that human beings can create. (In our culture wine is often associated with luxury, but in Jesus' day it was universal—and probably not nearly as tasty, the fermentation being both natural and needed to prevent spoiling.) We do not sit down at the table to enjoy a fancy meal with all the fixings (Paul rebuked some members of the church at Corinth who thought that might be a good idea); we do not even eat enough to physically nourish us. A communion wafer and cup are about as far from a supersize Happy Meal as you can get. And yet we believe that what we eat and drink is the bread of life (JOHN 6) and the fruit of the true vine (JOHN 15). If we indeed taste and see that the Lord is good, how can we rise from the communion table and go back to a life of frenzied consumption? { ⊗ *BRIAN D. McLAREN: This insight is, for me, the jewel in Andy's piece. So well said. I would also add that a life of stewardship (of resources, money, time, energy, talents) must follow as we rise from the communion table, with a renewed awareness that the whole earth is the Lord's, and we are created to be caretakers of God's world.* }

The Eucharist is the place where the church practices postconsumerism. { ▷ *MICHAEL HORTON: What an important point! Think of how this would transform our praxis. One of the reasons for the low view of the sacraments in our day is undoubtedly a failure to see their practical role, and yet, as Andy clearly points out, without baptism and communion being central practices beside the preached Word, the church is left without resources for a genuinely Christian way of being in the world.* } The communion table levels those of different economic means—poor and rich get the same portion. It effaces our carefully cultivated tastes—there is no menu, no list of options, no "good, better, best!" hierarchy of products. { ▷ *MICHAEL HORTON: Exactly. Whereas so many of our methods invite, "Come and try this! And if you're not completely satisfied, simply return the unused portion for a full refund," baptism invites, "Come and die, so that I can raise you in newness of life," and communion feeds us with Christ and all his benefits. We came wanting sweets because we had never actually been to a feast, but if the feast is actually spread, we can never go back to Egypt.* } In many churches that take communion most seriously, we do not even, properly speaking, "take" communion—the wafer is placed on our tongue. We receive a banquet, "without money and without price" (ISAIAH 55:1, NRSV). As the promises of communion become more real to us, we see the promises of consumption more and more as the insubstantial nothings that they are.

My point here, as with baptism, is not to argue for one of the many theological positions on communion that have emerged over the centuries. Rather, it is to observe the way that a more regular practice of the Eucharist—however it is exactly understood—has the potential to do what the culture is certainly not going to do for us: make disciples who practice the presence of God's economy and thus equip themselves to resist the consumer economy. { ▽ *ERWIN RAPHAEL McMANUS: I love and appreciate your passion for the centrality of baptism and Eucharist. Certainly the central metaphors carry with them the memories and convictions necessary to remain a truly apostolic movement, yet I find it impossible to agree with your conclusion that these two practices solve the problems that the church faces. Even if we reduce everything to individualism and consumerism, there is simply too much evidence to prove that even these two corrupting elements are not effectively dealt with through the practice of these rituals. While risking the danger of being insensitive and politically incorrect, could there possibly be a more dramatic proof that more is needed than the current crisis in the Catholic church? Those priests not only continuously participated in the Eucharist but in fact were the dispensers of this grace, yet they could not restrain themselves from consuming the fragile, innocent bodies and spirits of young children, especially the boys who were entrusted to their care. Certainly if the Eucharist gives us victory over consumerism, this tragedy would have been averted. }*

IN THE PRAGMATIC ATMOSPHERE of the American church, all this can seem rather unsatisfying. In order to be relevant to the postmodern culture, don't we have to talk about preaching styles, candles, video imagery, Narrative, Mystery, Nose Rings? { ❀ *BRIAN D. McLAREN: Again, contrary to Andy's critical tone here, many of us are talking about baptism and communion much as he is, and in fact, his insights (minus the critique) will enrich us in our discussion.* }

But if one wants to talk about relevance to postmodernity, it is hard to imagine a better place to begin than the sacraments. Take nose rings, along with the flip side of the postmodern coin, Botox and other forms of cosmetic surgery. What is being expressed by these forms of body modification if not the idea that our bodies are sites of meaning, even transcendence? Both tattooed teenagers and Botox-injected thirtysomethings are enacting their dissatisfaction with modernity's studied disregard for the body.

It is in modernity, after all, that increasing numbers of people work at jobs that require nothing of our bodies except that they be support systems for our brains. Postmoderns, even as they are fully implicated in the height of modern disembodiment in information technology, still know that bodies matter, not least because our bodies are, ultimately, all that we have. { ❀ *BRIAN D. McLAREN: Oops. It almost sounds like Andy thinks that postmodernity really exists here, as something distinct from ultramodernity. But ultramodernity should be even more body-unconscious than plain modernity, I would think, based on Andy's earlier comments.* } They also know that our bodies are capable of glory—of revealing something greater than themselves. And—again illustrating the way in which postmodernity both depends upon and reacts against modernity— they know that the very modern sterility and precision that make both Botox and tattoos acceptable for mainstream America also misses some- thing essential about our embodiedness: that we must be wounded to be fully healed.

The sacraments speak this embodied language in ways that words never will. In baptism, we subject our bodies to both burying and washing, to both death and rejuvenation, uniting the pain of piercing with the relief and restoration of surgery. In the Eucharist, we touch, taste, smell, see, and hear a story that then enters us as food and drink—a story of a body that was pierced and then glorified. In modernity's early stages it may have seemed possible to offer the gospel in disembodied form—though even that high modern form of evangelism, the stadium crusade, asked the convert to come forward bodily or at the very least to raise a hand—but in post-modernity, embodied forms of Christian practice will be essential.

The sacraments answer the postmodern hunger for a true story after modernity's impoverished recital of facts and figures. Week after week, they allow us to revisit the story of the Christian gospel—another's death for the sake of our life. But they do so in a uniquely comprehensive way, bringing us the words, images, sounds, tastes, and smells of that story—the splashing of water, the sound of a breaking loaf of matzo, the pouring of wine. (One of the deficits of grape juice as a communion element is that, unlike wine, it has essentially no aroma.) The sacraments are a "multimedia" experience orders of magnitude more powerful than a Hollywood production because they are enacted with real water, bread, and wine—not pixels, tweeters, and woofers—and because, most of all, they tell the world's truest story.

And when regularly practiced, the sacraments liberate us from the addiction to novelty that is the postmodern counterpart to modernity's quest for information. Baptism and the Eucharist do not convey any "news." They are accompanied by the same literal words each time. "For I received from the Lord what I also handed on to you," says Paul (1 CORINTHIANS 11:23, NRSV)—and what follows are words that, in some form, are present in almost every celebration of the Eucharist around the world and throughout history. "I baptize you in the name of the Father, Son, and the Holy Spirit"—these words say absolutely nothing new even while they compress all of salvation history into three personal names. The sacraments—and the liturgy that surrounds

them in many traditions—offer us a chance to detoxify from (post)modernity's clamor of newness; they are a declaration, astonishingly subversive to modernity and postmodernity alike, that all that truly matters in the world has already happened. { *⟡ERWIN RAPHAEL McMANUS: I would agree that what matters most has already happened. But I pray that all that truly matters in the world has not already happened. I'm reminded of the words of our Lord through Isaiah to Israel, "Forget the former things; do not dwell on the past. See, I am doing a new thing! Now it springs up; do you not perceive it?" (Isaiah 43:18-19). From Adam to Jesus, God points us forward. It shouldn't surprise us that he created us as time travelers with only the capacity to move into the future. I woke up this morning believing, perhaps hoping, that something I would do, something I would join God in, something that truly mattered, was about to happen.* }

THIS LIBERATION FROM NOVELTY has an important side effect. Second only to the Atlantic slave trade, no force in history has more effectively dissolved family relationships than modernity. The separation of parents from children in the modern West is justified by the demands of "progress"— which moves so quickly that only the young can keep up. The arrival of postmodernity has brought an intensification of this generational consciousness. Postmodern institutions like MTV go far beyond "generations," which demographers used to define as 20-year groups—they have cradle-to-grave marketing plans that segment their audience into five-to-ten-year cohorts, offering each group customized experiences that both create and perpetuate a sense of progressive distinctiveness from one another. ("Not your father's Oldsmobile" becomes, in its postmodern intensification, "Not your older brother's Oldsmobile.")

Following the postmodern cue, many churches now offer specialized worship services that depend for their intelligibility on fluency in a particular set of cultural codes. { *⊕FREDERICA MATHEWES-GREEN: How strangely these things loop is indicated by the comment made by a Southern Baptist friend. She said that her church had instituted a Celtic service on Sunday mornings before the "contemporary" service because "the old people want an early service, and the young people, of course, want something more traditional." Old and "traditional" young gravitate toward the Celtic service, while the midyears are "contemporary."* } Music, humor, forms of dress, styles of speaking all communicate more or less subtly that certain groups are in and others are out. Indeed, casual or contemporary services can be just as fascist as their formal or traditional counterparts—I once was told by a leader of a contemporary church that if a guest speaker wanted to wear a tie, he would not be allowed to speak. Anyone not already inducted into the relevant subculture who somehow wanders into such a service will feel strangely self-conscious. In their zeal to make friends in a certain generation or cultural niche, such churches make strangers of most of humanity.

And yet the sacraments, especially when surrounded by a traditional liturgy, make strangers of us all. They come to us from another time, place, and culture that none of us experiences as home; they do not flatter us by being new, current, trendy, or hip. But as the Greeks knew—their word for "hospitality," *xenia*, was cognate with the word for "stranger," *xenos*—it is only where there are strangers that there can be hospitality. The sacraments dispense with an easy familiarity. Instead, they say we are all strangers here, yet we are all welcome too. In that hospitality we meet across our differences and are caught up in a journey in which none of us is privileged, none of us knows the way any better than another, and yet all of us are finding ourselves accompanied by another who is explaining the Scriptures to us, revealing himself in the breaking of bread. It is perhaps not a coincidence that in many (though certainly not all) liturgically oriented churches that stress the sacraments, you can find worshipers in suits and worshipers in sneakers passing the peace in a crosscultural, multigenerational expression of community. { ▷ *MICHAEL HORTON: I have firsthand experience to illustrate this point. When Kim Riddlebarger and I planted a church in Anaheim, California, we were surprised at the rapid growth, fueled mainly by young people burned out on area megachurches. They wanted to be fed, both in terms of teaching or preaching and sacrament, and cared for (the spiritual direction of elders and temporal care of deacons). We failed in many ways, but Christ Reformed Church, with Kim as pastor, is a remarkably diverse community—the most ethnically diverse, in fact, in our mostly Dutch denomination. Elderly folks in suits and dresses sit beside professional women and surf rats in shorts—and not only in the worship service but also during various other events. I've seen many other examples substantiate the point that "product driven" (Word and sacrament) rather than "market-driven" (demographic niches) ministry builds genuine community that defies worldly measurements.* } If Americans ever become disillusioned with postmodernity's false familiarity, constructed entirely on the basis of tastes in clothing and entertainment, they will be hungry for the hospitable strangeness that the sacraments can provide.

But with all the attention American churches pay to everything from the fonts on the PowerPoint® to the greeters in the parking lot, it amazes me that I can think of only a handful of American { ⊕ *FREDERICA MATHEWES-GREEN: Don't you need to insert the word* Protestant *here? If you add up Roman Catholic, Orthodox, Lutheran, and Episcopalian churches, that's a lot of congregations. This confusion points to one of my questions about this book: Are we addressing questions of "Christ and culture" or "current American Protestantism and culture"? If the latter, why should we propose that "current American Protestantism" follow a principle of relating to culture different from what churches in other times and places should follow or different from what Christ himself is doing?* } churches that seriously practice both baptism—as a normative experience of death and resurrection that ushers us into a new community—and the Eucharist—as the definitive weekly source of nourishment for our myriad hungers—and structure their life around them. { ✳ *BRIAN D. McLAREN: Again, Andy will be glad to know that many of the churches associated with the "p-word" in this piece practice both sacraments with deep sincerity, reverence, awe, and value.* } I can think of many, especially in the low-church traditions, that hardly practice either one. I can think of many more that emphasize one but effectively neglect the other. Among the traditions most likely to be represented by readers of this book, the most common pattern is for the communion service to be tacked on periodically (sometimes unpredictably), with minimal teaching about its significance, and for baptism to be practiced more regularly but with little explanation of the radical transaction that occurs there. In almost no church that I know of are baptism and communion regularly the source for whole sermons, sermon illustrations on other topics, or Christian education—even though the New Testament itself would fall apart if you removed all the allusions to these two foundational practices in the life of the early church.

If we are not observing the two practices that reflect what the Bible says the church is—the Body of Christ that is nourished on his body broken for us—is it any surprise that our churches do not look like the Body of Christ but instead look like the clientele of one or another shop at the Mall of America, whether Brooks Brothers or the tattoo parlor? Is it any surprise that when our members change jobs and leave town, they give less notice to their small-group leaders than to their former employers—demonstrating their failure to understand that they no longer belong to themselves but to a body of which they are indispensable members? Is it any surprise that churches full of well-paid young professionals struggle to meet even lean budgets—demonstrating that the heart and treasure of the members are still more driven by *Cosmo* than by the communion cup?

I FEAR THAT IN THE CHURCH'S ZEAL to strain out the gnat of our culture's challenges to Christian belief, many are swallowing the camel of our culture's challenges to Christian practice. { ▷ *MICHAEL HORTON: This is why we should have trouble, I think, with any thick line of demarcation between faith and practice. Whether we are speaking of the torah in the Old Testament or the teachings in the New Testament, both law (command) and gospel (promise), things to be done and things to be trusted, are integrated. In conservative settings, the gradual devaluation of well-prepared sermons and liturgies can be, over the long haul, just as dangerous to the health of the church as attacks on the inspiration of Scripture. It is not just the doctrine of the covenant but the praxis of the covenant that must be maintained in each generation.* } Undoubtedly many crucial beliefs are at stake. Ultimate truth is threatened by relativism; the universal claims of the gospel are threatened by pluralism; the authority of Scripture is imperiled by the friction-free play of transgressive and suspicious readings. But the truth is that all of these challenges were well underway in the modern era—the skepticism of faith's avowed enemies (Hume), the reductionism of faith's alleged friends (Locke, Kant), the cacophony (or was it the cornucopia?) of the World's Parliament of Religions in 1893, the "nothing but" theories of Marx, Darwin, and Freud. Indeed, for much of the twentieth century, the modern united front cowed or converted most of American Protestantism—a feat postmodernism, with its chastened ambitions and self-consuming fragmentation, seems hardly likely to repeat. { ⊕ *FREDERICA MATHEWES-GREEN: Don't you mean "seems likely to repeat"? That is, postmodernism is no more likely to support faith than modernism, precisely because it is so fragmentary. It will not repeat modernism's united attack on faith, but it undermines coherence and prefers irony to any conviction. Sounds like all we can do is try to pander to and please its mercurial moods and hang on for the ride.* }

At any rate, there has rarely been a time or place in which the intellectual climate was sympathetic to the improbable fundamentals of Jewish and Christian belief. When or where has it ever been plausible that God acted most decisively in the history of an insignificant nation that spent most of its existence trying to avoid becoming roadkill on the interstate highway of commerce and conquest that was Palestine? When has the prevailing philosophical zeitgeist been willing to accept the idea that the divine absolute was disclosed in a thirtysomething vagabond with a pronounced Galilean accent? The Byzantine Empire and medieval Christendom secured a relatively friendly atmosphere for Christian belief only at the cost of an accommodation with imperial power { ⊕ *FREDERICA MATHEWES-GREEN: Actually, the church regularly suffered because of its resistance to imperial power, the iconoclast controversy being just one example. It was the distress at repeated Muslim attacks that led an emperor to first destroy an icon, in hopes of placating a God who apparently favored attackers who used no images. Christians died defending icons until empresses stopped the persecution—not once but twice.* } that inevitably poisoned the well for Christian witness outside of the Empire's borders—an unholy alliance that bears bitter fruit in the Muslim world to this day. We cannot be nostalgic for a time when Christian faith could be easily defended against its intellectually sophisticated critics—there is no such time to be nostalgic for.

And in fact, Christian belief has thrived when it has encountered challenge. It was critiques from pagans and heretics that led to the articulation of the creeds. The fall of Rome prompted Augustine to write *City of God*; the vigor of Islamic Aristotelianism spurred Aquinas to write *Summa Contra Gentiles*. Modernism, which seduced figures like Bultmann and Tillich into ultimately sterile theologies of accommodation (not to mention whole churches—think of 1930s German Protestantism or the Dutch Reformed Church in South Africa), also called forth the electrifying and challenging work of Kirkegaard, Barth, Bonhoeffer, and Niebuhr. We do not need to swallow any of these thinkers' work whole to see that it was the very adversity of their intellectual surroundings that produced their vital rereadings of Christian faith.

There is every reason to believe that postmodernism is calling forth new ways of reading the Scriptures and the Christian tradition that expose vitality in the unlikeliest places. "O the depth of the riches and wisdom and knowledge of God! How unsearchable are his judgments and how inscrutable his ways!" (ROMANS 11:33, NRSV). Why should we not hope that our generation, prompted by the new challenges of postmodernism, will discover new depths and previously uncharted territory in the gospel? From the "discovery" of irony in the gospel of Mark—something no postmodern Christian can fail to see and that no premodern Christian seems to have noticed— { ⊕ *FREDERICA MATHEWES-GREEN: If Mark's community did not use irony, it's not likely to be there, is it? I don't know the answer to that question; perhaps they did use irony. Ponderousness has historically prevented Christians from seeing the essential hilarity of images like a camel trying to squeeze through the eye of a needle. (Surely, they say, there had to be a gate named the "Eye of a Needle"? Such earnestly literal speculations, I hope, make Jesus laugh all over again.) Still, humans are inevitably disposed to read ancient documents through the lens of their own prevailing culture—in this case, a culture that is entranced by irony. I'd like to see whether irony was employed in other Christian and secular documents of the Middle East at that time and whether commentators who lived closest to the time of Mark observed irony in his gospel. If, Andy, you are claiming that Mark did not intend irony but it is nevertheless there, hidden by God like an Easter egg for us to discover 20 centuries later, that leads to an entirely different theological discussion.* } to the reclaiming of the political and historical dimensions of the Christian gospel in the work of thinkers like N. T. Wright, we are in the midst of an intensely exciting period in which the church, under the duress of new questions, is finding new languages and new songs. { ⊛ *BRIAN D. McLAREN: I hope other readers can hear me cheering for the preceding paragraph.* }

But the Scriptures warn us that getting belief right is hardly sufficient. Even demons have an adequate working theology (JAMES 2:19). The much more pressing question, in my view, is whether we have communities capable of receiving and incarnating the gospel. And this is a question of practice, not belief. The distinction between practice and belief is ultimately too easy, of course—no one would dare to practice the life of Christian faith if they did not have some reason to trust that the gospel were true; no one can sustain belief in the gospel for any length of time without practicing a eucharistic, baptized life. But the real danger to the church in the twenty-first century will be practical—the danger of succumbing to a way of life that renders even the most orthodox beliefs vestigial at best. To put it another way, the danger is the culture of postmodernity, not the ideology of postmodernism—the way postmodernity brilliantly sublimates modernity's frustrated ambitions into the addictions of consumption, compounded by the perennial temptation for the church to try to beat the culture at its own game.

Does the church have anything to gain by imitating the Mall of America and its ever more refined successors, whether the virtual (and increasingly commercial) communities of the Web or new temples like Chicago's Niketown, New York's Prada, or Seattle's Experience Music Project? No more than it did by imitating imperial power at the height of the Holy Roman Empire or modernistic science at the height of modernity. We will have something worth offering the world only if we joyfully and stubbornly observe the practices that make the church the church. { ✼ *BRIAN D. McLAREN: I don't want to be a killjoy (because I enthusiastically affirm Andy's second-half emphasis on Christian practices), but I must admit at least mild discomfort at elevating baptism and Eucharist as essential practices while neglecting love, reconciliation, peace-making, caring for the poor, generosity, joy, and service, for example. I know it's not really in the Gospels, but in my imagination I faintly hear someone saying, "Lord, Lord, didn't we practice the sacraments in your name?"* } **For the sacraments are, and have always been, the only practices that exert a strong enough gravitational field to attract and elevate the basic elements of human culture—water, food, drink, and ultimately our very bodies and souls—into a divine drama that transcends, judges, and redeems the world.**

{ ◇ *ERWIN RAPHAEL McMANUS: Andy, I, like you, long for the church to become the church Jesus Christ died for and dreams of. It seems to me, though, that we have nearly 2,000 years of evidence that the practice of the sacraments not only fails to bring this result but also clouds us from the reality of our situation. The rituals seem destined to form themselves as Christian superstitions, creating an improper relationship between cause and effect. They have all too often allowed the church to become a hollow shell while pointing at the sacredness of its practices. Isn't this where Christianity as a world religion and the movement Jesus Christ began 2,000 years ago part ways? The practices are not enough. Only Jesus has power enough to free us from the weight that holds us. The practices must point to the presence, but they are not the presence, nor do they guarantee the presence. At the same time, whenever he is present, he grows in us a great longing to follow his practices.* }

The church's job, Stanley Hauerwas says, is to remind the world that it is the world. Our calling is to expose the false promises of modernity's machinery of production and postmodernity's machinery of consumption.

{ ✼ *BRIAN D. McLAREN: I would want to add that we owe the world much more than critique of its false promises: love, service, care, understanding, grace, gentleness, and respect, for example. I fear we too often stop at critique and fail to practice the gentleness and respect modeled by Jesus and called for by Peter (1 Peter 3:15).* } And how will we do that? By reminding ourselves, week by week, that we live a story that does not conform to the way of the world. By dying to ourselves and being raised into a new community and by proclaiming the Lord's death until he comes again. By splashing, drowning, and breathing again; by breaking, taking, eating, and drinking; by affirming, against all the evidence, that only in these practices do we become truly human. By becoming together a "spiritual house" (1 PETER 2:5, NRSV), a "holy temple" (EPHESIANS 2:21, NRSV), small and seemingly lost in the midst of the world's massive buildings, but in fact the first and only outpost of the one kingdom that keeps its promises.

{ ⊛ *BRIAN D. McLAREN: Andy plays rhetorical hardball; he pitches some fast sentences, and he has a wicked curve that I find myself swinging at and missing once, twice, three times. (I feel like more of a Frisbee kind of guy these days.) On the brighter side, as my comments in the text make clear, although I found Andy's piece frustrating in many places (almost everywhere in the first half), there is much I agree with in the second half. I believe that consumerism (*greed *is probably the best biblical word for it, or "the lust of the eyes," or, with the poor of the world in mind, *theft*) is every bit as shabby as Andy says it is and worse. And I heartily agree with him on the value (this is an understatement) of practicing the sacraments much more passionately than we have in much of Protestant modernity (or whatever). So I say amen to so much in Andy's article, but with two recurring provisos. ⊛ First, regarding consumerism: Buying and selling aren't evil. They're part of God's world, and Scripture gives us moral guidelines to protect us from letting these good parts of life (a.k.a., "good work") go bad (don't lie, don't cheat, don't steal, do unto others, for starters). Andy himself makes and sells a magazine, and I'm sure he hopes to sell more copies of it. I would add that if you make canes, you are probably going to market them to older people and those who have been injured, not to parents of infants, to whom you will market diapers and rattles, which you will not market to teenagers, and so on. Andy's magazine, I'm sure, has some-thing like a target audience, and I'll bet some demographic discussions take place in his office, or at least in his head at times. (Meanwhile, Andy and I are participating at this moment in making a book to be marketed and sold—could we even say consumed?) So just as Andy is careful to warn "postmodern prophets" about oversimplifying or overstating their case, I want to join Andy in condemning the greed that seems to be one of the prime engines of our culture (post, ultra, or whatever), but I would also take care not to paint all commerce (creating, crafting, announcing, selling) as consumerism. ⊛ Second, Andy's punchy writing style makes it so clear what he's against; I wish I knew more about what he is for. As a mediocre (but trying hard) pastor who has tried to shepherd critics both old and young (many of whom seem to have been given the gift of discouragement), as a pastor who works in the trenches with good but imperfect people* *(who can sometimes be cranky and hard to please, demanding that their needs—or consumer preferences—be validated and met), I find myself wondering what Andy wishes would happen in our churches. And not only that, I wonder how we can talk about our wishes for what the church can be while avoiding cynicism and disillusionment about what the church now is. Dietrich Bonhoeffer talked about the destructive power of "wish-dreams" in the church, where our idealism about the church creates in us a disdain for it as it now actually is. I am reminded that a theologically refined and idealistically demanding taste in churches and their practices can subtly become a kind of religious consumerism in itself. Our dreams for the church are dangerous, yet dreaming is necessary. ✿ So I wonder: What kind of church does Andy dream of, beyond practicing believer's baptism and weekly Eucharist? If using contemporary music (or whatever) creates marketing segmentation in churches (because young people like it or older people don't), what style of music (or architecture, or preaching, or liturgy, or whatever) would he recommend, or how would he recommend making a choice about styles (since dominant styles of music, liturgy, preaching, or whatever are preferred by older or established market segments)? These aren't rhetorical questions. I respect Andy's mind and heart, and I think we'd all benefit from what he would offer by way of more positive recommendations. That's why I keep listening to Andy with respect and anticipation. ✿ In the meantime, I think Andy would agree with Michael, as I do: "Sweeping endorsements or sweeping denouncements make for light work," but leading into the future (which is always uncharted, whatever we call the epoch!) is a much tougher assignment, one which we're all in together.* }

Andy Crouch's Rejoinder

I'M GRATEFUL FOR—and humbled by—this conversation and sorry that it comes to an end, in book form at least, so soon.

I think I can address the concerns of Frederica and Erwin by emphasizing that it is not just some American Protestants who have lost hold, in my view, of the transforming power of the sacraments. Self-confessedly sacramental churches, too, while guarding the centrality of the Eucharist, have in too many cases hollowed out baptism so that what is left signifies no more than membership in the community. Indeed it often signifies, not least in the Orthodox churches, no more than membership in the culture. Attempts among the sacramental churches to reclaim baptism as a countercultural sign are always going to come up against the limited symbolic import of splashing a little bit of water over a baby's head (as opposed to, say, circumcising a male baby's foreskin or symbolically drowning an older person in water). Surely the right response to baptism, as seen, for example, in John the Baptizer's ministry, should be closer to awe than, "Aww, isn't that cute?"

But I am well aware that the sacramental combination I am proposing is, strictly speaking, available nowhere, even though it was (with due respect to Michael) the normal experience of the earliest Christians. Because no community of Christians changes its sacramental practice lightly, some creativity is required. I think the prospects are some-what better for churches that practice believer's baptism to rediscover the Eucharist than the reverse. But it is certainly possible for all churches to heighten their awareness of the dynamics at work in the sacrament that their tradition has, sometimes for good historical reasons, deemphasized.

Would a recovery of the sacraments solve our problems with assimilation into consumer culture, including its virulent expressions like pedophilia? Erwin (with Brian) doubts this—and so do I, if only because there is no such thing as a simple "problem" to be "solved." (There is no shortage of Protestant pedophiles, alas, though they tend to be youth ministers.) But put the question the other way around. If we are to be exercising the kind of faith that equips us to resist the lure of consumer culture, what practices will best strengthen our faith, hope, and love? Is such resistance to be entirely a mental or emotional exercise, or are there things we can do with our bodies to discover and dwell in God's new creation? Christians throughout history declare that there is something in being washed and in sharing a feast that assists in this process. Without encountering Jesus and being filled with his Spirit, no religious practice is anything but empty. But what person with faith in Christ would not want to practice that faith in bodily ways? That is what the sacraments are for.

Brian suggests that in equating postmodernity with ultramodernity, I have created a straw man that allows me to dismiss the creative possibilities of truly postmodern faith and practice. He is further concerned that I have unfairly lumped him personally, along with many of his fellow travelers, together with equally strawy representatives of a *consumeristic Christianity.*

All I can say is, if the shoe fits, wear it. And in Brian's case, the shoe clearly does not fit. He is one of my favorite writers on these topics, and my wife and I have more than once wistfully talked about his church as a remarkable expression of the kind of Christian community we would like to spend our lives in, not least because of its sacramental commitments. I beg forgiveness if I've said anything that implies otherwise.

But does the shoe fit when it comes to lining Neo's postmodern catalog up against expressions of consumer culture like the Mall of America? Is it not true that late consumer capitalism is profoundly postobjective, postanalytical, postcritical, and so forth? Is there not a strange disjunction between the first eight categories in Neo's list, which we see all around us right now and the last two (postindividualistic and post-consumeristic), which we see almost nowhere? I have specific friends (not Christians), sophisticated exponents of Neo's first eight values, whose life choices have embodied postmodern consumerism to devastating effect. And while I wish it weren't true, I have encountered many self-proclaimed postmodern Christians whose church practices reflect, often unwittingly and with the best of intentions, the enshrinement of personal choice and preference in all its gilded postmodern, or ultramodern, glory.

In this book, Frederica, Michael, and I—all occupying the more conservative half of one axis—zero in on consumer (indeed, bobo!) culture as one of the defining features of our "postmodern" moment, while Brian and Erwin (and also Len) say almost nothing about consumerism or, for that matter, postmodernity by name. Partisans of one camp might infer that we are reactionary conservatives fighting straw men; partisans of the other might conclude that our counterparts are naive arrivistes who are unwittingly propping up the worst features of the culture. Both sets of partisans would be wrong. We are, all of us, seeking the shape of faithfulness in an era that is both profoundly new and "nothing new under the sun." We are blessed to have life together at this time in history, when the illusions of modernity are so thin and the promise of the gospel once again so tangible. It is a great treasure to have these brothers and this sister as companions on the way. I look forward to the end of the story, when we will all laugh with amazement at what God did with our little efforts to see his will done on earth as it is in Heaven.

MICHAEL
HORTON

Michael Horton

Better Homes & Gardens

AN AD HAS RECENTLY APPEARED in a number of evangelical magazines for yet another Bible translation. In this ad, a woman, looking smart and sophisticated, stares intently at the reader. The caption says, "If you want to attract me, you'd better watch your language." The ad relates how busy this young professional is and demands that the Bible be tailored to her lifestyle. In many respects, this ad captures the mood of mission these days: unswerving devotion to the adage that the customer is king. Furthermore, this woman is "postmodern." The unstated question is, Are we postmodern? Should we be?

Naming "Postmodernism"

WHAT IS "POSTMODERNISM"? IT DEPENDS. To an architect, sculptor, painter, or novelist, it may be the reaction against the International Style and High Modern art and literature; to political theorists, it's the end of utopian ideologies; to philosophers, a transition from Cartesian foundationalism; and to economists, the shift from an industrial to an information economy in capitalism's global phase.

Reflecting the sloppy thinking in many of the hyperbolic announcements of a postmodern age is the failure of definition. Most often postmodernism is simply a code word for something new, a supposed break with the past (modernity) and the dawn of a radically new era. Of course, a more modern description of an era could hardly be found, as academic postmodernists will be the first to point out. Radical breaks with the past just don't exist, pace Descartes, Lessing, the French philosophes, and Kant. More approved by at least some postmodern intellectuals is Hegel's developmental theory of history, although the more Marxian among them would prefer the revolutionary (left wing) school to Hegel's more conservative version. On a host of points that we cannot pursue in this space (notions of tradition, language, the critique of autonomy, progress, presence and absence, and so on), thinkers classed as postmodern have a lot to teach us about what popularizers of postmodernism fail to recognize is little more than "most-modernism."

For our purposes, it seems to me there are two types of postmodernism: academic and popular. There is great variety among the former: Heidegger; French poststructuralism; Gadamer, Ricoeur, and Levinas; not to mention the convergence of continental and Anglo-American schools in the later Wittgenstein, Austinian speech-act theory, and on we could go. Remarkably fruitful discussions and debates abound in these deep waters, and I find myself among those who enjoy swimming in them. Modern foundationalism is a dead end, as any premodern Christian writer could have told us. { *BRIAN D. McLAREN: I really appreciate Michael's acknowledgment of the many nuances in this ongoing conversation about postmodernism and postmodernity, including the conversation about what the terms mean!* }

Without denying the existence of intellectual, social, and cultural transitions, one discovers a rather clear if sometimes winding path from Kant to Schleiermacher to Hegel and Fichte to Schopenhauer, Feuerbach, and Nietzsche that leads finally on to Freud and eventually to French deconstruction. Schopenhauer, for example, was talking about "reality" being nothing more than objectified drives and irrational urges and Nietzsche was reducing truth to metaphor long before Derrida or Rorty appeared on the scene, and the latter sees himself as simply building on the pragmatism of William James and John Dewey—hardly to be classed as post-modern. { *FREDERICA MATHEWES-GREEN: Whew! It's all I can do in this blizzard of surnames to keep these guys straight. Boy, do I feel uneducated. Somebody should have been standing outside the first paragraph, handing out name tags.* }

In fact, the debate between "modern" and "postmodern" worldviews is in many respects the ongoing debate between conceptual realists and idealists. It was Kant, not Derrida or Rorty, who introduced the modern world to the view that the "world" conforms to the knower's conceptual categories rather than vice versa. There is just too much of the modern in the postmodern to be able to speak in sweeping terms of a major paradigm shift in culture. { ❦ *BRIAN D. McLAREN: I wonder if the same could be said about what we call the medieval world and modernity—that there is too much of the Middle Ages in the modern to speak of the modern? In other words, I can agree with Michael that in an ultimate sense, these epochal terms are imprecise and problematic, obfuscating one thing as they clarify another. But once we start critiquing words for their imprecision (ironically, by using other equally critiqueable words to make the critique), where do we stop? No doubt our packaging of the flow of history into epochs is a convenient fiction that must be deconstructed so we don't take ourselves too seriously. But that's not to say there's no value in doing so. ❦ As Andy does in his chapter, Michael seems to me to be beating a horse that, if it's not dead, at least nobody is riding: I don't hear anybody calling the postmodern world a utopia. True, many of us do see new and exciting opportunities opening up, though "unprecedented" is probably an overstatement. But like Michael, none of us believes we'll find any unmixed blessings this side of Heaven!* } As Peter Berger and John Milbank have shown, much of the social theory that has underwritten both modern and postmodern thought is motivated by deeply theological factors—namely, the attack on God and on discourse that is grounded in his existence and sovereignty.

There is also great variety among popular versions of postmodernism, but I cannot bring myself to acknowledge that they are either sufficiently distinct from modernity or that they are sufficiently coherent to identify under one label. That much has changed since the storming of the Bastille and the invention of television, I do not doubt—some for the better and some for the worse. But the cheerleading for the idea that we have entered a radically new era, a utopia of unprecedented opportunity, fails to move me. I do not think it's because I am a stodgy conservative. (For the record, I enjoy "extreme" skiing and the Dave Matthews Band, fully aware that both may be passé by the time this goes to press.) Rather, it's because I just don't believe the hype. I think that every period has its pluses and minuses and that typecasting periods leads to demonizing or equally impulsive lionizing. This makes it hard to conduct cost-benefit analyses in particular cases because we have either bought postmodernism hook, line, and sinker or spurned it. But history as well as Scripture reminds us that no era can be regarded as either an unmixed blessing or wholly a curse. Human sinfulness { ⊕ *FREDERICA MATHEWES-GREEN: As Koppenhuffermeier would have said, "Yes."* } and God's common grace coincide throughout the ages. Conservatism and progressivism can easily become cop-outs for serious evaluation.

Call me dismissive, but I cannot get beyond the notion that post-modernism in the popular sense is little more than the triumph of popular culture, with its obsessions with technology, mass communications, mass marketing, the therapeutic orientation, and consumption. { ⊕ *FREDERICA MATHEWES-GREEN: And "hear, hear!" I believe Flugelhappner was once heard to remark.* } Hasn't the invention of the automobile, for instance, had more of an impact on the way the world looks (and thinks) today than just about any ideological paradigm shift? { ⊛ *BRIAN D. McLAREN: It's useful to distinguish between postmodernism as a philosophy and postmodernity as a cultural experience. The automobile, a product of modernity, thus can help produce a world that is different from the world that created it. This "different than because of" is precisely what I understand the prefix post to mean. Postmodern is not antimodern. The hormones produced by a child produce a "postchild" adolescent, and the disciplined study engaged in by the student produces a "poststudent" graduate; in the same way, it seems clear to me that the technology produced by modernity (including cars and computers) can produce something that is beyond modernity. That seems clear enough to me, but I realize that to Andy and Michael (and many others), it sounds like nonsense.* }

Neither an economist nor the son of an economist, I don't have the expertise—or the interest—to offer a critique of capitalism in that sphere. But I will say that capitalism, like socialism or feudalism, has its price. It is not a merely benevolent dictator. Especially when allowed to reign over all spheres of human culture and even our life together as God's people, it becomes a demon. And it is not satisfied until it has brought low everything that cannot be made profitable and efficient. The market trivializes. Nothing is sacred. The problem, of course, is that there are a lot of things in life—the most important things in life—that are financially unprofitable and terribly inefficient, things like marriage, family, leisure reading, Lord's Day observance, opera. Unlike MTV, the kind of programming one might see on PBS can exist only because federal tax money props up what commercial interests can only regard as unprofitable and inefficient. "All that is solid melts into the air" sounds like a description of postmodernism, but in fact it was Marx's description of modernity. Francis Watson remarks, "Capitalist ideology applauds dynamism, the restless dissatisfaction with the way things are and the quest for the new...to such an extent that that which endures and does not change becomes a troubling enigma that must either be passed over in silence or denounced as inflexible, outdated, and dogmatic." That dominant { ⊕ *FREDERICA MATHEWES-GREEN: "Excellent," to quote Montgomery Burns.* } church-growth ideologies and ministry paradigms cater to these all-consuming criteria seems obvious, at least to me.

Postmodernism—or whatever one wishes to designate our brief moment in history—is the culture in which *Sesame Street* is considered educational; sexy is the term of approbation for everything from jeans to doctoral theses; watching sitcoms together at dinner is called family time; abortion is considered choice; films sell products; and a barrage of images and sound bites selected for their entertainment and commercial value is called news. This general trend in culture translates into hipper-than-thou clubs passing for youth ministry, informal chats passing for sermons, and brazen marketing passing for evangelism, where busyness equals holiness, and expository preaching is considered too intellectual. This trend can account in part for homes in which disciplined habits both of domestic culture and instruction in Christian faith and practice give way to niche marketing and churches becoming theaters of the absurd. { ⊕ *FREDERICA MATHEWES-GREEN: I am standing on my chair applauding. Okay, I'm getting down now.* }

If the image of modernity is the crusty tyrant, wrinkled with the fatigue of old age and faded dreams, the postmodern visage is that of a child who refuses to grow up and accept the challenges as well as the opportunities of wisdom, truth, righteousness, and responsibilities, in addition to having a good time. Stated in such simplistic terms, one can hardly distinguish post-modern from boomer, that postwar generation so aptly described by David Brooks as insisting on having its cake (the fruit of hard labor and genuine community) and eating it too (absolute freedom of individual choice). { ⊕ *FREDERICA MATHEWES-GREEN: To give the bobos their due, doesn't Brooks at least allow that they work hard? That's* *the bourgeois side of the balance; the other "bo" is that they spend their earnings in ways that appear superficially bohemian. His piquant example is that they would look down on someone who paid $15,000 for a giant-screen TV but would spend $15,000 on a slate-lined shower because it proves they are in touch with the earth. But we should admit that they work hard to pay for whatever kind of cake they want to eat (the kind made with organic, stone-milled flour). }*

This take on postmodernism is hardly new. Marxist intellectual Alex Callinicos' illuminating analysis of postmodernism concludes that it is little more than the result of the self-obsessed "flower children" of the revolutionary '60s now taking their place in the professional "new middle class." In other words, postmodernism and boomer go hand in hand. There is no epochal change in Western culture, Callinicos insists. "Moreover, much of what is written in support of the idea that we live in a postmodern epoch seems to me of small caliber intellectually, usually superficial, often ignorant, sometimes incoherent." One must carefully distinguish poststructuralism, which does exist, from postmodernism, which probably does not. Fellow Marxist Terry Eagleton adds, "Radicals, for example, are traditionalists, just as conservatives are; it is simply that they adhere to different traditions." This appraisal fits perfectly with what I see in my experience of contemporary evangelicalism. Postmodernism is the new code word for mission, a new way of enforcing not just change but particular changes that have particular ideological assumptions. One can even detect a note of fatalism in challenges that verge on bullying: "Get with it or get left behind." { ⊕ *FREDERICA MATHEWES-GREEN: In the 1970s we Episcopalians in the charismatic renewal used to say similarly that parishes would be "charismatic or dead in 10 years." Boy, were we wrong. A totally unanticipated third thing happened.* } This is just the way things are now, so we had better adapt. Sweeping endorsements or sweeping denouncements make for light work.

Fatalism or Reformation?

IF A CHURCH STILL THINKS that the means of grace appointed by Christ as the Lord of his church are sufficient for the conversion of sinners and the edification of the saints, the burden of its critics is to show from Scripture why that shouldn't be regarded as true after the dawn of space travel. Why must change in the faith and practice of Christians parallel change in technology? Is there really a direct connection between changing the patterns of ministry established in Scripture and the surrender of dial-up providers (AOL) to broadband Internet? If there is, I fail to see it.

Even the most superficial appeal to the fact that we inhabit "the postmodern era" too often suffices to force a capitulation before that greatest of all threats: obsolescence. Frank Kermode calls postmodernism "another of those period descriptions that help you to take a view of the past suitable to whatever it is you want to do." One is reminded of the Dark Ages, which, despite their wealth of discoveries, advancing technologies, the founding of universities, and so forth, were effectively so nicknamed by the scions of the Renaissance ("rebirth") who sold subsequent generations on the spin that they were in fact breathing new life into Western civilization.

In modernity, psychological categories overwhelm confessional ones; managerial models of ministry outstrip the pastoral; categories of consumption, sometimes brazen and at other times indirect, reign over a more discipleship-oriented paradigm. Furthermore, ministers are constantly told these days, repeating a mantra in business, that they must be market driven rather than product driven. The pragmatic takes precedence over the deliberative, autonomy over authority, the individual over the community, and the new and improved over the tried and tested. { ⊛ *BRIAN D. McLAREN: If it's of any comfort to Michael, I for one would side with all but one of the categories he prefers here: confessional over psychological, pastoral over managerial, discipleship over consumption, deliberation over unthinking pragmatism, authority over autonomy, community over the individual. (I find it impossible to choose between the tried and true and the new and improved—because in order for something to be truly improved, it would have to be tried and shown true.)* }

It is not so much the modern versus the postmodern but the capitulation to pop culture that John Seebrook identifies as "the culture of marketing and the marketing of culture." Evangelicals obsessed with family values in a vaguely moral context often reflect the opposite values in the practice of their faith, as niche marketing breaks up the generations, entertainment drowns out catechesis, and the attraction of the customer edges out the communion of saints across all times and places. And I'm just talking about the youth group!

One benefit of such typologies as modern and postmodern is that we are able to at least fancy ourselves spectators of a bygone era. Whether or not modernity lives on, it is heartening that a certain hegemony of rationalism, utopian ideology, autonomy, and arrogant secularism now appears to be not only *capable* of being criticized but also *required*, by a new edict of the academy, to be criticized. When one just is modern, it is difficult to know how much one is an accomplice to it. But I do not discern the same willingness to critique what passes for postmodern. In a rather modern way, pop postmodernism assumes that "is" implies "ought" that "the way things are" is itself neutral, benign, or perhaps even an unmixed blessing. We do not take the trouble to analyze the ways in which, for example, the culture of marketing is fraught with peril for both culture and church because being "cutting edge," "effective," "successful"—or in more pious terms, "missional"—simply requires it. { ✱ *BRIAN D. McLAREN: I hope that Michael does not completely dismiss the important conversation that has sprung up around the word* missional *(thanks in large part to the Gospel and Our Culture Network, www.gocn.org) as a synonym for successful. As he said earlier, that kind of sweeping denouncement would be "light work."* }

C. Peter Wagner argues, "Traditional church models no longer work in our fast-changing world. A commitment to reaching the lost is driving new apostolic churches to find new ways to fulfill the Great Commission." In this outlook, "our fast-changing world"—which the Bible knows as "this fading age"—becomes the norm, and church models are viewed in thoroughly relativistic terms, as if the Lord had left the twenty-first-century church to find "new ways to fulfill the Great Commision" other than Word and sacrament. And just how does a faith that is passed down "from generation to generation" survive being marketed by a pop culture that entices with the line, "This is not your father's Oldsmobile"? { ⊕ *FREDERICA MATHEWES-GREEN: It's interesting that this Oldsmobile ad is cited by two of our authors; the slogan obviously had great impact as an evocative expression of youth defying stodgy old age. However, joke's on us, because the ad itself is old now; it debuted way back in 1988. Though this slogan still has the snap of generational rebellion, it was developed half a generation ago. Rebellion magically always sounds daisy fresh. To compound the irony, though the copywriter succeeded in penning an indelibly memorable slogan, it was a failure for*

Oldsmobile because its premise was that everybody thinks of Olds as the older generation's car. } According to George Barna, it is "critical that we keep in mind a fundamental principle of Christian communication: the audience, not the message, is sovereign." Is this the same evangelical movement that castigated the World Council of Churches for its slogan, "The church follows the world's agenda"? { ✦ *BRIAN D. McLAREN: Michael, like Andy, is clearly against something worth being against: superficial statements, overstatements, clever but misleading marketing slogans, and the like. But as one who will no doubt be critiqued for these faults in my own chapter, I have to admit that these statements are very easy to make. "As if the Lord left the twenty-first-century church to find 'new ways to fulfill the Great Commission' other than Word and sacrament" strikes me as one such statement. For example, the Lord didn't tell the church whether (or how much) to use organs, drums, telephones, the Internet, credit cards, automobiles, magazines, radio broadcasts, printing presses, icons, or computers to fulfill the Great Commission. Yet decisions about using these technologies, while trivial in some ways, are far from trivial in others. As Michael celebrates later in this chapter, Luther felt it good to use the new printing technology of his day, yet many of Luther's descendants today seem upset when other of Luther's descendants seek to follow his example of technological appropriation.* }

A Different Typology

IN SCHOLARSHIP, THE DEBATE over the nature of postmodernism and its relation to modernity has resulted in so much lost energy and meager results that the whole business has been largely abandoned. And yet in the church this typology seems so definitive in driving the rhetoric of relevance. What if, instead of adopting the division of history into modern and postmodern, we followed the New Testament distinction between "this present evil age" and "the age to come," the reality of "life in the flesh" versus "life in the Spirit"? { ✦ *BRIAN D. McLAREN: In answer to Michael's rhetorical question, I would say, "We're talking about two different things." Those of us grappling with the need for change in the church are seeking to proclaim, in the power of the Spirit, the good news of the age to come in this present evil age, in which people live lives of quiet desperation in the flesh. Medieval, modern, postmodern, or whatever all occur in the present evil age—which is also, by the way, the age Jesus promised to be with us to the end of—in a world God created and still loves. Perhaps I or others have given the impression that we think postmodernity means "the eschaton" or "the millennium." If so, I'm sorry—especially because some of us are amillennialists!* } Jesus frequently referred to this contrast, as did Paul even more emphatically. Whatever the generation presently in ascendance, its inhabitants are defined either by "this passing age" or "the age to come." In fact, a good mark of being "pressed into the world's way of thinking" rather than being "transformed by the renewing of [our] mind" (ROMANS 12:2) is that we think of ourselves (and our generation) more highly than we ought (v. 3).

In the New Testament typology, "That's postmodern" no longer becomes a get-out-of-jail-free card, a justification for all sorts of deviance from historic Christian norms in the name of evangelism, mission, and outreach to the postmodern culture. Both the ancient businesswoman Lydia and today's believer belong neither to ancient Rome nor to contemporary America but to "the city which has foundations, whose builder and maker is God" (HEBREWS 11:10 NKJV).

God has promised that by his Spirit working through Word and sacrament, he will slay us and raise us up to newness of life. If the age to come is breaking into even this present evil age through the preaching of the cross and the Resurrection, we really are in the presence of the one who has the power to disrupt our vain plot, to rescript us and take us "nowhere" people—"aliens and strangers"—and give us a place around the Lamb's table with Abraham, Isaac, and Jacob, as well as with the covenant people of today and tomorrow. And if not everybody likes us (perhaps our greatest insecurity these days), that might confirm that we are on the right track again. Oddly enough, it might even attract a new generation to take the Christian faith seriously, as fake and cloying attempts to impress those who are "dead in trespasses and sins" give way to genuinely satisfying richness: that gospel which alone is "the power of God unto salvation." { ✾ *BRIAN D. McLAREN: Again, just to clarify, I should say that at least some of us who disagree with Michael's downplaying the need for change in relation to culture nevertheless stand with him in decrying "fake and cloying attempts to impress" and that we in no way want to relativize Christian truth by any historical or cultural category. None of us doubts that God's story dominates the horizon of expectation. We're just trying to play our role in the part of the story we happened to be born into, and to do so faithfully, as Michael and the rest of the writers in this volume are seeking to do with all our hearts. Some of us are particularly interested in this additional goal: to seek to relativize the ways in which Christian truth has already been captured and confined by modernity. In that project I think we're all allies, right? }*

What if instead of allowing the categories of modern versus postmodern to relativize Christian truth, we allowed the latter (with its own eschatological categories of this present age versus the age to come) to relativize the former? What if the Christian has yet another place to stand "outside" both modernity and postmodernity? What if both are seen as part of this passing evil age and are relativized by the age to come, which even now is breaking in on a decadent world? I'm postmodern enough to realize that nobody really stands outside of his or her own culture and language. My intent here is to suggest that faith gives us confidence to believe that Scripture provides new glasses through which to view the world from God's perspective, albeit accommodated to our capacity, and that through those lenses we cannot help but laugh at the kings and their kingdoms arrayed against our God and his Christ. Through these glasses we see God's own testimony regarding what he's doing in history and not just what Michael Eisner or the ecclesiastical equivalent is doing. In that way God's redemptive plan, his story, dominates the horizon of expectation instead of any era "under the sun."

In fact, the current trends touted as unique and unprecedented have marked declining civilizations (and the churches that follow them) throughout history. Near the beginning of the twentieth century, writer and social commentator Walter Lippman wrote, "The philosophy which inspires the whole process is based on the theory, which is no doubt correct, that a great population under modern conditions is not held by sustained convictions and traditions, but that it wants and must have one thrill after another." Steinar Kavale { ⊕ *FREDERICA MATHEWES-GREEN: Man, it's getting crowded in here! Hauerwas, maybe you can get on top of that bookcase over there. Steinar, you're going to have to sit on Walter's lap. And if any more intellectuals ring the doorbell, we're going to turn out the lights and pretend nobody's home.* } has written more recently, "Fascination may take the place of reflection; seduction may replace argumentation." When Lippmann wrote, it was called the modern age; now Kavale calls it postmodernism, but either way it's the same cultural captivity. { ⊛ *BRIAN D. McLAREN: Michael treats us to some impressive quotations that imply that convictions and traditions, reflection and argumentation, are good, but thrills and fascinations are bad. That's easy enough to agree with on one level. But it's also easy, thinking this way, to turn everyone into intense, serious, scholarly northern European stereotypes perpetually reflecting on their traditions, arguing about their convictions in a most unthrilling and unfascinating way. I'm a northern European myself, but even my*

Scottish blood enjoys a good genuine thrill or a true fascination from time to time, and if the emerging culture is capable of pursuing a both-and here, rather than an either-or, I'll be most happy. How about being thrilled by our conviction, fascinated by our traditions? I'm sure Michael would agree that's not a bad thing at all. }

One piece of good news is that despite the boomer generation's fascination with itself, the coming generations exhibit a renewed interest in roots, the very thing that our age, whatever one wants to call it, treats with hostility when its values of autonomy are called into question. A host of recent studies confirms that the ecclesiastical ideology of "mission to postmodern culture" works least among the people who are supposed to be the most impressed: the so-called Gen-Xers and younger. Even aside from the all-important challenge of biblical fidelity, not even the demographics support the hype that almost tyrannically controls contemporary approaches to mission and worship. { ♡*ERWIN RAPHAEL McMANUS: Michael, this is a great observation. The average age of Mosaic is 24.4, and 82 percent are single. It is not accommodation that is attractive, but revolution. The church, even with her best efforts, is not the best place to placate self-indulgence and nurture narcissism. Jesus in the end continuously gets in the way of pandering to the flesh. One of our greatest struggles is the desire for absolute certainty in areas where God leaves mystery. Our challenge is to live with absolute certainty in the trustworthiness of God as God calls us to a life filled with uncertainty. In other words, we need to know that we don't know and move forward with confidence in the knowledge of him. }*

The obsession with the modern-postmodern typology not only fuels an uncritical embrace of everything currently marketed as important and interesting. It is problematic also because it fosters an antimodern despair that cripples our witness on the more conservative side of the fence. Sweeping generalizations concerning postmodern relativism and the "paradigm shift" from rationality to irrationality may not only be technically inaccurate; they can create an almost nostalgic longing for "the good old days" that were dominated by some other offspring of the spirit of the age. Why not abandon this obsession altogether and recognize that the real contrast is between the "age of the Spirit" that dawned with the resurrection of Christ from the dead and the spirit of the age, which has throughout history dominated the nations in their rage against the Lord and his Anointed One? Whether we are talking about the businesswoman Lydia, whose heart the Spirit opened as Paul preached Christ, or today's businesswoman in the ad referred to earlier, the real divide is between the kingdom of Christ and the kingdoms of this world.

One of the remarkable achievements of the Reformation was that instead of capitulating to the ignorance of the people by relying on pictures and icons as "the books for the unlearned," the Reformers insisted that they be elevated in their abilities so that they could read Scripture, { ⊕ *FREDERICA MATHEWES-GREEN: The invention of the printing press and the unprecedented availability of books and spread of literacy made this a much more possible goal, of course. Before the invention of the airplane, people made a fatalistic accommodation that they must travel everywhere by land or sea.* } understand sermons, and find new opportunities to advance their own calling and their neighbor's good. Instead of fatalistic accommodation, the Reformers resisted and in fact turned back the night. { ▽ *ERWIN RAPHAEL McMANUS: Michael, it seems that this achievement by the Reformers makes the opposite point. To imagine a society in which everyone could read, in which the commoner was literate, was extraordinarily futuristic. They were in essence creating a new culture, and we are the beneficiaries of that vision. For them to have expected the Reformation to erupt out of literacy rather than literacy erupting out of the Reformation would have been a tragic mistake. They did in fact accommodate to the ignorance of the people. They communicated the message in a manner they could understand. It seems to me that part of the problem in the Western church is that we want everyone to understand our highly tuned academic rhetoric, and then we condemn them for their ignorance if they just can't get it. It is not beneath us to begin with the pictures. It certainly wasn't beneath Jesus. And isn't it possible that one who is illiterate could walk in the light while one who is renowned for their scholarship could grope in the darkness?* ⊛ *BRIAN D. McLAREN: As I implied earlier, I think nearly all of Michael's critiques of those in our day who are working for change could be put in the mouths of Luther's critics five hundred years ago. They would have said that Luther was accommodating to the spirit of his age, seeking "new possibilities" when he should stay with "the tried and true."* }

It may be that one is an entrenched conservative who experiences vertigo at the thought of change: the "if you build it, they will come" philosophy of church growth. And if they don't come, you can reassure yourself with the thought that you are too faithful to be successful. This I would regard as an unhealthy nostalgia or, worse, lazy negligence in one's ministry, although it is far too characteristic of many churches today, where getting the gospel right somehow justifies the failure to get it out.

Therefore, the various ways in which discussions like this are framed may not always be helpful. Leonard Sweet has offered a colorful and evenhanded metaphor in his introduction. The view represented in this chapter corresponds in Sweet's typology to a garden, carefully manicured and with high walls. { ⊕ *FREDERICA MATHEWES-GREEN: The chief problem with this metaphor is that it implies a desire to protect the church from evil influences outside. Instead the classic position claims that there is no outside; the whole earth is the Lord's and all that is therein; classic Christianity encompasses all and speaks to every age. It is instead those positions anxious to address transitory times that seem constricted and narrow and inevitably failing at their goal by going swiftly out of date.* } I take it that he would say there are different ecologies, and we need them all. But metaphors aren't window dressing; they are the windows themselves. I do not believe we need all of the approaches represented in this volume in the way that we need gardens, glens, parks, and meadows. All of us writing for this book are convinced that we have something to learn from each other, but we are equally convinced that the approach each is defending is the most faithful to the Great Commission and that other views are on balance inadequate or even pernicious. The ecological typology seems a bit too innocent to me. Further, I do not think that the view I am encouraging us to embrace is so easily though respectfully reduced to that single environment.

What if it's less like different ecologies—all of which are essential, despite personal preferences—and more like, say, different architectural environments? Although my version will not be as ostensibly neutral as Sweet's, I would offer two rival approaches. One is a centuries-old building or plaza that has been extended, remodeled, and improved over successive generations, so that it has lived through time and ties together past, present, and future. Accordingly, this complex of edifices is neither nostalgically stuck in the past, refusing any tinkering with its Gothic glory, nor is it narrowly stuck in the present, given to innovations that pass into ridicule as quickly as they rose to fame. Rather, it brings the past and the present together in conversation, as if to wave its hand to future generations to indwell it, care for it, repair it, and make their own contributions to its completion. { ⊕ *FREDERICA MATHEWES-GREEN: The flaw in this otherwise appealing metaphor is that it brings to mind arrogant, insensitive, "modernizing" additions to timeworn older buildings. An expanded building can be a cacophony unless new additions honor the existing building and setting and aim to harmonize with them. See Stewart Brand's excellent book* How Buildings Learn: What Happens after They're Built. } Scripture itself appeals to this analogy, speaking of a foundation laid once and for all by the prophets and apostles and a building that subsequently rises upon it to the end of the age.

The contrasting picture is a suburban strip mall, which replaced a dilapidated older structure deemed unworthy of upkeep, and destined itself to be replaced in a matter of years rather than centuries. These distinct architectural analogies have more direct connections with the historical epochs within our horizon than Sweet's ecological analogy supplies. Modernity sought to level everything, to begin anew. The past was an impediment to progress, and the future held the real promise. Cities would now be rebuilt with efficiency and convenience in view. No more winding footpaths or rambling colonnades but direct thoroughfares and broad avenues radiating from the bureaucratic and commercial center. Particular enclaves, ghettos, and neighborhoods would surrender their generations-old habitat and habits to "real life" in the city of mass consumption, mass transit, mass communications, and mass marketing. The results of that way of thinking today are obvious, not only in architecture and city planning but also in every part of our lives. And the consequences are seen not just in the shape of our cities but in the shape of our lives, our hopes, our praxis—and increasingly, our churches.

Each of these transformations has a corollary in religious history. One thinks of Charles Finney, who in one easy stroke swept away the entire system of doctrine to which he had promised allegiance and with it the entire covenantal structure of Christian nurture in favor of "excitements suffi-cient to induce conversion." By the end of it all even Finney was discouraged and wondered whether people would eventually just get burned out on it all. In fact, they did. The area in which he most frequently labored is now called "the burned-over district." The debates over the church-growth movement, psychological manipulation, the transformation of worship into a form of pop-cultural entertainment, the replacement of the proclamation of law and gospel with moralism and politics, as well as the substitution of seduction for persuasion are merely repeats of past performances.

While past discussions of ministry in the church and in the world might have concentrated on the different approaches that Roman Catholic, Orthodox, Baptist, Lutheran, Reformed, Pentecostal, Anabaptist, and Quaker theologies entail, our present discussion focuses more on different personalities or styles. And this makes sense in the present milieu. After all, even among brothers and sisters in my own tradition who profess a strong commitment to their confessional standards, divisions such as those explored in this volume threaten discord even more perhaps than interconfessional strife. Today, evangelicals who are Reformed and Presbyterian may find themselves closer in many ways to those outside their ecclesiastical ambit who represent a "resistance movement" to modernity within their respective communions. A new ecumenism along those lines may be perceived even now, and if it is true to its aspirations, we can only hope that it will resist a nostalgic conservatism as well, adding in its small but important way to that edifice that Christ is still building from generation to generation. But we have to be careful to observe Jaroslav Pelikan's distinction between "the living tradition of the dead and the dead tradition of the living," assiduously avoiding the latter.

Is Luther's Question the Question for Today?

IT MAY BE WORTH CITING a case study to see how past achievements of the church are frequently treated as irrelevant for today. These days we are frequently told by biblical scholars and theologians, as well as pastors and church-growth consultants, that the creeds and confessions (not to mention the liturgies and worship principles) of centuries past can hardly be suitable to the questions of today. Presumably, God is no longer triune—or if he is, it no longer matters since the invention of the cell phone. Forgive me for not seeing the connection. It reminds me of Rudolph Bultmann's infamous non sequitur about how those who use electric lights and the wireless radio cannot possibly continue to believe in a supernatural realm. As Peter Berger remarked, it may be more difficult to believe in the supernatural in a technological age, but belief in the one is hardly affected causally by the other.

On one end of the hermeneutical debate are those who reduce the influence of a given context to a bare trace. Truth is timeless. It may, of course, put in more of an appearance in some periods than in others, but the historical factors at work in any given age have no serious effect on the emergence of the truth in question. On the other end is historicism, the view that truth is constructed by these factors. While we will differ on specifics, Christians should agree that both of these extremes are unavailable options. "The Word became flesh" dismisses any Platonic or Cartesian love affair with disembodied ideas. Scripture itself reflects all of the peculiarities of diverse human authorship. And yet the narrative of God's saving purpose in Jesus Christ spans the many centuries, languages, cultures, and styles. The Christological formula *finitum non capax infiniti* (the finite cannot fully contain the infinite) emphasizes that although Jesus Christ was fully God the Son, he nevertheless continued to transcend time and space even as he nursed at Mary's breast. In the same way, truth is a cultural artifact and yet transcends every cultural context. Even while it bears the marks of its bodily existence, it cannot be captured and reduced to any set of historical factors. Naturalism is the metaphysical theory that rejects transcendent truth and lodges meaning only in the various uses to which individuals and communities put it.

One of the implications of historicism is the isolation of each period (and the ideas most obviously associated with it) in a hermeneutically sealed compartment. Just explain how the dogma of the Trinity was the result of the "acute Hellenization" of the original Jesus movement (à la Harnack), and you have made it irrelevant to the modern age. Provide a suitable explanation of how the Reformation could not have happened apart from certain social, political, philosophical, as well as ecclesiastical and theological trends, and you have successfully stood outside of the tradition. You have maintained objectivity, and you are not personally responsible for casting your vote for or against the claim that God justifies the wicked by grace alone through faith alone on the basis of Christ alone. The belief that there is no such thing as truth that transcends all times and places is as old as the Sophists and was advanced by modern thought long before it became a cardinal dogma of postmodernism. Yet for Christians, at least, whose God is "from everlasting to everlasting," this cannot be so. And this should come as the best possible news. In Hebrews 6 the writer appeals to God's oath to Abraham.

In the same way, when God desired to show even more clearly to the heirs of the promise the unchangeable character of his purpose, he guaranteed it by an oath, so that through two unchangeable things [God and his promise], in which it is impossible that God would prove false, we who have taken refuge might be strongly encouraged to seize the hope set before us. We have this hope, a sure and steadfast anchor of the soul, a hope that enters the inner shrine behind the curtain, where Jesus, a forerunner on our behalf, has entered, having become a high priest forever according to the order of Melchizedek. (vv. 17-20 NRSV).

While the historicist approach is a serious challenge in historical theology, it is far more dangerous if we apply it to Scripture. While no teaching in Scripture is timeless (for reasons mentioned above), the truths taught by the mouth of God in redemptive revelation endure through all times and places. So the real question is not, Is Luther's question our question? but, Is Luther's question Scripture's question? How are sinners reconciled to a holy God? While that question does not consume the horizon, can we honestly say that it is not central to the biblical narrative from Genesis to Revelation? And that narrative spans centuries, cultures, distinctive personalities, and generations. "What must I do to be saved?" is hardly the question of a neurotic individualist obsessed with his or her own condition as a result of a sacramental system gone wrong. It is the recurring question of Scripture, whether directly or indirectly stated. { ⊗ *ANDY CROUCH: First of all, Michael, as is made clear by my own essay, I am with you in almost every respect up to this point in your assessment of (post)modernity and its dangers. Your reframing of the issue in terms of "the spirit of the age" versus "the age of the spirit" is invaluable. Just to put the question this way reminds us how little Christian attention is given to truly theocentric readings of history, rather than glorified sociological analysis. ⊗ But at this point in your essay I think we part company and not only because of our theological inclinations (mine, Wesleyan; yours, Reformed). I am postmodern enough to think that it is far too simple to speak of "the" question of Scripture. "What must I do to be saved?" is, of course, a scriptural question in the most literal sense. "What is your only comfort in life and death?" (Heidelberg Catechism Q. 1) is equally scriptural, though not a direct quote. The answers to these questions are of profound importance, and the five of us would disagree only about minor details as to the answers Scripture provides. ☺ But I'm not convinced that "What must I do to be saved?"—at least as that question is so readily refracted through modern, Western lenses—is "the" question of Scripture. I would suggest at least one other major question, identified by P. T. Forsyth at the beginning of the last century and by Milton, St. Paul, and Job before him: the question of God's—rather than our—justification. How are we to "justify the ways of God to man" (Milton)? Why do the wicked prosper and the good suffer? How will God prove that he himself is righteous (Romans 3:4, 26)? These questions are of particular urgency when many of our contemporaries lack, for better or worse, awareness of personal guilt or sin but have an exquisite sense of the injustices of this world. Christian attempts to reframe their questions—Why do the good suffer?—into more Luther-friendly form (by, for example, arguing that there are no "good" people in the first place) are of limited evangelistic value. (See Brian's story about his neighbor Louie.) ☺ Another recurring (and related) question of Scripture: What are God's plans for his people Israel? This is the question that recent scholarship sees at the heart of Romans, for example, climaxing in Romans 9–11, chapters that, strangely, were neglected in my Protestant instruction, which consistently skipped straight from Romans 8:39 to Romans 12:1. It is also the question that N. T. Wright has discovered at the heart of many beloved parables of Jesus that have long been interpreted exclusively as stories of individual salvation. If God has chosen these people, and if they have indeed rebelled against him, what is he going to do? And what is the relation between this special people and the rest of the nations of the earth? Our answer will be inescapably relevant to current geopolitical realities, as well as to the global religious pluralism that is posing a fresh, if not unprecedented, challenge to Christian witness. Like the question of justification of God, this question is not easily subsumed under the categories of individual sin and redemption. ☺ Brian has put it well in his essay: Scripture's narrative is "many versioned, many faceted, many layered"—or, we might say, polyphonous. Our forebears have not served us well by boiling it down, even to questions so beautifully phrased as "What is your only comfort in life and death?" The ecumenical creeds are of paramount importance, and I believe every word of them—yet they too, because they are embedded in a particular history, fail to acknowledge questions (like the nature and destiny of Israel) that are self-evidently at the heart of the Bible and the ministry of Jesus. Affirming that truth is enduring—as we all would—is not the same as fixing upon "Luther's question," or any question, as "the" question of Scripture. }*

This case study, then, suggests that truth is neither timeless nor time-bound but enduring. The Protestant Reformers did not seek to be revolutionaries, reinventing the faith for a new generation as a model for us in our own time. Rather, they sought to recall to the ancient and apostolic faith a medieval church that had in a number of respects compromised its very identity as the church of Christ. They believed that they were being

faithful to Scripture—in their time and place but not to their time and place. It is just as true today as it has always been since the resurrection of our Lord and the sending of his Spirit that where the gospel is rightly preached and the sacraments are rightly administered according to Christ's command, we are not to doubt that there is a true church. And the reverse still holds as well. {♡*ERWIN RAPHAEL McMANUS: I think this is such an important point. Certainly our goal is to become the church God had in mind as he was crucified on our behalf; yet with that comes the question, What does this true church look like? And perhaps more poignant, What does it mean to rightly preach the gospel and rightly administer the sacraments? How is it that so many churches—even Reformed churches—are so convinced of their rightness, and yet their congregations look very little like the church in the book of Acts? Why is it that others who would agree with this position have tragically led the church to become more of an institution or even a world religion than a movement?* }

It is important to add, all too briefly, that the enduring character of faith cannot be pried from the enduring character of practice. It is not as if what we believe remains the same, while how we believe and live out our beliefs are always in transition. In both cases—our knowing and doing—we find ourselves growing in grace, individually and corporately. But it is organic, like the growth of a plant or a person. There is always much of the old in the new, not only in doctrine but also in the way truth is experienced and lived in the church and in the world. "An unchanging message through ever-changing methods" marks a divorce that is alien to Scripture and debilitating to the church's life and witness. We must find ways to avoid slavery to both human traditions and human innovations, preferring to anchor both our faith and practice in God's Word. We may send taped sermons through the mail rather than write them on parchment, but we can never replace the preaching of the Word with an alternative medium. Numerous other examples suggest themselves that we cannot explore here. God has prescribed how he will be worshiped and how he will bestow his saving benefits. Further, it is just at the point where Christian faith and practice collide with the spirit of the age that things finally get interesting. What could be more boring than a religious affirmation of boomer narcissism?

Critics who suggest that ancient creeds and historical confessions lose their relevance with time bear the burden of demonstrating their case from the creeds and confessions themselves. It was with the emergence of a group of young pastors whose faith had been renewed by a fresh encounter with the Reformation confessions that the Confessing Church took its stand against the domination of Nazi ideology in the churches. Could such a witness occur in modern evangelicalism? Is it occurring? Or might it be the case that our cultural captivity is entirely consistent with our modern arrogance in thinking ourselves sufficient to the task without the cumulative resources of our forebears? Weren't the "German Christians" just translating the gospel for their time and place, contextualizing their ministry in the light of the felt needs of the young and upwardly mobile generation?

The covenantal mentality of the Scriptures ("unto a thousand generations"), especially inasmuch as it enrolls us in "a new and better covenant," must have priority over allegiances to any ethnic group, generation, culture, or class. When Christ promised to continue to build his church even up to and through the very gates of hell, he was saying neither that the church would be once and for all built in the first five centuries nor that it would be razed and rebuilt in each self-infatuated generation. Rather, he promised that it would endure and prevail under the perpetual guidance of the Spirit through Word and sacrament "until the end of the age."

I suppose this means that I can accept at least some aspects of the garden typology alongside the architectural metaphor. After all, it takes time to cultivate roses and people. One does not have to work very hard to maintain a glen or a meadow, although a park can be a nuisance if it's a mere "letting be" that one has in mind. Scripture calls us to convert the world, not to be converted by it. In contrast to the fatalism of so much contemporary mission, Paul declares, we destroy "arguments and every high thing that exalts itself against the knowledge of God, bringing every thought into captivity to the obedience of Christ" (2 CORINTHIANS 10:5 NKJV). Paul, I take it, was a good gardener.

Think of the great gardens that are handed down from generation to generation and lovingly held in trust by those who realize that it is not just their garden. Isn't it more likely that people who honor their inheritance in this way can be especially trusted to pass it down with improvements rather than in ruins? Like poorer parents who want to give their children even better opportunities in the world by providing the best education and the richest experiences, "garden-variety" churches—at their best, at least—can be expected to give a rich treasure to their future generations by passing on what they themselves received. None of this means, of course, that immutability is a mark of ecclesiastical nobility. A rigid conservatism can keep a church from making changes that are more in conformity with God's Word. Unfaithfulness comes in conservative and liberal packages. It is never change itself or conservation itself that qualifies as faithfulness but fidelity to Scripture.

SO WHICH IS IT? Is postmodernism the big new thing? Or is postmodernism the same old thing? For mission, at least, it just doesn't matter. Whatever postmodernism is, it belongs to the fading dreams that cannot compare to the solid joys of Zion. Deep down, God's people know that the "Song of Myself" must give way to the Song of Moses:

I will sing to the LORD, *for he has*
triumphed gloriously;
horse and rider he has thrown
into the sea.
The LORD *is my strength and my might,*
and he has become my salvation;
this is my God, and I will praise him,
my father's God, and I will exalt him.
(EXODUS 15:1-2 NRSV)

{ ⊗ BRIAN D. McLAREN: *Michael has given here a very clear presentation of an intelligent, articulate Reformed view. I can't think of any Reformed writer who could have written this chapter more gracefully and graciously while being as persuasive and incisive as Michael has been.* ⊗ *I believe that the Reformed system is the highest and best theological system in modernity. This is a sincere compliment. But it also invites reflection on the ways in which the Reformed system must be* semper reformanda *to be faithful to its roots in history and, more important, in Scripture—especially if modernity fades and something new emerges. (Perhaps this helps explain why some people, not necessarily Michael or Andy, don't want* to admit or even consider that a postmodern world may be emerging.) At the end of the day, even though I agree with so very much of the content of Michael's tradition, and even though I find myself standing against so much of what the best of the Reformed tradition stands against, I suspect that there is a good bit of modernity in at least some of the Reformed tradition. Michael may even agree, to some limited degree at least. ❦ That strong connection between the modern Western way of thinking and the Reformed tradition is a sign of the tradition's success, in my view. Calvin stepped into the void left by the collapse of the medieval theo-political power structures in northern Europe and (as an amazingly young man!) offered a new way of systematizing the faith—a way that brilliantly filled the void and met the need of a newly literate emerging modern world. His system affirmed the lordship of Christ over all creation in a powerful and motivating way and thus propelled godly men (and occasionally women) into the construction of new modern institutions (such as the Constitution of the United States) that, while not perfect, were and are some of the grandest creations in human history, serving God and man long and well. ❦ I would never expect Michael to be disloyal to this rich tradition that has given millions of Christians high and deep access to the "solid joys of Zion" and of "the age to come." Rather, I hope that he will continue to bring those joys, as uniquely seen and savored and flavored by the Reformed faith, to everyone he can, including those of us who are more sanguine about the "unprecedented opportunities" presented by these times, whatever they're called. Some of us will no doubt emphasize the semper reformanda of the Reformation more acutely than he would wish: We will seek to reform things he doesn't believe need to be reformed. Even so, I hope that he will see us not as enemies but as missional and worshipful allies. Where he feels we're wrong or going wrong, I hope he will offer his sagely advice and brotherly suggestions. I know that I, for one, will listen with respect and gratitude and prayerful consideration to what he says, just as I have received the many rays of wisdom shining in his chapter. ❦ I would also hope that magnanimous souls in Michael's tradition would avoid caricaturing those who are asking questions and exploring answers that differ from traditional formulations. I believe Michael could help us all avoid needless disunity in the body of Christ by discouraging "sweeping denouncements," as he has done so well in this chapter. ❦ I also hope he and his tradition will not assume the worst about us and will instead respond to our mistakes (real or perceived) with grace. Some of us speak harshly and brashly and without sufficient thought at times. (Of course, Luther himself launched a few zingers in his day, didn't he?) Sometimes we're just plain ignorant, few of us having the advantage of Michael's scholarship and native brilliance. And while none of us (as far as I know) would endorse all the wild extremes he rightly critiques in this chapter, still many of us (myself included) say and do stupid things here and there—far more often than we'd like or should. I hope that all who, like Michael, believe strongly in the sovereignty of God will beseech the Lord to guide those of us who stand convinced by Scripture in our minds, hearts, and bones that our cultural matrix is changing and that something perhaps as profound as the reformation is needed once again. God knows these waters are deep and dangerous, and any people (intrepid or foolhardy, time will tell) venturing into them need prayer as they need the air they breathe. }

Michael Horton's Rejoinder

THIS HAS BEEN a fruitful exchange, and I am grateful to have been included. In my rejoinder to the other writers' reviews of my chapter, I would like to express thanks for the charity they exercised. Perhaps the best way of responding is to draw together the comments of Brian and Erwin on the one hand and Frederica and Andy on the other.

In my estimation Brian overidentifies Reformed theology and modernity. My chapter is a defense not of Reformed distinctives per se but of a position that could be held by adherents of other traditions. That there is a lot of modernity in our Reformed circles is indisputable but also (it seems to me) unexceptional, given the fact that there is a lot of modernity everywhere—especially in the West—and I think I discern it even in Brian's thoughtful chapter. However compromised our churches might be at present with modernity, the basic form and substance of Reformed theology emerged in the premodern era. In addition to the ecumenical creeds, all of our confessions or catechisms were drafted before the dawn of the Enlightenment. Whatever our conclusions about this project, Karl Barth's "thunder-bolt" was precisely the claim that modern Protestantism is not the faith articulated by the reformers.

Part of my contention is that very often what is advertised as postmodern today is in fact "most-modern." Autonomous individualism, an insatiable appetite for innovation, suspicion of the past, and other marks of modernity persist in a more radical form in much of postmodern discourse. While I am certainly not implying that Brian endorses these marks of modernity, I wonder if modernity all too easily becomes for many of us a catchall term for whatever it is that we do not like or find no longer relevant. I would much rather talk about the specific and concrete questions before us in our time than rest a great deal on whether something is modern or postmodern.

Brian is concerned also about tone, and this leads me to Erwin's similar caution. All of this is well taken. Both appear to be wary of separating truth from love, and what could be more scriptural and needful than that? I wince sometimes at comments I've made in hasty generalization. At the same time, radical claims are being made about what the church should be or become, and objections to those claims cannot simply be dismissed as stirring division in Christ's body. Erwin is rightly concerned that we explain the faith in terms the average person can understand. However, I disagree with his suggestion that we begin with pictures—not because it is somehow beneath us but because the Old Testament saints, Jesus, and his apostles refused the idolatry of the eye and instead concentrated on the preaching of the Word. "So then faith comes by hearing, and hearing by the word of God" (Romans 10:17, NKJV). It is hardly for elitist reasons that Christians are called people of the book. To be sure, the book is not an end in itself but is meant to lead us to Christ. Jesus certainly used colorful metaphors and parables, but these are figures of speech and genres of discourse, not pictures. Further, Erwin is worried that some who hold the views I have set forth have led away from the model of the church in Acts 2 toward a view of the church as "more of an institution or even a world religion than a movement."

Yet it is precisely in Acts 2 where we read that the growing church "continued steadfastly in the apostles' doctrine and fellowship, in the breaking of bread, and in prayers" (v. 42, NKJV). It was a Word-and-sacrament ministry, and the church did grow as an institution. Although we Americans are anti-institutional almost by definition, we ought to beware of separating the soul of the church (as a movement) from its body (as a visible institution).

Brian and Erwin both remind us that we need to exercise humility in the task of theology and church practice. It is indeed all too easy to treat the truth as a flag for our team instead of as the finger pointing to the Lamb of God. At the same time, I would caution against overreaction at this point. If modernity was arrogant in asserting its mastery, postmodern skepticism is no better. There is that line of John Cusack in the movie Say Anything: *"I don't know, but I know that I don't know. You know?" Or there's that charming confession from a long-gone Top 40 song: "I don't know about too many things. I know what I know, if you know what I mean...Push me in the shallow water, before I get too deep." We need to guard against a type of anti-intellectualism that masquerades as humility, a perennial temptation in our evangelical circles. G. K. Chesterton complained, "What we suffer from today is humility in the wrong place. Modesty has moved from the organ of ambition...[and] settled upon the organ of conviction, where it was never meant to be. A man was meant to be doubtful about himself, but undoubting about the truth; this has been exactly reversed. We are on the road to producing a race of men too mentally modest to believe in the multiplication table." John Stott adds, "The corridors of the New*

Testament reverberate with dogmatic affirmations beginning 'We know,' 'We are sure,' 'We are confident.'" While we must distinguish between God's Word and our fallible interpretations, "when the biblical teaching is plain," writes Stott, "the cult of an open mind is a sign not of maturity, but of immaturity."

Our old theologians used to make a lot out of the distinction between God's knowledge (archetypal) and ours (ectypal). At no point do God's knowledge and ours coincide exactly, they insisted, barring the door to any rationalistic blurring of the Creator-creature distinction. In fact, they distinguished for that reason between a knowledge of God in himself (a theology of glory), which was unavailable to us, and a revelation of God accommodated to our weakness (a theology of the cross). They called "our theology" theologia viatorum, "the theology of pilgrims." It seems to me that pilgrims is a remarkably apt analogy. While pilgrims haven't already arrived, they know where they're headed and are even now on their way by God's grace.

And now to the responses of Frederica and Andy. First, Frederica's observation that "there is no 'outside,'" pace the walled-garden metaphor, seems to me to be right on the mark. I agree wholeheartedly that "classic Christianity encompasses all and speaks to every age," while "it is instead those positions anxious to address transitory times that seem constricted and narrow and inevitably failing at their goal by going swiftly out of date." What does it mean to be genuinely catholic? One thing that it certainly cannot mean is that we divorce ourselves from the wide-open spaces marvelously seeded and cultivated by brothers and sisters across all places and times. Being preoccupied with relevance is its own form of narrowness.

As one who appreciates his writing, I found Andy's contribution and response to my chapter illuminating. Andy challenges my claim that Scripture is centrally concerned with our reconciliation with God—more specifically, the question of personal salvation. While I have spent a lot of time myself criticizing the individualistic tendencies of evangelical approaches that undermine both the ecclesial and cosmic aspects of redemption, I remain persuaded that the gospel of God's grace in and through Jesus Christ is the plot that unites the diverse biblical canon. That plot can be explained in terms of the history of redemption (the promised seed of the woman crushing the serpent's head, for instance) or the order of individual salvation (election, calling, justification, sanctification, glorification). Scripture does both, and so should we, but in either account it is the gospel that is the recurring refrain.

Andy suggests that theodicy (justifying God's ways with the world in light of the problem of evil) is more central in Scripture than the question of personal salvation. However, Isaiah 59 illustrates in my mind the reversal that needs to take place in our day: Instead of putting God on trial, we need to realize that it is we who are on trial. In the language of a covenant lawsuit, the chapter begins, "Behold, the LORD's hand is not shortened, that it cannot save; nor his ear heavy, that it cannot hear. But your iniquities have separated you from your God; and your sins have hidden His face from you, so that He will not hear" (vv. 1–2, NKJV). The prophet, as covenant prosecutor, lays out the evidence against the people until the latter finally, with one voice, confess that it is they who are in the wrong. Justice, righteousness, and truth are "far from us" because of our own transgressions (vv. 9–15). But the good news comes in verses 15b–21, where Yahweh himself dresses for battle, is upheld by his own righteousness, and saves his people from their sins. I haven't yet found a satisfying theodicy, but precisely because the judgment for sin has been dealt with by God at the cross, I can at least take comfort that it has been settled in practical terms and that this will one day be clear to everyone.

I am far less impressed than Andy with the revisions of Paul and his theology as articulated by James Dunn, E. P. Sanders, N. T. Wright, and others. The jury is still out on the methods as well as the conclusions of the so-called new perspectives on Paul. In suggesting that Luther's question was in fact Scripture's question, I mean not that it is the only question or that all other questions pale in comparison but that the question itself is central in Scripture even when it is not explicitly asked or answered. My point is that we need to abandon the historicist assumptions of modernity that let us see only discontinuity across times and places. Whether Luther's question is a scriptural question has to be decided exegetically and historically; it cannot be dismissed merely as the question of a sixteenth-century monk caught up in historical circumstances quite irrelevant to our concerns today. Still, Andy is correct to caution us against reductionism, as if the Bible were little more than an evangelistic tract.

▷ ▷ ▷ ▷ ▷

FREDERICA
MATHEWES-
GREEN

Frederica Mathewes-Green

Under the Heaventree

Why is this essay written in question and answer format?

It is intended to reference the penultimate section of James Joyce's *Ulysses*. This section, called "Ithaca," concerns a late-night conversation between Leopold Bloom and Stephen Dedalus. It is cast in the form of a series of objective, impersonal questions and answers; for example, "What seemed to the host to be the predominant qualities of his guest?"

Why is "Ithaca" written in question and answer format?

{ ⬦ *ERWIN RAPHAEL McMANUS: Frederica, is it possible that here we find our greatest evidence of our relationship to the Creator? How is it that children must be endlessly schooled with answers but come to questions quite on their own? We must force them to master who, what, when, where, and how. But they are unrelenting in their pursuit of why. Could this in some small way reflect Jesus' command to come to him as little children? The child asks, "Why?" The adult responds, "Because I said so." In the pluralistic environment in which I live in Los Angeles, there is an endless cacophony of answers. But everyone asks the same questions. Is it possible that God places within the human spirit questions that presume answers?* }

Joyce's monumental novel employed many experimental forms. While some twentieth-century artists experimented in haphazard or even deliberately destructive ways, Joyce's work is carefully constructed and frequently beautiful.

Give an example.

When Bloom escorts Dedalus to the door, well after midnight, they see "the heaventree of stars hung with humid nightblue fruit."

Give an example of an artwork deliberately destructive of aestheticism.

The *Fountain* of Marcel Duchamp, which consisted of a urinal signed "R. Mutt."

What did these experimenting artists share?

They shared an impulse to go beyond traditional forms of art to use new methods to express messages that, they believed, were also new.

Were these messages in fact new?

Probably not.

Were these methods new?

They were certainly experimental and original.

Were these methods more effective in communication than previous methods?

Probably not.

When was *Ulysses* written?

Between 1914 and 1921.

When did Duchamp present his *Fountain*?

In 1917.

**Why was there an impulse to experiment with new methods
and new messages?**

Because the old messages and methods seemed exhausted. Previous generations'
optimistic and orderly view of the world seemed artificial and incapable
of expressing the confusion and darkness artists sensed. These artists hoped
that brutal realism would enable contact with something more true.

How did Joyce scholar Stuart Gilbert analyze this ferment?

Joyce scholar Stuart Gilbert wrote in 1950, "Writers and artists of that
bygone age [the 1890s] had the advantage over the present generation
[1950] that there was a citadel of organized propriety on which to drop
their incendiaries, and the ensuing blaze filled them and their admirers
with mischievous delight." That is, these artists challenged propriety
and styled themselves revolutionaries. They felt particular exhilaration
when their works outraged stuffy, proper people.

What was Joyce's own hope?

Joyce wrote, when he completed Dubliners, of "the special odour of
corruption which, I hope, floats over all my works."

How did Gilbert characterize this statement?

"That 'hope' was typically 'ninetyish.'"

And he meant by "ninetyish"?

The 1890s.

Was this love of challenging and questioning restricted to the arts?

No. In *The Quest of the Historical Jesus*, Albert Schweitzer found that attempts to revise the view of Jesus had been going on since the middle 1700s.

What characterized these attempts to revise the view of Jesus?

These attempts were characterized by rejection of the prevailing view and proposal of a substitute Jesus filled with whatever virtues were most valued at the time. Schweitzer termed this "a uniquely great expression of sincerity."

When did Schweitzer write his book?

In 1906.

What did Schweitzer conclude was the only way we could know Jesus?

He concluded that we can know Jesus only by following him.

What did Philip Jenkins assert in *Hidden Gospels: How the Search for Jesus Lost Its Way*?

Jenkins asserted that although Jesus-revision has been going on for centuries, revisers were for the most part ignorant of the revisers that preceded them. They believed that they were uniquely bold and felt particular exhilaration when their works outraged stuffy, proper people.

Jenkins asserted that the reviser's self-dramatizing narrative follows the classic lines of legend: A brave rebel uncovers—or uncovers new meaning in—an ancient document and brings about something liberating and new.

What two things do Jesus-revisers, past and present, share?

A restless desire to overthrow the past and do something new and a conviction that Jesus is all we can admire or desire.

Is Jesus all we can admire or desire?

Yes.

{ ▽*ERWIN RAPHAEL McMANUS: Is Jesus all we can admire or desire? Was Eden desirable for Adam? Of course we know one tree was. But what of the others? Is there a subplot hidden within the name of paradise? The name* Eden *literally means "pleasure." Everything God created was desirable—even the tree that was forbidden. Certainly all of creation was admirable. Can we admire or desire what God has created for us? Was Adam created with desires beyond God? Did Adam desire Eve when she was created by God? Was the first woman undesirable? Did God create us to desire and delight in a passion satisfied? What does it mean when the psalmist instructs us, "Delight yourself in the Lord and he will give you the desires of your heart"? Are there things in this world in which we live that are desirable?* }

How, then, do these revisers go wrong?

By failing to question the assumptions of thought fashion, which seep in and control them unaware. By mistakenly identifying the eternally admirable and desirable with passing popular ideas of what is admirable or desirable.

Give a contemporary example.

A contemporary example is the present age's romantic fascination with rebellion and the Jesus Seminar's preference to see Jesus as a political revolutionary, to the extent of rejecting as ahistorical any Gospel sayings thought inappropriate to a revolutionary.

{ ✸ *BRIAN D. McLAREN: Frederica addresses an important tension here, and she addresses it without resolving it, which is (in my opinion) exactly the right thing to do. The tension in question is between loyalty to tradition and willingness to break with tradition. Some in our culture are quick to applaud any questioning or defiance of tradition, as if tradition is the root of all evil. Others are as quick to defend tradition and condemn every questioning of it, as if innovation is the root of all evil. Somewhere in the midst of this tension, I believe, is the way of wisdom, neither underestimating the rich inheritance we have in our traditions (and in our shared Christian traditions) nor overestimating their present perfection. Interestingly, in every instance I can think of where I believe our churches today need to change (in method and in message), we can look back into our tradition and find resources to help us move ahead in innovation.* }

Give a second contemporary example.

In 1999 a British ad agency produced a black-and-red Easter poster for the Anglican church depicting Jesus in the likeness of Che Guevara. Both method and message were typically "nineties-ish."

Was this revised message and method successful?

Probably not. People under 50 did not recognize the allusion to the Guevara poster, which had been popular in the 1960s. Nor did they know who Guevara was. A vintage copy of this poster is now a valuable semiantique collectible, in the category of "paper ephemera."

What happened to Duchamp's urinal?

It was exhibited in an admiring retrospective of Duchamp's work in 1962.

How did Duchamp react to the art establishment's embrace of his work?

With anger and frustration. He said, "I threw the urinal...in their faces as a challenge and now they admire [it] for [its] aesthetic beauty!"

What do stuffy, proper people do with revolutionary objects?

Enjoy them. Acquire them. Turn them into collectibles.

Are they, then, not outraged by them after all?

Powerful people are exhilarated by works intended to outrage powerful people, whom they apparently think is someone else.

Why is this?

Contemporary culture honors the rebel above all other authority. The rebel enjoys highest status and greatest power. The rebel is the establishment.

How does cultural critic Thomas Frank describe this phenomenon?

Thomas Frank wrote in *The Conquest of Cool*, "Today there are few things more beloved of our mass media than the figure of the cultural rebel, the defiant individualist resisting the mandates of the machine civilization. Whether he is an athlete decked out in a mohawk and multiple-pierced ears, a policeman who plays by his own rules, an actor on a motorcycle, a movie frat boy wreaking havoc on the townies' parade, a soldier of fortune with explosive bow and arrow, a long-haired alienated cowboy gunning down square cowboys, or a rock star in leather jacket and sunglasses, he has become the paramount cliché of our popular entertainment, the preeminent symbol of the system he is supposed to be subverting."

Is the rebel figure, then, not truly subverting the status quo?

The rebel figure preserves the status quo. He possesses preeminent status. He is our culture's authority, while so-called authority figures, if they exist, are despised and mocked.

Do authority figures no longer exist?

Frank wrote, "On the other side of the coin, of course, are the central-casting prudes and squares (police, Southerners, old folks, etc.) against whom contemporary advertising, rock stars, and artists routinely cast themselves."

Who has power in that conflict?

Not the prudes and squares. They are props controlled by the rebels, brought out when necessary for dramatic purposes.

Why does our culture adore the rebel identity?

It's complicated.

Explain.

The affluence and ease of post-World War II America pooled into a growing sense of anxiety. The fear was that the seductive appeal of abundant, attractive, affordable mass-produced goods was turning us into a nation of mere consumers. The term for this was *conformity*. Though now forgotten, the soul-deadening danger of conformity was a topic of widespread discussion, from intellectual journals to *Reader's Digest*. This dilemma is now forgotten because it was resolved.

What solution was developed and by whom?

Advertising developed the brilliant solution of presenting the consumer as rebel. Customers could prove their independence by buying goods that demonstrated defiance of fashion. Such fashionable goods were akin to talismans, keeping the specter of conformity at bay. Especially fashionable were those products that appeared to repudiate fashion, implying that you were too cool to care whether you were cool. Yet because these goods could still be identically mass-produced, they remained affordable and of reassuringly familiar quality. The goods had never been the problem; anxiety about consuming them was the problem. This problem was eliminated through the magic of marketing, by invention of the consumer-as-rebel persona.

Did this rebel persona arise due to the hippie movement?

No. Frank finds the origin in Norman Mailer's 1957 essay "The White Negro." Mailer proposed that the "Hipsters" combat the "squares" by living the kind of sexy, jazzy, freewheeling life that whites fantasized belonged to blacks. Frank notes that Mailer was the first to take an option previously enjoyed by the intellectual elite, that of contempt for common culture and a self-elevating image of rebellion, and democratize it. At last the common man could feel superior to the common man.

Who first implemented this solution?

Doyle Dane Bernbach's brilliant Volkswagen antiads began appearing in 1959 and the "Pepsi Generation" in 1961. If the hippies hadn't arrived, it would have been necessary to invent them.

How many pages are in the current Birkenstock catalog?

Seventy-seven full-color pages, offering aggressively simple, unself-conscious footwear that thumbs its nose at fashion, costing up to $259.95 per pair.

Why is this essay written in question and answer format?

Because our age reverences questioning. Questioners are thought to be rebellious, which superior status exempts them from interrogation. The mechanism is similar to the "preemptive irony" of advertising and television, which makes it invulnerable to ironic critique.

What, then, must we conclude about the prescription that we should subvert, rebel, question, and revise?

We must ask whether we embrace this prescription because it has been diligently marketed to us.

Why has it been marketed to us?

So we'll buy stuff.

What must be suspected?

That we exercise this rebel persona most often not by actually rebelling but by purchasing status items that we have been told will make us cool.

What might real rebellion look like?

Standing outside an abortion clinic on a cold Saturday morning wearing really uncool sneakers and an uncool cardigan, praying.

What must we do with a reflexive-conformist stance of questioning authority?

Question it.

What happened to Duchamp's urinal?

It continues to gather authority as a prized and priceless artwork. In 1993, while it was on loan to a museum in Nimes from the Pompidou Center in

Paris, artist Pierre Pinoncelli revised its meaning, expressing a new message via a new method.

How?

He urinated in it.

What did this do to the urinal, or perhaps artwork?

Pinoncelli said that this liberated it. The museum said that this vandalized it. Courts sided with the museum, and Pinoncelli was assessed a heavy fine.

Is a sense that current methods and messages are exhausted a new phenomenon?

No. It would be possible to trace this dissatisfaction back for centuries, perhaps, depending on the criteria used. Modernism is by nature restless, always questing for the next new thing, and in rebellion against the present.

Is there such a thing as postmodernism?

There is no way to tell. Dissatisfaction with the current times is an old phenomenon. Flux is modernism's stasis. Yet times will eventually change, so it is possible that they are changing now. If so, however, the future would not call this period postmodernism. They would name it by whatever distinctive features emerge, and these are not yet perceptible.

What is new under the sun?

Nothing.

What is old under the sun?

A fear that all is vanity and striving after the wind. Weariness. Frustration. Impatience. Futility. Loneliness at the deepest levels. Two friends, after a long late-night conversation, still puzzles to themselves and each other, earthbound and aging, side by side and miles apart, looking up at the cold blue heaventree.

{ *ERWIN RAPHAEL McMANUS: I slipped into bed late one night and lay flat on my back staring mindlessly at our ceiling. To my surprise, as my eyes adjusted to the dark, I found myself staring at a constellation of stars. My wife, Kim, had glued fluorescent stars to our ceiling, bringing the heaventree indoors so that I might enjoy it before my sleep. This was somewhat ironic, living in a place where modernity and consumption have swallowed the stars in a blanket of smog and pollution. Much like we've lost the stars in a man-made haze, we have lost the place where we see the questions clearly and stop long enough to reflect on the majesty that is really there.* }

Is this ridiculous or contemptible?

No.

Is it sad?

Yes.

Will some new thing alleviate it?

It has not been shown to do so.

Why is this essay written in question and answer format?

To use an unfamiliar, though not new, method to disrupt the reader's expectations and disarm him to receive an unfamiliar, though not new, message.

Why does it appear that the questions anticipate the answers?

Because "Ithaca" is not written in the form of simple dialogue. Joyce's format in the "Ithaca" sequence is catechism. In a catechism, questions have answers. The answers unfold what is already known, rather than speculate freely or end in uncertainty. The questions presume that answers exist. The questions presume that it is possible to know these answers or partial answers.

Do the questions presume that the answers are exhaustive?

No. The questions presume that answers are necessarily fragmentary. However, those fragments may be reliable.

Does reliable mean "objectively true"?

Reliable means that there is an objective truth who is a person, not a proposition. He is reliable; he is trustworthy.

Can we not know objective truths?

We can know some objective truths. Some objective truths we do not, or cannot, grasp because they are beyond our comprehension or because we dislike them. These truths nevertheless exist. Someone knows the number of hairs on your head, though you do not. We don't know ourselves very well, but he does. We see ourselves in a mirror dimly, but one day we will know ourselves and him as well as we are known by him right now.

Why does life seem like great weariness, vanity, and striving after wind?

Because although he knows us, we do not know him very well. We are lonely and empty because we do not know him very well. We are vacant inside, deafened by the continual wind of our emptiness, and only his presence can fill us. Yet we fail to know him well. Sometimes this is because we don't want to know him and sometimes because we don't know how.

Why do people continually want to revise the prevailing view of Jesus?

To relieve the pain of this dilemma by changing Jesus into something we can understand.

What is Jesus' alternative plan?

To change us into something that can understand him.

{ ✿ *BRIAN D. McLAREN: This is, I think, my favorite (of many favorite) lines in this chapter. It reminds us that the kind of knowing that applies to God is not simply a matter of objective neutrality plus proper tools of research, plus the right text to be researched, plus due diligence. Knowledge of God involves being transformed into the kind of person—humble, inquisitive, teachable, obedient, practiced—who is capable of knowing the holy.* }

Do we misunderstand him because our message or methods are outdated?

Perhaps in part. But the main reason is that he is scary. Another factor is that he is deep.

How might misguided messages or methods impede, in part, our knowledge of him?

Inept responses to prevailing culture in the past may have resulted in institutionalized misunderstanding and misrepresentation. As cultures change and efforts are made to adapt and revise, these mistakes may be compounded or overcorrected. Well-meaning attempts to keep pace with culture can result in desperate faddishness that looks lame a decade later. The doctrine of ceaseless adaptation to superficial culture must be interrogated. The dogma of suspicion must be critiqued.

Does adapting to varying cultures enable us to better know him in some ways?

Yes, for example, by translating the gospel into a local language. Changes to make the faith merely appealing, however, backfire. The gospel is inherently not appealing but challenging, or as St. Paul said, an offense and a stumbling block. People who are coaxed into buying it for its charming qualities are apt to feel deceived and to quit altogether when the going gets tough (see the parable of the sower). Adjustments to reflect local or temporary culture have a net trivializing effect. They focus attention on the superficial rather than on those more difficult elements that pertain to all humans everywhere and to the unchanging God with whom they must deal.

How does a doctrine of cultural adaptation impede our knowledge of him?

By not going deep enough and halting at the superficial level of culture. By failing to touch the transcultural, transhistorical, and ultimately cosmic reality at the source. By failing to know Christ himself.

How can we know Christ?

I don't know where to begin.

Begin.

The place to begin is with the Scriptures. You must not see this book dropping leather-bound from Heaven. Don't think of it as a book at all. Picture the living words and deeds of Jesus and the people who saw him. Imagine how they told and retold these stories and eventually wrote them down. The distinctive feature of this life, whether told, written, or painted, was its dynamic and transformative power.

How then shall we use this book?

See again the context and the listeners. This budding community heard and saw this life and was charged and changed by it firsthand. When they heard and discussed the events that became the Scriptures, they had a simple advantage over us and rather a mundane one: The stories were told in their native language. We fall into turmoil over fine points of translation, but they used no translation; they heard the stories in the same Greek that they used in the home and the marketplace. The analogies and jokes were those of their time and common culture. Things we puzzle over were clear to them. They knew how to weigh and value things that confuse us, two thousand years and half a world away.

{ ANDY CROUCH: I confess I am not completely persuaded by this argument. First, is the presence of the Holy Spirit not a more reliable guarantee of understanding than temporal or cultural proximity? I have seen Scripture in a fresh light thanks to African brothers and sisters who first heard the gospel from Americans, who in turn heard it from Europeans—three times or more culturally removed from its source and yet closer in many ways to the heart of the message than their own teachers. We have plenty of evidence, above all from the evangelist Mark, that the disciples of Jesus, who could have been presumed to get all his jokes and understand his allusions, in fact were utterly unable to understand what Jesus was saying and doing—even after the Resurrection. No Christian can be anything but grateful for the efforts made in the first centuries of Christianity to discern truth and refute heresies. We are in every sense dependent on those who came before us. And yet—what they delivered to us was not most of all their own conclusions and formulations but the Scriptures themselves, texts which speak eloquently about the potential for God's people to be deceived and also about the possibility that God will do dramatically new things (the Exodus, the Exile, the Restoration, the ministry of Jesus, the inclusion of the Gentiles) that no amount of tradition could have prepared us for. Precisely because it is a living word, the Bible has the ongoing capacity to disclose things that have been hidden for ages (Ephesians 3:9). Scripture says, "I am about to do a new thing; now it springs forth, do you not perceive it?" (Isaiah 43:19 NRSV). Is there no category of newness that reflects God's new creation rather than humanity's rebellious attempts at novelty? What does it mean to allow that new creation to work itself out in the history of the church? These questions have not always been answered satisfactorily by those who anchor their faith and practice in the consensus that emerged in the middle of the first millennium. "Two thousand years and half a world away/Dying trees still grow greener when you pray" (Bruce Cockburn, "All the Diamonds"). There is plenty of dead wood throughout the history of the people of God, but isn't it possible that the overall direction is toward a more and more comprehensive understanding of the gospel as the news spreads through time and cultures rather than the reverse? }

Were these people better Christians than we are?

It seems that they held themselves to higher standards of morality and integrity than we currently expect, and they demonstrated courage under persecution that might make us quail. But God was not closer to them than he is to us. He doesn't prefer them, and they didn't get a bigger share of him.

Was the church of that time holier than the church today?

No.

Why not?

Because weeds and wheat grow up together till the last day. An enemy has done this.

In what, then, is their advantage?

Their advantage is that they heard the message first, in their own cultural language, and were more able to understand it clearly. When we are puzzled by bits of the message or disagree about its meaning, we may be able to settle things by looking up what they wrote in explanation. When they are in broad agreement, across many times and cultures, it is a witness that should arrest our attention.

Do such works exist?

On the shelf behind me are two such collections, one in 54 volumes and one in 38.

Are all these writings from the time of the New Testament?

No. They range through the first centuries. We give precedence to those beliefs that were agreed to over the broadest geographic range, from the earliest times, and attested to by the greatest number of writers. The summary test is "everywhere, always, and by all."

Do all early writers and early communities agree?

No. We look for broadest consensus.

Give an example.

These Christians came to agreement on which books should be considered part of the canon of the New Testament. The question was strongly debated, and some books (the epistle to the Hebrews and the Revelation of St. John) required centuries to win full approval. Our older brothers and sisters in faith trusted in Jesus' promise that "When the Spirit of truth comes, he will guide you into all the truth" (JOHN 16:13, RSV). Whenever we open the New Testament, we demonstrate in turn our trust in their discernment and leadership. Whenever we read the New Testament, we affirm that they had authority to make decisions like this.

Give an example of another decision.

These Christians also wrote the Nicene Creed (A.D. 325) to correct a popular idea that Jesus was a mere human and not God from all eternity. Some questions, like this one, seemed unclearly addressed in Scripture and open to the interpretation of the individual Christian. Believers met in council to decide such questions, prayerfully seeking the Spirit's guidance. This method of discernment was in use even before the New Testament was written, as shown by the Council of Jerusalem in Acts 15. It became, in fact, an article of faith to believe that the community had discerned accurately when it was "with one accord" (Acts 15:25). In the Nicene Creed, we say that we believe in four things: God the Father, Jesus Christ, the Holy Spirit, and the church.

May any quotation from any early church writer be taken as gospel?

No. We look for broadest consensus. Individual writers of the early church could be as flawed as they are today. Most have occasional trouble spots. Despite this, they may be called "saints." Even saints aren't perfect on earth. Some whose writings are still treasured departed from the consensus at significant points—more likely to be points of theological speculation than points of devotion.

Give three examples.

Origen, most eloquent and intoxicated with the love of God, was censured for his assertion of universal salvation. Augustine, confessor of touching intimacy and humility, was criticized for his views of free will and original sin. Tertullian, acerbic Mark Twain of the early church, drifted from the faith community into a cult. Yet all may be read profitably today.

May we use this threefold test in looking for consensus among Christians today?

No. That would be to omit one of the three elements, the requirement that the earliest belief, the one held for the longest amount of time, takes precedence. When this element is abandoned, variant doctrines emerge that are held by ever-smaller numbers of believers, and continual disagreement and splintering results.

Give an example of an original, then replaced and splintered, belief.

In the sixth chapter of the gospel of John, Jesus said that we must eat his body and drink his blood or we will have no life in us. He used emphatic words—not "eat my body" in the Greek but "chew my flesh." It was a confrontational statement and to "many of his disciples" so disgusting and distressing that they ceased following him.

What was the consensus of the early Christians on this disturbing passage?

The consensus of the early Christians was that this passage is to be taken literally. They believed that the bread and wine of the Eucharist genuinely become the body and blood of Christ. They did not venture to explain how this could be so but simply believed it on Jesus' word. The earliness of this belief is evident in the writings of St. Ignatius (about A.D. 105), the Didache (perhaps A.D. 80), and St. Paul (the description and warnings of 1 Corinthians 11:23-30). It is the plain meaning of the Scripture in John as well. This view was held in unanimity for the first millennium and a half of Christian faith.

{ ▽ERWIN RAPHAEL McMANUS: *Here, of course, I must respectfully disagree with you. Putting aside all the rest, I cannot see how "it is the plain meaning of the Scripture in John as well." Even while growing up in this theological tradition, I find it to be imposed on the text. To have acted on the literal nature of Jesus' words, Jesus' listeners would have roasted him and enjoyed him for dinner that night. Instead, Peter concludes, "Only you have the words of eternal life." In the same context Jesus emphatically declares, "The Spirit gives life; the flesh counts for nothing. The words I have spoken to you are spirit and they are life" (John 6:63). Even more troubling are the words of Jesus where he equates our eating him with his life in the Father. He says, "Just as the living Father sends me and I live because of the Father, so the one who feeds on me will live because of me." Isn't the clearest reading that as the Son feeds on the Father, so we are to feed on the Son?* }

Is this still a hard saying today?

Yes. It continues to be capable of distressing and disgusting the followers of Jesus even as during his time, and in some quarters individual interpretations of the passage arose. These interpretations may be currently widely spread, but they do not have the attestation of being held from earliest times.

Is the church an institution, or is it summed up in a single earthly leader?

No. The church is the body of Christ on earth. All members are equal. All together guard the faith. The leadership of the church does not create or impose beliefs. Instead, all believers, including those in leadership, are under the authority of the common faith.

Which denomination possesses this treasure?

The early consensus is the heritage of every Christian of any denomination. It is something that we all go back to.

May we go back to it, retrieve the things we like, disregard those we don't, and create Christianities that suit our times and temperaments?

No. This places unwarranted confidence in one's own wisdom and ability to discern. It underestimates how brainwashed we are by our surrounding culture, as we affirm what is currently fashionable and recoil from, or fail even to perceive, what is not. The wisest course is to submit to the accumulated faith of our older brothers and sisters, to immerse ourselves in it, and gradually to comprehend more as we ourselves are changed.

Is this best done by reading theology and history?

No. It is best done by praying. This can include using the ancient prayers in private and standing in the flow of corporate worship. Prayer should also be the context for reading Scripture or other works. We are transformed by the renewing of our minds. This takes time. It includes the whole self, reason, emotion, and body. It happens slowly, by immersion in the living faith.

Is nothing to be gained by choosing and implementing ancient elements we like?

Elements plucked out according to taste are like flowers in a vase. They are more lovely than no flowers at all, but they have no roots and will wither. It is like sewing an old patch on a new garment. It is a better solution than having a hole in your pants, but it is not a lasting solution. It will not bring you to the goal.

Is the goal to develop spotless doctrine?

No. The goal is to know Christ.

{ ♡ *ERWIN RAPHAEL McMANUS: Frederica, I choose this place to simply say how often your words resonate in my heart. You speak of Jesus with an intimacy that is all too lacking in Christian literature today. Throughout your dialogue I have found surprising resonance again and again. I find it strange to so strongly disagree with your process of determining orthodoxy and at the same time to find such profound agreement with the essence and texture of your faith.* }

Do we know Christ in order to possess correct ideas?

No. The goal of knowing Christ is to be healed and transformed. It is to partake of the presence of Christ, to dwell "in him." It is to take on his fire like a coal in the furnace.

Is there any value to correct doctrine?

Correct doctrine is indispensable because otherwise we will fall into delusion. This is why the guidance of older brothers and sisters in the faith is so vital. Not one of them is dead. They are alive in Christ, in continual prayer in the presence of God. They pray for us, and we can ask their prayers. They worship the Lord in the beauty of holiness where seraphim shield their faces and cry, "Holy." They invite us to join them. This is the church we must enter, which has been formed and proved by the Spirit, and can safeguard us from delusion and teach us how to know Christ.

How can we know Christ?

I don't know where to begin.

Begin.

The place to begin is with the cross. You must not picture this as a static legal transaction whereby a debt was canceled. You must see this, as the early Christians did, as a continuing, vigorous victory.

Over whom was Christ victorious?

Over death. The wages of sin is death, which is more than a condition; in its personification, death is related to the Evil One from whom we ask deliverance in the Lord's Prayer. The desire of our ancient foe is to enslave us by luring us through temptation into sin and thus into his trap. Because all humans inevitably sin, all are bound over to death.

How was Christ victorious?

By becoming human, Christ took on human nature. By dying, he brought human nature into the kingdom of death. By rising, he demolished the gates of death and conquered the Evil One.

Did Christ then pay the ransom to his Father in his own blood?

No. The early Christians knew that it couldn't be the Father who received a "ransom," because the Father was not holding us hostage. The Evil One, who did hold us, was unworthy of such a ransom for freeing us; "this [idea] is an outrage!" said St. Gregory the Theologian (died A.D. 389). What's more, if Christ's blood "paid" the ransom, he took back that payment when he was resurrected. No, the Evil One was not merely bought off; he was defeated.

Was Christ's death not a ransom but a payment to his Father?

The early Christians would not have said so. St. Gregory continues, "Why would the blood of his only begotten Son be pleasing to the Father, who would not accept even Isaac when he was offered by his father?"

{ ▷ *MICHAEL HORTON: First, I would challenge the claim that the early church rejected the notion of ransom. But more importantly, the New Testament uses the verb* lyo *(to free by ransom payment) and the noun* lytron *(ransom payment) more than 40 times. In view of related terms, such as propitiation, expiation, sacrifice, it is impossible to exclude the idea of God's wrath against sin being absorbed by Christ in our place. With all due respect to St. Gregory, Isaiah prophesied that "it pleased the LORD to bruise Him; he has put Him to grief. When You make His soul an offering for sin, He shall see His seed, He shall prolong His days, and the pleasure of the LORD shall prosper in His hand. He shall see the labor of His soul, and be satisfied. By His knowledge My righteous Servant shall justify many, for He shall bear their iniquities" (Isaiah 53:10-11 NKJV). The Father was pleased with the Son's sacrifice and interrupted Abraham's sacrifice of Isaac because Isaac was not the Messiah. I never have understood why contemporary Orthodox brothers and sisters have trouble accepting the notion of substitutionary atonement. It seems as if it is treated as an either-or—substitution or conquest over the powers—but why not both? Surely Scripture is rich with both metaphors for Christ's work (and others besides).* }

Doesn't the wrath of God demand payment for our sins?

Our actions deserve God's wrath, but early Christians would say that instead he pours out on us compassion. Though the prodigal son deserved wrath, the father did not punish him. While he was yet a long way off, the father ran to embrace him. The father did not ask who would pay the son's bills. The father did not say he would pay them by killing the blameless older brother.

Doesn't the ancient Hebrew temple sacrifice foreshadow Christ's sacrifice on the cross?

Early Christians considered those parallels evocative and moving but did not press them in a literal or mechanical way. As Athanasius (died A.D. 373) explained in *On the Incarnation*, the chief sacrifice was in Christ's becoming human in the first place. The Incarnation was the great act of obedience to the will of the Father, the initial act that set all else in motion. The entire drama, from beginning to end, is what saves us, not just three hours on Friday.

{ ▷ *MICHAEL HORTON: A salutary reminder. But what three hours those were! We dare not forget that Jesus himself (as reported in Matthew, Luke, and John) repeatedly refers to the cross as his "hour"—the climax of the drama.* }

If God intended to forgive us, why was it necessary for Jesus to come and die?

Because the Fall, and our continuing complicity in sin, had worked fundamental damage in human nature. Though we are not born bearing Adam's guilt, we are still so bent that we will inevitably fall into sin and earn our own captivity by death. This tendency is something we share, which flows among all humans.

How did the Incarnation address this problem?

Think of human nature as a corporate reality rather than something individuals possess in little pieces. When Jesus became human, he represented, or embodied, all of us, everyone who ever has lived or ever will. That is what he carried into hades and out again; that is what he raised from the dead. This means that every human who ever has lived or ever will is going to live forever.

Will everyone spend eternity in the presence of God?

Everyone will spend eternity in the presence of God. No place exists apart from God's presence, even now. There is no separate corner in the afterlife where demons will be allowed to torture humans forever because that would be a reward for the Evil One. He is not rewarded but defeated. God is love, and there is no darkness in him. We will all live forever in the light of God's love.

What, then, is hell?

Our God is a consuming fire. Those who have turned to Christ and prepared themselves in this life will experience that river of fire as light, warmth, and life. We see a glimpse of what this is like in Christ's transfiguration on Mount Tabor. This life is a process of turning increasingly toward Christ, learning to bear that uncreated light, getting the impurities out of our lump of coal. We must grow stronger and learn to bear his fire. Those who have not accepted Christ will experience his presence as burning and darkness and gnashing of teeth. All the misery of this life and the next is due to not knowing Christ.

How can we know Christ?

I don't know where to begin.

Begin.

The place to begin is with repentance. You must not picture this as despair or masochism. Instead, you must see a sick person who wants to get well. We are sick, world-sick, self-sick, and even our ability to comprehend our sickness is damaged. We abandon ourselves into the hands of the healer, who loves us, who won victory for us and freed us from bondage to death.

Does he pronounce us cured, though we are not, by imputing to us his wholeness?

No. What he offers us is not merely legal acquittal. It is more alarmingly intimate than that. He offers himself, his very life, he in us and we in him. He is already here, filling all things, overflowing all creation with his breathed-in presence. In him all things hold together. Wretched, fragmented, and lonely, we can barely perceive him, and we may not consistently want to know him, so addicted are we to our sickness. But it is his will that a sinner not die but come to repentance, his will that we become partakers of the divine nature, his will that we increasingly receive the light of Christ. Thus we become light-bearing saints, destined to live for the praise of his glory.

{▷ *MICHAEL HORTON: It all comes down to the diagnosis. If Adam's children are merely sick, then salvation is a matter of healing and improving. But if they are "dead in trespasses and sins,"(Ephesians 2:1, NKJV) incapable of receiving the things of God because of their sinful condition, and "suppress the truth in unrighteousness,"(Romans 1:18, NKJV) then salvation depends entirely on divine mercy and radical grace. The announcement that we can be saved by cooperating with God in our moral transformation is not good news to those who see in Scripture a deep, pervasive, and radical diagnosis of the human problem. While affirming a large place for talk of sanctification and glorification (theosis), the churches of the Reformation (once again) do not thereby deny the legal aspect, which is so clear in the language and metaphors adopted by the biblical writers in both testaments. Why should the affirmation of sanctification and glorification cancel the affirmation of a purely forensic justification?* }

What has this to do with repentance?

If we are to be transformed, we must be changed. That is tautological. If we are to change, we must recognize where we need to change and begin to do so. It is not a matter of allowing a divine spark within to gently bloom. The kingdom of Heaven is taken by force. You must be perfect, as your Father is perfect. The sickness is real and will require a skilled surgeon. All things come from God in this process, even our rudimentary and vacillating desire to be healed. We cooperate with the surgeon but do not earn healing or anything else thereby. It is a free gift. It is a gift we can refuse. Many do.

What dissuades us from embracing healing?

A powder-puff gospel that invites people to get comfortable instead. A cupcake gospel that invites people to like themselves just the way they are and to stay that way. A self-pity gospel that is afraid to reprove, though the Father will chasten every son he receives. A soft, enculturated gospel that is so dazzled by the prevailing culture's valuing of self-affirmation and self-esteem that it cannot call it to repentance. Thinking, "I am rich, I have prospered, and I need nothing," not knowing that you are wretched, pitiable, poor, blind, and naked.

How do we cooperate with the surgeon?

A patient cooperates with a surgeon by allowing him to work. We make room for his healing; we exercise kindness toward others, curb our tongues, avoid gross sin, discipline our minds and bodies. We get to know our familiar sins and train ourselves to defeat them. We train like athletes competing for a prize. The athlete works out not in order to pay for past failures but to prepare for future contests. We learn from our older brothers and sisters what exercises they have tested and found most useful, such as fasting and continual prayer. We learn from them how to do these exercises in ways that fit us personally, which will make us stronger rather than break us. As we grow in strength, we can take on more.

At what point are we legally saved?

This is not a matter of legality but of health. { ▷ *MICHAEL HORTON: There is a lot of dismissal of legality these days, not only from our historical challengers (Orthodox and Roman Catholics) but from many evangelicals as well. Nevertheless, the burden of proof is on critics to offer some account of the obviously legal terms and themes that are pervasive throughout Scripture: covenant (with its stipulations and sanctions), sacrifices, law, the covenant lawsuits God brings against the people in the prophets and the courtroom scenes in which God judges and justifies, the unmistakably legal terminology used by Jesus ("acquitted," "stands condemned already," "testimony," "judge," "judgment," "justified") and by the apostles (especially by Paul). It is one thing to say that we have so emphasized the legal aspect that other important aspects of salvation have been neglected, but to simply dispense with the legal aspect assumes an enormous burden of proof in the light of the evidence. By the way, I would recommend Thomas Oden's* The Justification Reader *(Eerdmans, 2002), which culls citations from the early Christian writers defending an evangelical understanding of justification.* } At what point is the patient fully cured? It may be possible to tell from the end of the story, but while in process we must be humble and aware of the half-hearted, feeble quality of our discipleship. Be sober, be watchful. There is always danger of relapse. Christ always wills to save us, but we, like Judas, can reject that at any point. He who endures to the end will be saved. Yet if Christ did not move us to desire him and give us his strength, no one could endure.

Do sins accumulate as debts that must be paid?

No. Sins are akin to drops of poison. They make us sick. We want to be full of radiance as he is and so try to wean ourselves from these temptations. Sin is infection, not infraction.

{ ▷ *MICHAEL HORTON: Sorry to butt in again, but why the either-or? Surely Scripture represents sin as both infection and infraction. There is simply no way to understand the covenantal relationship of God and his people as fleshed out in Scripture apart from the recognition of sanctions, curse and blessing, judgment and justification.* ⊗ *BRIAN D. McLAREN: Frederica may have little or no interest in (and maybe, instead, a high degree of revulsion against) translating the gospel into terms more understandable to postmodern men and women. But she is doing so beautifully in this section. Because she is walking in a path of discipleship that is decidedly premodern and because almost every common Protestant and Catholic elucidation of the gospel is expressed in ultramodern thought forms and language (the kind of thing I fret about incessantly in my chapter in this volume), Frederica's imagery and language offer rich resources for postmodern people who are seeking to understand the gospel but find our modern or ultramodern articulations banal, flat, or dishonoring to God and humanity. Modern concepts of salvation are almost exclusively legal; the dominant metaphor is the courtroom; God's deepest identity is judge. The imagery that comes naturally to Frederica is no less potent and is even more primal: poison, health, light. This more primal imagery (not to exclude legal imagery but to end its exclusive dominance) will "season our speech with salt," in my opinion, as we move out of modernity and into postmodernity.* }

Don't sins offend God?

Our sins must bring God great grief, but nothing shocks him. He needs no one to tell him what is in man, for he himself knows what is in man. Rather, misuse of our bodies or each other will damage us and carry us far from his healing presence—he, the only Light, the only Life. To be far from him is to be in darkness and death. This is a direct effect, rather than the result of storing up points toward punishment.

Give an example.

If a person uses tobacco and becomes ill, we see that this illness is a direct result. This is the case even if the person did not realize that tobacco would harm him and even if the use of it continued to feel pleasant. These negative results can even spill over and damage innocent family members and the general culture, due to secondhand effects. Yet these effects are simple and direct. We would not say that tobacco use angers God, which in turn creates a debt that must be paid and that God receives this payment by punishing Jesus or the ill person. The concept of merit is wholly irrelevant because the process is direct and simple. Sins sicken us and alienate us from God, and we fight against them, pommel our body and subdue it, because we want to be well.

{ ▷ *MICHAEL HORTON: It seems to me that sin is reduced almost entirely to actions in this account, giving insufficient development to sin as a condition. Could this not be at the heart of the differences between the East and West over original sin?* }

Give another example.

In the case of adultery, likewise, the action damages participants and estranges them from God, even if they don't realize that adultery will harm them and even if it continues to feel pleasant. These negative results can even spill over and damage innocent family members and the general culture, due to secondhand effects. The process is a direct one, not based on external merits or demerits. The result is damaged souls and alienation from God—a direct result rather than a calculated punishment.

Is homosexuality an infraction against God's holy code?

The early Christians would not categorize any sin in such terms. However, they would identify homosexuality as sin. They would say that it, like adultery, is subtly damaging even to those who enjoy it and see no harm in it. We may be puzzled as to why they make this diagnosis, but they are consistent and emphatic on this from one generation to the next. They also saw virginity as a source of spiritual power, something we likewise find hard to grasp. We should recognize that our comprehension in the arena of sexuality has been damaged by the distortion of the prevailing culture and admit that our ability to evaluate these things is not trustworthy. We can recognize that our older brothers and sisters were unanimous on these things and hope to come to see what they saw so clearly as we grow in Christ and our damaged sexual understanding is healed.

Mustn't each person test and establish his own ethical standards?

No. We have inside a conscience informed by God; we also have desires and selfish impulses that can do a very good impression of that voice. Further, we are confused by the prevailing culture's opinions and fashions. We must learn to have humility about our limited perspective and question our reflexive prejudices. Humility, in fact, is the single most important exercise.

How does humility change us?

When we see ourselves as the chief of sinners, we no longer take offense at wrongs done to us. We forgive others as we ourselves are forgiven. We love even our enemies. We no longer judge.

How can there be justice without judgment?

There is judgment; it's just not our job. God is the judge, and all will be judged one day. { ▷ *MICHAEL HORTON: But that's legal language. It was earlier asserted that sin was an infection, not an infraction. On what basis can a judgment be made where such procedures are absent?* } But because we have been forgiven so much, we pray that others will come to repentance and receive forgiveness as well. The best way to help someone come to repentance may not be to indulge them; it may be necessary to intervene and confront. This may be what justice requires. But we never seek vengeance. Vengeance is the Lord's. Our hope and goal, our great commission, is directed toward bringing all to salvation and knowledge of the Lord.

With this goal in mind, how should the church relate to the culture?

Both categories are deceptive. Instead, picture the Lord filling all things. The church is the company of people who know this truth, living and departed, those of us who struggle and the unseen cloud of witnesses who pray with and for us. We who persevere in this life are in the process of getting well.

What of others who are outside, in the secular culture?

There is no outside. There is no place where God is not, even now. Even those who do not know the truth of Christ are also created, beloved, and known by him. He is closer to them than their own breath, though they do not know him. We work together with God so that every person can come to saving knowledge of Christ and be healed and transformed alongside us.

What has the culture to do with this?

Christ has compassion on those who are harassed and helpless because they do not know their shepherd. The culture is the ever-changing weather conditions that these sheep must endure, which they try to respond to as best they can, though they are confused and wounded. Protection and rescue of individual sheep is our primary goal. It is less worthwhile to try to change the weather. We may occasionally have isolated success, but it appears that every weather pattern will have both good and bad elements, and weather itself is bound to be a perennial phenomenon.

How can we convert the culture?

A culture cannot be converted. { ✿ *BRIAN D. McLAREN: I agree, yet I think of the words of the Apocalypse (11:15): "The kingdom of the world has become the kingdom of our Lord and of his Christ, and he will reign for ever and ever." Cultures (which may be what Paul had in mind when he spoke of "principalities and powers"), as real parts of creation, must be included in the redemption and restoration of all things, don't you think? Aren't cultures the dark spaces that we light through our good deeds and the meat that we salt through our Christlike lives (Matthew 5:13)?* } Only individuals can be converted. God knows how to reach each individual; every conversion is an inside job. We cooperate by listening attentively for God's directions and speaking the right words at the right moment, doing a kind deed, bearing Christ's light and being his fragrance in the lives of people we know. This is the level where things change, one individual at a time, as one coal gives light to another. When enough people change, the culture follows—though, again, the hope of ever having a perfect culture is futile. Our effectiveness as witnesses is tested not on the public stage but by our private daily conduct. If we are not being healed at those levels, all we do for public display will be garbage. "But only acquire the Holy Spirit" and you will save a thousand around you (St. Seraphim of Sarov, died 1833).

{ ♡ *ERWIN RAPHAEL McMANUS: Yes, only individuals can be converted. A resounding yes. What does it look like when two converted individuals walk together? Or perhaps three or more are gathered in his name? Is this the beginning of community or specifically a community of faith? How would we describe the result of when the participants in this community grow in social, political, and cultural influence? What impact on culture would they have? Would something new emerge from the ancient? Conceding there will never be a perfect culture, is it possible to have a healthy one? It would seem a given that evil men and women have been the epicenters of emerging nefarious cultures. Is it possible that a part of the overflow of the transformative movement of Jesus Christ is the creation of a new culture?* }

What kinds of questions are worthless?

Ironic, smart-aleck questions; questions designed to reinforce a self-image of being a rebel and questioner; rhetorical questions; questions designed to trap or humiliate another person.

What kinds of questions are worthwhile?

Questions that open to yourself your own vast ignorance; questions that reveal your smallness and weakness; questions that cast you down in awe; questions that raise you up in worship.

{ ▷ *MICHAEL HORTON: This has to be one of the most succinct and edifying statements of godly questions I've come across. It certainly comports with Paul's rhetorical scheme: argument, question, argument, leading to doxological outburst.* }

What is the most important question?

"Who do you say that I am?"

{ ▽ *ERWIN RAPHAEL McMANUS: Yes, I agree without question. This is the most important question. Thank you for raising it.* }

Why is this essay written in question and answer format?

Go outside after midnight and look up at the heaventree of stars.

{ ✿ *BRIAN D. McLAREN: We Christians have always struggled with authority. When Jesus walked Galilean roads, our brothers the disciples repeatedly doubted him and even tried to correct him at times, not having full confidence in his authority. Jesus' opponents repeatedly asked, "By what authority?" and ultimately judged him a fraud and so appealed to the authority of Caesar to have Jesus executed. He was labeled a king only in mockery on the cross. After the Resurrection, Jesus said that all authority had been granted to him (even then, some doubted), but he didn't explain how that authority was to be extended to his disciples, and so power struggles soon enough erupted among them. By Paul's time there were "pseudo-apostles" afoot, and bitter debates arose about whose voices should be heard in the churches and whose voices should be ignored. ✿ The Western church eventually "solved" this problem by creating a structure that mirrored the Roman Empire. But even so, heretical sects continued to arise, questioning the authority of the church, and at times the church responded to dissent in ways that ultimately undermined ecclesial authority, even while imposing temporary control through violence or threats of violence. Eventually, the Protestant Reformation broke the church's practical authority over many of her previous members, and since Protestants let the authority cat out of the institutional bag, we haven't been able to get it back in. ✿ Protestants often claimed that the Bible was their authority but acted (too often) as if the Bible could wield that authority without interpreters. This created a situation in which interpreters, scholars, and teachers often exerted covert authority that neither they nor their followers were even aware they possessed. Sometimes, like wizards in Oz hiding behind the curtain, they pretended not to be there. "Don't argue with me—argue with God. I'm just preaching the* }

Word," they would say, as if their preaching involved no interpretation at all. This "solution" to the problem of authority satisfied some but not all. ❈ Frederica offers another potential solution to the authority problem, or perhaps more modestly, an element of that solution: Authoritative beliefs are attested to "everywhere, always, and by all." I wish it were that easy, but even this ancient prescription involves interpretation, it seems to me. And so one must ask, Whose interpretation of "everywhere, always, and by all" do we accept? Which parts of the "by all" are excluded and which are included? Her formula is helpful, but I don't think it solves the problem as neatly as some might conclude. ❈ Actually, I don't believe this problem ever will be resolved, or should be resolved, this side of the eschaton. I believe that the kind of world God made requires a mixture of form and freedom, a mixture of limits and possibilities, a dynamic tension between God's power and God's creatures' power. This requires God's authority to be deniable, unobvious, subtle, and apparently weak. As Dietrich Bonhoeffer said, God "wins power and space in the world by his weakness" (Letters and Papers from Prison, *July 16, 1944). I am writing these words a few weeks before Christmas, which displays the weakness and vulnerability of God's coming into our world in Christ, a display of powerful weakness matched only by the cross. ❈ This potent weakness, this understated authority, is displayed by the apostles at their best moments when they realize that God's power is perfected in their weakness (not when they're jockeying for positions of power, as they did in their worst moments). The great missiologist David Bosch said it like this: "The people who are to be won and saved should, as it were, always have the possibility of crucifying the witness of the gospel"* (Transforming Mission, 485). *❈ This crucifiable authority doesn't shout, "Resistance is futile! Submit and be assimilated!" like the Borg on Star Trek. It doesn't convert by the sword but rather says, "Put up your sword, Peter." Jesus empties himself, becomes a servant, suffers, dies, and eventually, raised and glorified, wins the heart, so that every knee bows and every tongue confesses the authority of the crucified. ❈ This is the authority of the Desert Fathers of Frederica's tradition, which is also our shared tradition in Christ. It's a kind of authority that needs to be rediscovered, in my opinion, as we leave the world of modern authority (scholarship, degrees, bureaucratic savvy, media savvy) and enter a new world seeking a voice that is not raised in the streets but is heard all the more because of its softness, gentleness, and uniqueness: "He who has ears to hear, let him hear," this voice says. ❈ Although I am not convinced the Orthodox path is the right one for everyone, I do believe that it offers all of us radically different resources—old, but new for many of us—to deal with the problems that confront us on all sides. I think in it we will hear the gentle voice in ways that many of us have too long neglected.* }

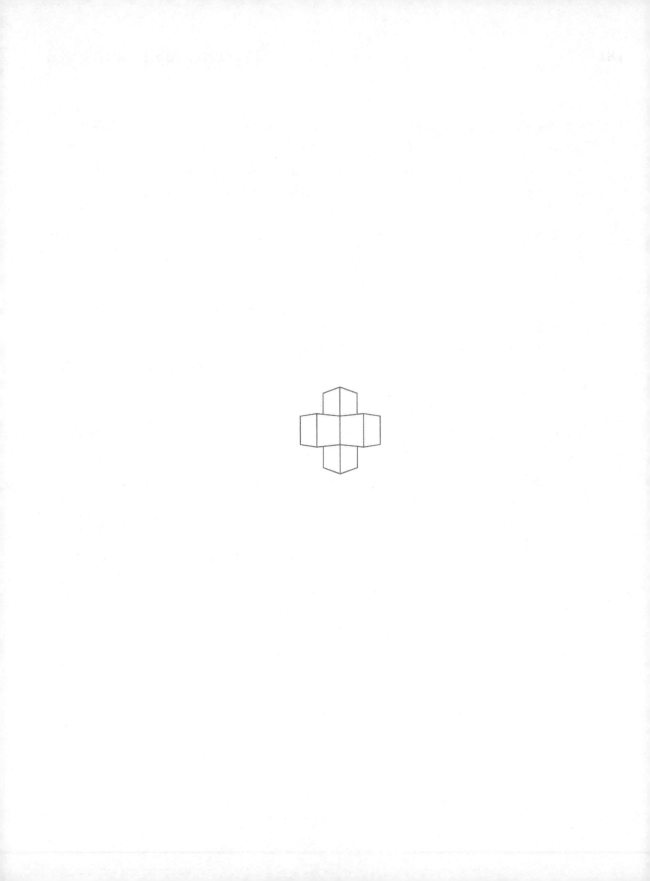

Frederica Mathewes-Green's Rejoinder

I APPRECIATE MY FRIENDS' PATIENCE with my essay and find that, in response to many of the comments, I would just repeat what I've already said. The central question is whether we should conform to the morals, theology, and worship of the church of the first centuries. The only further point I'd want to make is that we must not think of "the early church" as a single culture; even in the same city a culture changes radically over time, and we're talking about peoples all over the then-known world. What you can catch in a sieve, what has stayed strong through so many cultures over so much time, is reliable truth, the presence of the Holy Spirit.

Of course, most Christians today hold to a reduced version of that view, recognizing in other believers at a minimum a quality of being captured by the living, powerful presence of Christ. But there is a great deal more that we can access, which has already been "table tested" by a wide variety of cultures. We don't have to settle for the lowest common denominator. We don't have to make up new stuff because what we made up a decade ago is starting to feel lame.

That's the central question, as I say, but I'm also concerned about two other questions. One is, Does the Orthodox church accurately perpetuate this original biblical faith? Is this the place to go if you want to be part of the original family? I am convinced that it is. But the next question is harder. Do I accurately understand what the early church, and by extension the Orthodox church, teaches? Have I done enough reading? Have I stood long enough in worship, listening to the ancient hymns? I don't know what "enough" could possibly mean, but there's no doubt that I will never be able to comprehend it all. So what I've said in my essay, and will continue to explore here, I say in fear and trembling. I may fall far short of understanding what the church teaches. It's certain that I will always fall short of comprehending the mystery of my Lord Christ, who is the beauty at its center.

Despite my likely incompetence, I want to take a turn at the questions Michael raises about substitutionary theory, sacrifice, and ransom. First, let's notice that sacrifice and ransom don't mean the same thing. A ransom is paid to a kidnapper or slave trader. A savior redeems a captive from his captor. Ransom and redemption language concerns Christ's dealing with the one who was holding us hostage—that is, the Evil One, not the Father.

Sacrifice language, on the other hand, aims at the Father. Here come into play all the beautiful images that grow from Old Testament temple sacrifice and how Jesus fulfills and completes them forever. How do these fit together? How is he both ransom and sacrifice?

An answer is not immediately obvious; we are dealing with a mystery beyond our comprehension. If Anselm's answer had been obvious, it wouldn't have taken praying, Christ-loving, Bible-memorizing believers a thousand years to get it. The Holy Spirit would not have been so cruel. He would not have deprived the martyrs, certainly, of an understanding of their own salvation. Truth can't be so hard to find.

I'm speaking of sufficient truth, all we need to live by, of course; we don't have to concern ourselves with things too great for us. Because the mechanism of salvation is not obvious, we can find a festival of fervent, grateful guesses in the early writings, but when consensus emerged, it was modest about its claims to intellectual conquest.

It was this. The Son offers a sacrifice to the Father. The sacrifice is the entire Incarnation, not merely the cross; though the cross is central, it is already fully present in Christ's decision to become human, like a jewel in a setting of gold. Look at Philippians 2:6–11, which you probably already know is the earliest extant Christian hymn. You'll notice that it focuses on the self-emptying act of the Incarnation rather than the cross, like a hymn of ours would today. The Philippians hymn imagines Christ choosing to become human, a choice that would inevitably mean his death, and praises him for that courageous descent.

This was obedience. The sacrifice Christ offers to the Father is like a sacrifice a brave soldier offers to his general when he volunteers for a deadly assignment. Father and Son are in agreement; the Son honors the will of his Father and undertakes this cataclysmic mission to please him. It is clearly a gift and an offering; what the early church would not see, however, is payment. A brave soldier is not paying the general.

Payment language—ransom, redemption—points toward getting us free from the

Evil One. And the early church was never quite sure about how that worked. It would be an outrage, as St. Gregory said, to picture Jesus paying the Evil One. Some speculated that it was a trick payment—the famous fishhook analogy. In the end, there was a desire to say that it cost Jesus his blood to enter the kingdom of hades; the only way in that door was to be dead. In that sense he paid the price of our redemption, paid it with his blood. But no one wanted to say that the Evil One had a right to that payment, fair and square. Instead, what we get is the victory language—that once Jesus was in hades, he broke down the doors and set us free. "Christ is risen from the dead, trampling down death by death, and upon those in the tomb bestowing life!" That's the hymn we sing hundreds and hundreds of times in Easter season. We can't know all the details of how he set us free—we just know in our hearts that he did.

The split between justification and sanctification just doesn't fit this context. That distinction answers a question that would not have occurred to early Christians, and "life in Christ" or theosis covers both terms and other things as well. It's just a wholly different formulation—a reality we understand only by our own obedience, by doing it, step by baby step.

⊕   ⊕   ⊕   ⊕   ⊕

BRIAN D.
McLAREN

Brian D. McLaren

The Method, the Message, and the Ongoing Story

I'VE HEARD IT A HUNDRED TIMES, and I've said it quite a few too: The methods may change, but the message never changes. That's a respectable belief, and in a sense I wholeheartedly agree with it and affirm all those who live by it.

Meanwhile, I guess I would agree with the alternatives too under the right conditions. For example, I'd say the methods never change if by methods you mean love, building friendships, being honest and authentic, treating others with gentleness and respect, praying, walking humbly with God while living justly and mercifully, becoming all things to all people. And I'd say the message never changes if by message you mean the story that begins with "In the beginning, God created..."

But the statement about the methods changing but not the message has been especially precious to, and oft repeated by, people (like me) with evangelical roots. Why? Partly because we often found ourselves in the company of those who believed that nothing in the mid-to-late-twentieth-century church could change, neither message nor methods.

Biblically Justified

IN THIS CASE methods would include style of music, order of service, structure of governance, gender of preachers, mode of baptism, requirements for membership, list of taboos, style of preaching, color of carpeting, projection technology, and the like. {▷ *MICHAEL HORTON: Is it really fair to class the color of the carpet with the order of the service, the structure of governance, and the gender of ministers? There is a certain tone (unintentional) of dismissal among many low-church evangelicals toward enduring practices that may be wrong but have at least been given centuries of mature Christian reflection on scriptural teaching. They should not be treated under a category of "remember when we were Neanderthals" in contrast to our "enlightened openness," one of the most modern tendencies still in vogue. Brian does not himself seem to wholly embrace this caricature (see the next paragraph), but I would still not want to belong to a communion that simply either "froze" its methods in one century or sought wholly new forms each new century. Shouldn't we prefer to be normed by Scripture in our worship and outreach insofar as Scripture speaks and allow freedom in other respects? In the Reformed–Presbyterian tradition this usually has meant the distinction between biblically required "elements" of worship (preaching, sacraments, the prayers, offerings, praise) and "circumstances" that are dependent on biblically informed common sense (time of worship, type of building, color of carpet). Furthermore, we believe that Scripture calls for a connectional government with local churches ruled by elders and ministers. We may be wrong, but we must be shown by Scripture. Brian seems to imply at points that our views are ineluctably determined by our socialization. If so, we are left with an extraordinarily weak understanding of Scripture and its normative authority as well as its transforming effectiveness.* } We wanted to change a number of these things (remember when getting guitars and drums in the service was a big deal?) and felt that we had biblical grounds for doing so. But many of our brothers and sisters who were more averse to change felt that each of the items on our "to be changed" list had been biblically justified with a chapter and verse (except the carpet color, maybe, but then there's that verse in Revelation...). For them, to change from doing it the biblical way (that is, our current, traditional way) was to become less biblical, so it must not be done. To assure them that the few changes we wanted to make were safe—merely cosmetic, tame, and superficial (methodological), not undercutting the foundations of the faith (the message) at all—we would repeat (passionately and often) our line about the methods changing but the message not changing. {▷ *MICHAEL HORTON: While this may be a tragic example of what all too often is the case (confusing our own comfortable habits with that which is biblical), we should not be dissuaded from doing our utmost to ground all of our faith and practice in Scripture. Should all such claims of biblical warrant be treated cynically as disguised attempts to simply reinforce what we already believe and practice? Further, on the question of changing message, not even the New Testament represents a change from the Old Testament in the sense of its core message. Jesus and his apostles repeatedly observed that the whole of the Scriptures pointed to Christ and redemption in him, and that is how apostolic preaching used the Old Testament, as promise whose fulfillment had finally come in the Messiah. What changes is the administration of the covenant of grace as this plan unfolds. The message gets clearer, but it does not change. }*

I did this for many years. But over the years the more I have acted on this belief and changed my methods while attempting to preserve my message, the more I have been struck by how intertwined method and message are. That's one reason I'm glad for the folks who (like some Amish, like some Calvinists, like all Orthodox) want to freeze the evolution of methods at different points in history (first century, fifth century, seventeenth century, 1950s, whenever). { ▷ *MICHAEL HORTON: Again, I'm not quite sure that sufficient nuance is provided here. While there are plenty of Calvinists who act as if worship could be frozen in a favorite "golden age," I don't know of any who actually articulate this view. According to "the regulative principle of worship," Reformed theology has sworn never to a particular historical form (unlike the Orthodox, for example) but only to the norm of scriptural simplicity. The goal is for worship to have as little of any particular century (including our own) dominate, to remove as many embellishments as possible, and to focus on prayers, praises, preaching, and the two appointed sacraments, with liturgies modeled as much as possible on Scripture. This is not to deny our cultural situatedness but to attempt to preserve worship as much as possible from our own idolatry, whether of the "traditionalist" or the "progressivist" varieties. The old and the young, people who prefer classical music and those who prefer alternative rock, should be able to worship together (indeed, joining their hearts to the praises of the church in all ages) without surrendering their consciences to the tyranny of one or the other. }* By so doing, they guarantee that their message will also remain more or less frozen—or better put—preserved. { ⊕ *FREDERICA MATHEWES-GREEN: Yikes! Frozen, preserved, dead! In our post-Enlightenment, post-scholastic culture, it's natural to think that everything boils down to ideas. In this view the Christianities of different eras appear like sections of a historical library, and we bow respectfully to each while deciding which most suits our taste. But when the way of the early church is allowed to speak for itself, the first impression is of great dynamism; it is all trans-figuration, transformation, divine energies, becoming partakers of the divine nature. It is not about getting the right ideas or the right emotions but about change at the core of being; it is not intellectual or emotional but ontological. This is the initial misconception that most people have about early-church spirituality, in thinking that it is a system of (old-fashioned) ideas. Instead, it is a confrontation with the power of God, and that can't be frozen or preserved any more than a fire can. }*

Make no mistake, I am deeply for old method-message systems to be conserved. The oldest things (things we almost threw away, not fully apprising their value) often turn out to be the most precious, the most worth preserving. And without preserving the whole message-method systems in our heritage, invaluable resources will be lost forever. (Many of these historic spiritual ways of faith and life could be compared to rain forests. For centuries we have cut them down and replaced them with monocultural farms and pastures, housing developments, slums, or whatever, and now we discover—almost too late—that they play an essential part in our planetary survival.)

Meanwhile, the more I have changed my methods in preaching, evangelizing, discipleship, leading worship, and so on, the more experience I have gained sharing the good news with what are often called "the unchurched," and especially those we might call "postmodern seekers." These people have asked me new questions, or old questions in new ways. The more I have interacted with them, the more questions I have had about not just my changing methods but my so-called unchanging message.

Questioning Intensified

MY QUESTIONING WAS INTENSIFIED by my interest in church history. The more I read about the patriarchs and Celts and anchorites and monastics and mendicants and scholastics and Reformers and Anabaptists and pietists and all the rest, the more I realized that the method-message system that I followed and believed was relatively new. Methodologically, I had to admit that Luther never asked anyone to say "the sinner's prayer." Calvin never issued an "altar call" or asked people to "come forward" for salvation. Augustine never invited anyone to "accept Jesus Christ as personal Lord and Savior." St. Francis didn't summarize the gospel in terms of "four steps" or "four laws." Menno Simons didn't use "the bridge diagram." Polycarp never asked "the two diagnostic questions," and Gregory of Nyssa never talked about "the born-again experience" or "the Rapture" or "plenary verbal inspiration and inerrancy." Aquinas never asked how many people "crossed the line" after his preaching, nor did Pascal wonder how many "made a decision for Christ" after reading his *Pensées*. The apostle Paul himself didn't even use "the Roman Road" when he preached in Rome or anywhere else!

These relatively new methods that I and my tribe practiced (sinner's prayer, bridge diagram, four laws, two diagnostic questions) fit the message as I understood it, while the differing methods of earlier times and places differed from mine precisely because their message differed from mine. For example, I had to admit that before Anselm, the theory of the atonement (penal substitution) that my tribe celebrated as the heart of the gospel was largely unknown. Could people have been true Christians without understanding penal substitutionary atonement? {▷ *MICHAEL HORTON: I am not entirely sure what these examples prove except that many of the methods that modern evangelicals regard as essential are in fact not essential and may even be erroneous. And I would agree with Brian's assessment regarding the examples cited. However, he moves immediately to Anselm's account of the substitutionary atonement without distinguishing between Anselm's arguments (perhaps too influenced by feudalistic categories, although that has been subjected recently to much scholarly debate) and the substitutionary atonement itself. If Christ's death as propitiatory, "in the place of" (hyper) sinners, cannot be described as substitution, it is difficult to know how to construe a host of passages that explain it in just those terms. But I am not sure in any case how a rejection of substitutionary atonement would signal a break with modernity in favor of postmodernism, given the fact that the doctrine has been held since long before the Enlightenment and has been subjected to relentless critique precisely by modernist theology. Surely people could have (and can be) saved without understanding a particular account of this substitution, but the belief that Christ bore God's just punishment in our place on the cross is the heart of the gospel itself. The sheer multiplicity of opinions, though existentially unsettling at times (especially if we were reared in parochial Christian circles), is not itself an argument for or against a particular view. If the diversity of opinions entirely relativized the possibility of accepting any one, we would never allow ourselves to be treated by a physician!* }

More: I had to admit that while the death of Jesus on the cross as the substitutionary atoning sacrifice for my sins was at the heart of my understanding of the gospel, for many Christians both ancient and contemporary, the Resurrection, not the cross, was the crux of the gospel. And for many others (such as the Eastern Orthodox), the Incarnation seemed more central than either the cross or the Resurrection. What gives? It got worse as I learned that for still other Christians, it was the life of Christ (or the teaching of Christ, or the moral example of Christ, or the community formed by

Christ, or the commission given by Christ), not his birth, death, or resurrection, that was closest to the heart of the gospel. This diversity of opinion was getting embarrassing. If the message never changes, which message was I talking about?

Of course, I could decide that the message had been properly understood by Paul for a few brief moments in A.D. 63, and then it got confused a bit until Constantine, and then it was forgotten entirely until Luther, and then only partially recovered until Darby or Campbell or White or the Azusa Street gang or Seminary X or Periodical Y or Evangelist Z or Radio Program Q or the FGBMFI or the ACE or someone else finally restored it to "our" pure, full message that (from now on) must never change. But that seemed implausible to me for too many reasons to detail here.

Irreducible Mere Message?

I WAS LOSING GROUND, I felt, but I hoped I could find some irreducible "Christian common sense" that I could discern, some essential truths shared by all (or almost all) Christians in all (or almost all) times and places. But then I realized that if I had sought such a Christian common sense in, say, 1450, it would have included the Ptolemaic view of the universe, including the notion that the sun rotates around the earth in one of 10 crystalline spheres: Nobody questioned that (although they would soon enough!). {▷ *MICHAEL HORTON: But we are not suggesting that our interpretations never change. This misunderstanding, it seems to me, is the result of the assumption that the text (Scripture) is a creation of the church and is itself lacking sovereign authority and clarity, so that the church (the community of readers) must have the last word. If we distinguish the text from its interpretation, we can distinguish the message from its capacity to be told, explained, explored, and experienced with extraordinary variety. The Nicene Creed does not require faith in a Ptolemaic cosmology or slavery. In fact, it is precisely because the message is unchanging that we can appeal to the last article of the creed, "He will come in glory to judge the living and the dead," in our opposition to such evil institutions as slavery. That we often misinterpret Scripture or, due to our prejudices, fail to come to terms with all aspects of its teaching says something about us.* } Or if I had sought a Christian consensus in 1550, it would have included ideas like the divine right of kings or the legitimacy of slavery. Even in 1950 Christian consensus would have included the common-sense or literal interpretations of Paul's writings that excluded women from leadership in ministry or an interpretation of Genesis that put the universe's birth at 4004 B.C., along with (probably) a consensus about the superiority of European culture too (depending on whom I consulted for my consensus). If I look for an unquestioned Christian consensus as of, say, 2005, won't it include things I would be similarly scandalized by if I lived in, say, 3005 (or more so, in 1005)?

Now this was getting more than embarrassing: It was downright scary. C. S. Lewis wrote *Mere Christianity*, which I loved (and love), but most of us would have some critique even of that. (For example, to my horror, I realized that Lewis himself didn't seem to appreciate my preferred penal substitution theory of the atonement!) Who would define the "mere" essentials?

Somewhere along the line, I remember meeting a card-carrying "liberal Christian," a Harvard-educated Methodist, as I recall. He mentioned, in passing, the obvious difference between the gospel of Jesus and the gospel about Jesus. I'd never heard that distinction and asked him about it. He pointed out how Jesus' own message was so different from, say, Paul's. It was obvious, he said, that the early church (largely guided by that Pharisee, Paul) had twisted the original message of Jesus (an inclusive message about social justice and compassion for the poor and needy here and now) and had created their own novel message about Jesus (an exclusive message about individual sin and forgiveness in the sweet by-and-by). { ▷ *MICHAEL HORTON: Not to get picky here with someone else's narrative, but we should bear in mind once more that this dichotomy between "the gospel of Jesus" and "the gospel about Jesus" is the product of the Enlightenment and reached its zenith in Adolf Harnack. In other words, it is deeply modern rather than postmodern.* }

Designer Gospels?

NOW MY HEAD WAS REALLY SPINNING because deep down, I had been noticing things in my own Bible study, unsettling things—like how in Matthew, Mark, and Luke, the gospel seems to be about something called the kingdom of God, and its operative words are *repent* and *follow*, but how in John, the gospel seems to be about something called eternal life and avoiding death or condemnation, with the operative word being *believe*. On top of that tension I also felt a certain tension between the style of Jesus (parables, questions, conversations) and the style of Paul (expositions, answers, monologues). And high on top of all that, of course, was the difference among popular contemporary versions of the gospel—a five-point Calvinist version versus a power-of-positive-thinking version, versus a name-it-and-claim-it-health-and-wealth version, versus a standard fundamentalist version or a therapeutic version or a classic Pentecostal version. Was this liberal guy right? Did the church (from Paul of Tarsus to TBN of Southern California) paste over Jesus' singular original gospel its own plural designer gospels?

That couldn't be, I reasoned. Otherwise, the gospel is just a cloud of smoke, swirling to conform to whatever currents it encounters. That's not good news; it's not even news.

Meanwhile, struggling with these kinds of questions, as a pastor I needed to continue preaching and practicing my faith, which I endeavored to do as faithfully as I could but which wasn't easy under these circumstances.

Four Ideas

OVER TIME FOUR SEMINAL IDEAS converged in my thinking that helped me reach a new and, for me at least, better understanding about the gospel across times and cultures, an understanding that leads me to believe that our message (like our methods) must change from time to time and place to place in order to remain truly the gospel of Jesus and the gospel about Jesus.

IDEA 1: THE GOSPEL AS STORY. First, I had to be "depropositionalized." Rather than seeing the gospel as propositions, mechanisms, abstractions, or universal concepts, I came to see the gospel as a narrative, a story, a "once there was a man named Joseph engaged to a woman named Mary" type of account. {▷ *MICHAEL HORTON: As at least one version of postmodern literary theory has it, the older (logical positivist versus existentialist) dichotomy between propositions and actions (or narratives) has been undone by the recognition that all speech is action and that it involves both propositional content and illocutionary force (promising, commanding, encouraging, warning, instructing, asserting, blessing, and so on). Authors do more than assert, but any event of communication involves propositional content. For recent attempts to appropriate this communicative theory for theology, see, in addition to the work of Nicholas Wolterstorff* (Divine Discourse*) and Anthony Thiselton* (Two Horizons*), Kevin J. Vanhoozer,* First Theology: God, Scripture and Hermeneutics *(Zondervan, 2002) and Michael S. Horton,* Covenant and Eschatology: The Divine Drama *(Westminster John Knox, 2002).* } The term *gospel* itself should have told me this: the term means not just "good information" or "good concepts" or "good mechanisms" but "good news," and news (whether in the newspaper or on a news broadcast or in sharing news across the back fence) comes to us as stories that answer this question: What happened? { ▷ *MICHAEL HORTON: But this was precisely what people like J. Gresham Machen argued against liberalism's tendency to cast Scripture as a collection of timeless moral principles instead of as an announcement, news, of what God has accomplished in history as narrated in Scripture. This point that Scripture is to be read chiefly as an unfolding plot of redemption rather than as a sourcebook of timeless ideas or morals has been emphasized by conservative Reformed theologians such as Geerhardus Vos, Herman Ridderbos, Edmund Clowney, and many others. But this realization of a depth and richness that is not always apparent in some "cognitive-propositionalist" accounts should not lead us to the opposite reduction. This chapter is as full of propositions as the others, as the use of "Idea 1," and so on, confirms.* } The answer is not abstract propositions but news: "At a certain time and at a certain place, God was uniquely revealed to humanity through a person born to a young peasant woman named Mary. Here's what happened…"

We cannot truly tell the gospel without telling a story. Our message is at heart a story.

IDEA 2: THE GOSPEL AS MANY VERSIONED, MANY FACETED, MANY LAYERED, AND CHRIST CENTERED. The story we tell comes to us not in one authorized version (apologies to King James!) but in many. Matthew gives us a version, as do Mark, Luke, and John, and in the book of Acts, we get to hear Peter's and Stephen's versions of the story along with Paul's. The church has continued to offer many versions of the story ever since. No one version is the whole story, and the expanding, deepening, resonant story that we encounter in ever-new dimensions seems to pulsate with more and more meaning, meaning that could never be contained in even the longest, most detailed single compilation we could attempt. Beneath any version of the story told with a certain configuration of words lies the story in its fullness that can be conveyed truly, but never exhaustively. That's what I mean by saying the story is many versioned. { ▷ *MICHAEL HORTON: True enough; we are more aware of the distinct styles and emphases of biblical writers than ever before. This should not be surprising, though, since they are eyewitness reports or are based on them and such reports are by definition given from the point of view of the witness. However, we cannot forget the divine authorship of these reports as well, not to mention the unity of the canon as an unfolding witness to God's judgment and salvation in Jesus Christ. But does any serious evangelical theologian or biblical scholar deny the multiple strategies, emphases, and perspectives of the writers? To say that a story is too rich to be exhaustively told in only one telling is different from saying that the biblical writers had contradictory theologies, much less that we should relativize the theological controversies of the past. I don't think that Brian is taking it that far, but one might.* }

This many-versioned story reveals many facets and many layers. For example, there are facets or layers of the story that deal with guilt and sin, others that deal with hope and the future, still others that focus on justice and compassion, some that are primarily addressed to individuals, and others that relate more globally to all humanity. There are political layers to the story and interpersonal layers, psychological-sociological layers and mystical-spiritual layers.

But all of these versions, facets, and layers center in Jesus Christ. If Christianity has anything to say at all, if it has a message that is worth repeating at all, then at the core is Christ. And not just a facet of Christ or an idea about Christ, not just a theory about Christ's birth or death or resurrection or teaching or deity or humanity, but Christ himself, Christ the person, Christ the figure who came to us in the story we call the gospel. { ▷ *MICHAEL HORTON: Evangelicals have long insisted, over against a "dead orthodoxy," that they want to know Christ and not just about Christ. I agree with the author that the temptation to reduce faith to mere assent to a few basic assertions (the spiritual-laws approach) should be resisted. Nevertheless, what does "Christ himself" mean apart from what we can discern from his birth, death, resurrection, teaching, and his person as the God-Man? Somehow we must avoid both the tendency to have faith in true propositions and a thoughtlessness about the personal object of our faith. Only the Holy Spirit can illumine us in this task as we meditate on his Word, and especially when we hear it preached.* }

Some of you are right now saying, "Well, of course. Tell me something I don't know." Okay. I will. You don't know how little the story of Jesus Christ matters to many of our tellings of the gospel, and you don't know how much something else, which we might call "the modern Christian worldview," does matter. If you did know, you wouldn't have said "of course."

Others are right now asking, "Just a minute. How do you know that the records we have of Jesus are what really happened?" I would have to say that I cannot know this with absolute, undoubtable, unquestionable certainty.

{ ◇ *ERWIN McMANUS: Brian, I sense you know more than you're saying—or at least your uncertainty in regard to this question is overshadowing a greater certainty. I am convinced that you genuinely know God in Christ, that the person of Christ is more than an idea or hope to you. Am I wrong to say that you have had an undeniable encounter with Jesus Christ? Isn't a part of our dilemma that what we cannot know through reason, we know through revelation? Isn't it the person of Christ and not the records of Christ that in the end overcomes our doubts? In the same way, we are left with far more than stories, however beautiful and precious the stories may be to those of us who believe. What is passed down to us are not simply the stories of Jesus but the person of Jesus—that is no small distinction.* } But I would also have to say that to be a Christian means I begin with these stories; I find something in them so precious, I do not want to begin anywhere else. Having begun with the stories of Jesus that are given to me by the community of followers of Jesus (who have validated them as enlivened with the Holy Spirit's breath), all kinds of reflection and study are open to me—whether through textual criticism or source criticism or redaction criticism or whatever.

{ ▷ *MICHAEL HORTON: Brian seems to side here with those who view Scripture as functionally normative rather than intrinsically normative (as possessing divine authority because of its role in the life of the community rather than by virtue of its existence as theopneustos, "God-breathed"). If this is a fair interpretation of these remarks, then it is the community of readers (the church: but which one?) that is sovereign, rather than God himself as he speaks through his prophets and apostles, thereby creating the church.* } But I must remember: When I show greater loyalty to the schools and tools of scholarship (whether they're so-called liberal or conservative schools and tools) than to the stories of Jesus themselves, then I act more as a scholar-critic of some particular school or methodology and less as a follower of Christ and believer in the many-versioned, multifaceted, multilayered story about Christ. That's no small distinction.

IDEA 3: THE GOSPEL AS CUMULATIVE. Our message, I am asserting, is a story that is many versioned, many faceted, many layered, and Christ centered, but it is also cumulative. By this I mean that the story of Jesus itself includes and continues other stories, the Jewish prequel—of creation per verbum, of human crisis, of the calling of Abraham to be blessed and

be a global blessing, the story of exodus and kingdom and exile and return, the story of priests and prophets and poets and sages, the story of law and rebellion and judgment and forgiveness and promise. The story of Jesus accumulates all of these stories within it.

And it extends beyond the years Jesus walked the dusty roads and rocky hills of Palestine. In our New Testament we call the document that follows the four gospels the Acts of the Apostles, but this may be a kind of misnomer. The author, Luke, begins by referring to "the first account I composed...about all that Jesus began to do and teach," and then he launches into this second account, which is, by implication, "all that Jesus continued to do and teach," now through his Spirit at work in the early apostles and the early church at large. Acts of the Apostles, yes, but also the ongoing acts of Jesus Christ through the apostles, by the Holy Spirit. And the story we find there is so much like the earlier accounts, Luke's and the others': Jesus guiding the disciples, the disciples making one mistake after another, the Lord patiently correcting and guiding them, the disciples goofing up again, and so forth. {▽*ERWIN RAPHAEL McMANUS: I am totally with you on the distinction between the acts of the apostles and the ongoing acts of Jesus Christ. The distinction between the apostles simply and Jesus Christ through the apostles by the Holy Spirit is critical and significant. Yet you make a subtle shift from acts to stories—an equally significant shift. There is a difference between stories and actions. We are more than simply a part of an ongoing story. We are part of God's ongoing activity. God is not just a storyteller but a passionate initiator. This is an important distinction in that we are all a continuing part of God's story, yet not all chapters are of equal weight. When God took upon himself our humanity in the person of Jesus Christ, when the Prince of Life allowed himself to be put to death, when he conquered death and the power of sin through his resurrection, this act of God stood apart from all the other acts and stories—even those that flow out of the power of this act and the wonder of the story.*}

And as you read church history, that's very much how it continues, until today. And so the gospel is not just about what Jesus began to do and teach between approximately 5 B.C. and A.D. 28; it is also about the continuing work of Jesus ever since, and (thinking now of John's Revelation) the story will continue until the consummation of all things. {▷ *MICHAEL HORTON: These last few paragraphs are rich with insight. I suspect that there are some who might really believe that* The Four Spiritual Laws *represents the timeless, unchanging truth of the gospel. With Brian, I see Scripture as one sweeping drama centered around Christ. Telling a story and asserting propositions are different illocutionary acts, and examples of both can be found in Scripture (think of the differences between the Gospels and the Epistles, for instance). Nevertheless, the simplistic and reductionistic methods of modern evangelism (especially ever since Charles Finney) have been a major source of uneasiness on the part of confessional churches toward such cooperation. But perhaps that is why I have trouble taking sides on the "unchanging message" versus "changing message." If this amounts to choosing between (a) The Four Spiritual Laws or (b) the gospel being radically indeterminate, I can only opt out of the false dilemma. The news is unchanging in the sense that it heralds what God has accomplished once and for all in Christ and will consummate in the age to come, but it is dynamic and multilayered enough to be proclaimed in a variety of ways, with a variety of metaphors (as the biblical writers themselves model). A further note: I would want to clearly distinguish the Spirit's unique work in gathering up the various pieces of the Jesus Story under the auspices of the prophets and apostles from the Spirit's ongoing work in empowering the postapostolic witness of the church.* }

From this comprehensive news story of Jesus at work in the past, in the present, and into the future flows our message, our gospel. In this sense, again, our message never changes: It is always this unfolding story of Jesus. But the fact that Jesus continues to work, and so the story continues to unfold, means that the unchanging story constantly changes and grows richer and richer! But note well: We are well-experienced at misunderstanding and miscommunicating this story, both the ancient and the more recent parts of it. Frankly, we're often quite baffled as to what Jesus is or has been doing. But even that bafflement is simply part of the story, as it was in the beginning. We tell it as best we can, and we admit that we don't do it very well, and by the grace of God, Jesus continues to work in spite of us as well as with and through us.

IDEA 4: THE GOSPEL AS PERFORMATIVE AND CATALYTIC. This story is not just told, heard, and affirmed. This story always accomplishes things: It is powerful. It performs, catalyzes, saves. The story does so, empowered by God's Spirit, by convening and sustaining a community that seeks to understand it, inhabit it, let it inhabit them, and thereby live by it. The story inspires action in this community, action carried out in faith, hope, and love. { ⊕ *FREDERICA MATHEWES-GREEN: I have a concern about story, that though it is valuable and powerful, we must not forget that it is penultimate, not ultimate. Story is not a stopping place but a door to someplace else. Yet if we expect that people will be merely inspired by the story, it's like the Abelardian atonement, isn't it? Instead story is an invitation to encounter Jesus himself. The danger is that we will be content and comfortable with story alone, with secondhand faith that merely talks about God, shadows on the wall of the cave. In John 12:20-21, somebody must have told these Greeks the story about Jesus, but they then came to Philip and said, "Sir, we wish to see Jesus." The story is just the appetizer. If you think story is performative and catalyzing, get a load of Jesus himself! "I had heard of you by the hearing of the ear, but now my eye sees you," says Job.* } As this community welcomes new people into its faith, vision, and mission, and as this community extends into new cultures, more and more people become part of God's story in Christ and abandon competing and conflicting stories—whether the stories of racial and ethnic hatred, personal or corporate greed, reckless and thoughtless pursuit of pleasure, dominance and power, or hopelessness and despair. More and more people become part of God's solution and cease being part of the human problem. As a result, the world changes, and God's will is increasingly done on earth (as it is in Heaven): God's kingdom comes.

And this is why the gospel message must change along with its methods. Its very success yesterday creates a new situation today—new opportunities, new challenges, new problems, new sticking points. The many-versioned, many-faceted, many-layered, but always Christ-centered gospel story must then draw from its resources in new ways to address this new situation. Its doing so will then create yet another situation, calling for yet new dimensions of the gospel to be summoned to the fore, and so on. {♡*ERWIN RAPHAEL McMANUS: I think the challenge here is what does it mean when you say "but always Christ-centered"? What is the criteria of evaluating all of the future stories that claim to be the ongoing stories of Christ? For example, the Church of Jesus Christ of Latter Day Saints (Mormons) claim that Christ's story continued far beyond the Middle East to the shores of America. From your scenario so far we would agree completely. Then it starts getting tricky. They mean Jesus physically walked on this soil and with him came a many-versioned, many-faceted, many-layered, but strangely Christ-centered gospel story drawing from its resources in new ways to address their new situation. From your vantage point how do we know which stories are authentic expressions of God's story?* }

For example, when Jesus came, his gospel was quite simple, clear, and direct: The kingdom of God is at hand; repent and believe the good news. This was the original gospel of Jesus. As he proclaimed it, his call to those who heard was, "Follow me!"

Jesus Succeeded

JESUS (WE SHOULDN'T BE SURPRISED) succeeded in his mission. He convened a group of men and women who repented and believed that the kingdom of God was at hand. They followed Jesus; in other words, they became his disciples to learn his way of life so they could then pass it on to others, much the way a young musician apprentices herself to a master musician—to learn the craft, to perform music, and then to become a master herself who passes on the tradition of the master to the next generation of players.

To achieve this success Jesus faced many problems and obstacles, among them gross misunderstanding among the Jewish clergy about God's heart and will, skewed expectations about the role and mission of the Messiah, and a distorted sense of identity among the Jews regarding what it meant to be the people of God, not to mention the general dullness of his own disciples. In response, Jesus' message included the innovative methodology of parables that aimed to subvert these misconceptions and replace them with new ways of thinking. And again, Jesus succeeded to a sufficient degree, at least among a few.

Jesus sent those few out to develop communities of disciples in every culture, to play the music of life, so to speak, and to invite others to learn it, so they too could play it and teach it and so on. But at this point, we have a fundamentally new situation. Jesus himself came only to the Jewish people. Although he made important moves toward Gentiles, all his disciples were Jewish, like Jesus. But now Jesus' success at training Jewish disciples and giving them a global, multiethnic mission changes the situation. How?

Jesus' Success Creates a New Situation

NOW THE GOSPEL FACES a problem that has never been faced before in history: How can Jews and Gentiles coexist and cooperate within the formerly Jews-only people of God? How should Jews regard Gentiles (and themselves) in this new arrangement, and how should Gentiles regard Jews (and themselves)? Paul is the perfect candidate to take on this challenge, Paul himself being a former Jewish Pharisee who has a special calling to Gentiles. And so this problem becomes a focal point of Paul's preaching and writing.

Of course his message is different in many respects from Jesus' message: He is working with new and different facets of the message because Jesus has changed the situation through his birth, teaching, life, and work (healing, training, dying, rising). It wasn't Jesus' job to bring the Gentiles and Jews into one multicultural community; Jesus set the stage for that but left its outworking to others, including Paul. { ▷ *MICHAEL HORTON: To some extent this point has merit: The gospel addresses both an enduring and universal problem (human sinfulness and a holy God) and particular challenges that arise in specific contexts (for example, the crisis between Paul and the "Judaizers"). In formulaic presentations of the gospel it seems almost entirely forgotten that God is himself, personally, encountering people here and now through our words. At the same time, this line of argument seems too dependent on a widely challenged interpretation. Although highly influential throughout the twentieth century, Adolf Harnack's "Hellenization" thesis has been subjected to sustained criticism from biblical scholars (such as James Barr, hardly a friend to evangelicalism) as well as historical theologians (such as David Steinmetz, Heiko Oberman, and Richard Muller). John's Gospel, for example, does not simply adopt Greek categories but uses them subversively. For example, the notion of the Logos becoming flesh was equivalent to saying that the principle of divinity and goodness in the cosmos became the principle of bodily, shadowy existence that thereby possessed at least less goodness (as in Plato) or was positively evil (as in Gnosticism and its precursors).* } (Remember how he told his disciples they would do even greater works?)

But Paul's success (a partial success, of course—problems always remain, like tares that grow along with wheat) also creates a new situation. With Gentiles now being welcomed into the people of God, the gospel spreads rapidly throughout much of the Roman world, a world deeply influenced by various forms of Greek philosophy. This rapid spread of the gospel creates a double problem. First, among those who accept the gospel, there is a real question of whether they are fitting the gospel of Jesus into their Greek categories of thinking (so that Christianity will just become an adornment of Greek culture) or whether they are revolutionizing their Greek categories of thinking around the centrality of the gospel (so that real disciples of Jesus will exist as agents of change in Greek culture). In this dangerous situation the apostles reached for the innovative methodology of dangerous new language, using terms rich with meaning in Greek-influenced culture, like the term *logos* we find in John's gospel or the term *pleroma* in Paul's writings. A few generations later, the methodology included referring to Plato and Socrates as "Christians before Christ." (And some centuries later, Aristotle would be granted similar status.) { ⊕ *FREDERICA MATHEWES-GREEN: Whoa, that's a multicentury broad jump! I'd point again to the possibility of perceiving consensus on essential points in the first millennium and that being a reliable guide to us today. Where there isn't consensus, that indicates that unity is not required and that we are free to decide for ourselves or to follow local custom. (St. Monica asked, "Should we fast on Saturdays, as in Milan, or not, as in Rome?" "When in Rome, do as the Romans do," said St. Ambrose.) }*

This message was evolving in many ways, still centered on Christ, of course, but different (as it should be, as it must be) to address each new situation that the gospel faced or itself created.

New Successes, New Problems

EVENTUALLY, THIS SUCCESS in communicating the gospel among Greek-influenced Roman citizens created more new problems: As the church grew, it was seen by some Roman leaders as a threat to the stability of Roman society. Soon church leaders found themselves making their apologia in very reasoned, dignified, and diplomatic terms, correcting misconceptions, arguing that the gospel was not a threat to the Roman system but rather that a good Christian would be a good citizen. This was a new twist indeed, a message that one can hardly imagine Jesus having proclaimed in his Jewish context some decades earlier, but a message that became a natural outworking of Jesus' gospel, which keeps transforming situations and creating new ones.

We could go on and on, thinking about the new situation after Constantine, or after the fall of Rome, or under threat from the Goths and Visogoths from the north, or Mongols from the east, or under threat from Islam from the south. We would eventually come to the complex new situation at the time of the Reformation and the Radical Reformation. In each case, from the many layers and facets of the Christ-centered gospel, new resources are drawn, and so the message itself changes because the message changes its context, which is to say that the message itself changes by addressing new situations and problems and opportunities in new ways— because the message keeps changing the situation, the world, the context wherever it is proclaimed and practiced. (In this light, it seems an insult to the gospel to deny that it has so much richness and power, so many resources to offer as we bring the Word of the Lord to our places and moments.) { ▷ *MICHAEL HORTON: Sorry to belabor this point, but why does the obvious fact that Scripture in general (and the gospel in particular) is so pregnant with meaning and hope that it cannot be exhausted in any one context entail that the message is ever changing? To be sure, the gospel addresses everyone in their universal context (children of Adam) and their particular context, and the latter has some effect on the questions we put to the text, but as I read Polycarp, Ireneaus, the Cappadocians, Augustine, Aquinas, the Reformers, the pietists, and a host of brothers and sisters today who belong to different communions, including ones considered seriously defective by our confessions, I find myself confessing precisely the same core faith laid out in the clearest terms in the Scriptures. Is it not true that all Christians across all times and places are united by the faith we confess in the Nicene and Apostles' creeds (even if those creeds are not regularly recited)? Is there no catholicity? No "faith once and for all delivered unto the saints" but multiple versions that disperse from the core like atoms? Multilayered does not entail either multiple or changing messages. ▽ERWIN McMANUS: I think this is such an insightful and important observation. The message, to be transformative, must change as it addresses the important issues of its time, and in a profound way, the context is changed through the power of the message. While you describe this as evidence for an ever-changing gospel, I would see this as the prophetic and redemptive ministry of the church. I still think that something is lost when our focus is either the message of Jesus or the message about Jesus or even the message from Jesus. Again, the person of Jesus is far more potent than the message. The impact the message has on its context is incremental compared with the impact the person of Jesus has on the context in which he is present. With the message, we are always in danger of coming only with words. With the person of Christ come both power and presence.* }

So today it's not that we restrict ourselves to saying exactly what Justin Martyr or Augustine or Patrick or Brigit or Aquinas or Teresa of Avila or Zwingli or Edwards or Graham or Bright or Teresa of Calcutta said as they brought needed resources of the multilayered gospel to bear on their situations. No, we don't display our respect for and loyalty to our fathers and mothers in the faith simply by repeating their words (although their words bear repeating). Instead, we go farther by imitating their example, by doing as they did: bringing (under the guidance of the Holy Spirit) resources from the gospel story to bear on the new situations that face us today, situations that have come to fruition in part because of the success of the gospel in undermining the status quo of the past again and again.

This also means that in each context, wise Christians must be asking themselves what the Spirit is saying to and through the churches—just as we find John doing in his Revelation. { ▷ *MICHAEL HORTON: The failure to distinguish the foundation-laying period of the prophets and apostles from the construction that built upon it (1 Corinthians 3:9-15)—the failure to distinguish God and his Word from the church and its interpretation—is a perennial weakness of Brian's approach. His separation of the Spirit from the Word by (a) reducing the Word to the story of Jesus (apparently, the gospel narratives) and (b) suggesting that we are able to be led by the Spirit apart from the Word is hardly postmodern. It was the position of the radical Anabaptists of the sixteenth century.* } The gospel of and about Jesus that is proclaimed among the affluent in Orange County, California, in 2006 must in this way be the special word of the Lord to that situation, just as the gospel proclaimed in London, Paris, Hong Kong, Calcutta, or Bogota will be the word of the Lord needed in those situations at the proper time. { ⊕ *FREDERICA MATHEWES-GREEN: I agree with this. But I suspect we're skirting the issue of what exactly is unchangeable. For example, even those who advocate change would say, "But we all agree that it is Jesus we're presenting to them, rather than trying to sell them shoes or designer coffee, right?" And those who resist change would say, "Of course, when you go as a missionary to a new land, you must change the language to one they can understand." Within those broad boundaries how much do we change? Everyone here agrees that we should implement change, within limits; it's the specific limits we disagree about.* }

Making Me Think

ALL THIS MAKES ME THINK—and rethink. For example, looking back over my lifetime, I think about what was called liberation theology, an articulation of the gospel for the poor in Latin America and elsewhere. { ▷ *MICHAEL HORTON: This, it seems to me, is an illustration of why this position just doesn't work. Liberation theology, for all of its strengths in reminding us that we do not get the gospel right if we read it only with the rich and powerful, is not an example of presenting the same gospel message in a different context. Liberation theologians themselves insisted that the gospel presented by the missionaries, whether Catholic or Protestant, was simply wrong. So we need to think about that. In some respects, the critique probably sticks: Can a gospel that claims a person's whole life be reduced to the inner life, as many of the mission-aries taught? Not at all. But in that case, the missionaries had a deficient message. On the other hand, liberationists come very close (they would say so themselves) to equating the gospel with Marxism. Surely the zealots of Jesus' day missed the point of the cross and the Resurrection because they were looking for a different kind of gospel, and we could say the same of those who confuse the liberation promised in this age with that fully realized liberation to come or, worse, with a purely human order of political liberation. We cannot be freed from having to investigate and adjudicate these claims. Either way, to say that the gospel is Marxism has little to do with what St. John says it is. Is it the gospel that changes in each new context? Or is it we who are changed by the gospel as it encounters us in each new context? Is it the message that is sovereign or the audience? I would suggest that our context affects the way we hear God's Word, the emphases we pick up on most quickly, the bits that surprise us and take us aback, but that the very fact that God's Word is described as the Spirit's medium of conversion, a powerful and effective word, entails that it is we who are converted to its message, not the message that is converted to our use.* } I remember how it was critiqued by eloquent and comfortable scholars in the United States. But I wonder—maybe it wasn't the gospel the scholars needed to hear? { ⊕ *FREDERICA MATHEWES-GREEN: This is another area where it does us good to step back from contemporary culture and observe how it might be coloring our reading of the gospel. Jesus had frighteningly little to say about achieving justice on this earth. Frightening because he left people defenseless (in terms of earthly power) before those who would abuse or persecute them. He didn't say to fight back, to kill oppressors, or to prize liberty more than life; he told them to turn the other cheek or carry the soldier's pack a second mile, to count injustice both joy and blessing. Though it was the hottest topic of his time, he never advocated Jewish liberation from Roman rule. I can't see any evidence in the Gospels for liberation theology or any other pursuit of earthly power—and it must be acknowledged that any scheme to redistribute power begins with acquiring power. However, liberation theology sure has a suspicious resemblance to pockets of American popular thinking a couple of decades ago (if liberation is good, and Jesus is good, Jesus must have been for liberation, right?). It's startling and disruptive to us to realize that Jesus could say, "Repent!" to the poor as well as the rich, to ponder the disturbing complacency of "You will have the poor with you always." Apparently "thy kingdom come" doesn't mean that. He made it clear that the kingdom he was talking about was "not of this world" but rather was "within you." The reason for these priorities is that this world is passing away, transient as a dream. Jesus was concerned to establish people in the things that are eternal. So instead of challenging the establishment, Jesus dealt with people, rich and poor, as individuals, aiming straight for their hearts and challenging them to live in his light for whatever the course of their brief earthly lives. This is how the kingdom comes, through transformed, God-surrendered individuals. Though God may in this way work great improvements in human conditions, earthly improvements are necessarily temporary. The part that counts is the part that will last forever.* } (Or maybe it was, and they didn't want to hear it?) I think about the issue of ecology and how it seemed to have nothing to do with the gospel that I heard as a child, but how it has so much to do with the gospel that I proclaim now as an adult.

I think about the issue of racial and ethnic reconciliation, barely a tiny footnote to the gospel that I grew up hearing, but so important to the gospel that I know I must preach today.

I think about the gospel that I heard as a child and that I preached for many years, which implied that the gospel's essential purpose was to answer this one question: How can an individual's soul be forgiven of its sins so it will go to Heaven after death? That question may have been exactly the question that needed to be answered in Europe in the late Middle Ages, when childbirth and feudal warfare killed women and men by the thousands; and plagues swept through every few decades, decimating thousands more; life seemed so cheap, so short, so meaningless, and death seemed larger than life for so many, nearly every day. But now I wonder if this gospel about how to get your soul into Heaven after death is really only a ghost of the real gospel that Jesus talked about, which seemed to have something to do with God's will being done on earth now, not just in Heaven later.

I think about how the sinner's-prayer gospel that I grew up with really addressed—with clarity and relevance—a misconception held by many nominal or non-Christians in the midtwentieth century that Heaven was earned and hell avoided through an economy of human earning: Heaven rendered for good works performed. Then I think about how few of my uncommitted friends today even believe in Heaven or Hell, and how futile it is to try to correct a misconception they do not hold or motivate them based on something they don't believe. As a result, I find myself unable to preach a gospel of what Dallas Willard has called "sin management." Yes, I believe that the gospel has facets that deal with forgiveness of sins, but I feel unfaithful to Jesus to define the gospel by that one facet when I see our contemporary churches failing to address so many other essential gospel concerns—justice, compassion, sacrifice, purpose, transformation into Christlikeness, and ultimate hope. { ▷ *MICHAEL HORTON: As with liberation theology, Brian's examples here (justice, compassion, sacrifice, purpose, transformation into Christlikeness), with the exception of ultimate hope, all point to our work, not God's. Therefore, by definition, they cannot be identified as the gospel. The gospel is what God has done for sinners in Jesus Christ. That involves forgiveness of sins and justification, but it also is the announcement that he has toppled the tyranny of sin and*

Satan over our lives, the promise that we will continue to grow in sanctification, and the promise that the whole creation will one day be liberated from its bondage. But the gospel is never anything that we do. To identify our struggles for justice, our compassion, our sacrifices, as the gospel is a confusion of law and gospel. This is not to say that we do not struggle for these things or that we do not respond obediently to God's law as renewed creatures who live in faith, hope, and love, but it is to say that the gospel is exclusively concerned with the announcement of what God has done in Jesus Christ, not what we have done for him. ⇨ *As for his claim that a concern for salvation from divine judgment is no longer on people's radar, I couldn't agree more. But that is due in no small measure to the fact that there is such a weak witness to the reality of sin and the holiness of God in our churches, much less the culture. If people do not know who God is and who they are in his presence, the question, How can I be right with God? will hardly occur to them. A lot of this depends on whether we really do believe that human beings by nature "suppress the truth in unrighteousness"(Romans 1:18, NASB), as Paul declared, or whether they are reliable judges of what is worth knowing. To reduce the concern with reconciliation with God to a midtwentieth-century question forgets not only that most of the great debates throughout church history and advances in missions have turned on it but also (more importantly) that it was the central concern (pace Dunn, Sanders, and Wright) to the saints in the Old and New Testaments. The psalmist cries out, "Have mercy upon me, O God, according to Your lovingkindness; according to the multitude of your tender mercies, blot out my transgressions. Wash me thoroughly from my iniquity, and cleanse me from my sin" (Psalm 51:1-2, NKJV).* ⇨ *And how often is this urgent concern to be accepted by a holy God placed in the foreground throughout the prophets? John himself states that the whole purpose of his gospel was "that you might believe that Christ is the Son of God and that, believing, you might have life in his name." What then must I do to be saved? is hardly a midtwentieth-century question but arises in the story of Jesus itself and in the subsequent preaching of the apostles. The gospel is "the power of God unto salvation for everyone who believes," Paul wrote, and one can hardly make sense of his epistles apart from that theme.* ⇨ *Brian doesn't like the sinner's prayer or other "canned" approaches. Neither do I, and there are many of us who get along quite well without* The Four Spiritual Laws *also. Telling the story of what God has done in Christ is the most originally "evangelical" way of witnessing. In my estimation, however, it is that very message that is in danger of being confused and obscured by some aspects of Brian's proposal.* ⊕ FREDERICA MATHEWES-GREEN: *There's no denying that Jesus' first and most consistent message was "Repent!" however, so sin has something to do with it. The problem with "sin management" is with seeing sin as infractions against God's code or debts that must be paid. If repentance is, instead, the first step toward healing and reunion with God, then when sin is recognized and resisted, "compassion, purpose," and the rest flow out as a natural result.* }

If you ask me about the gospel, I'll tell you, as well as I can, the story of Jesus, the story leading up to Jesus, the story of what Jesus said and did, the story of what happened as a result, of what has been happening more recently, today even. I'll invite you to become part of that story, challenging you to change your whole way of thinking (to repent) in light of it, in light of him. Yes, I'll want you to learn about God's grace, God's forgiveness, about the free gift of salvation, and if you want to say the sinner's prayer, I'll be glad to lead you in it (I haven't forgotten it). But for me that will just be a footnote to a gospel that is much richer, grander, and more alive, a gospel that calls you to become a disciple and to disciple others, in authentic community, for the good of the world.

So this is why to me the gospel must be a changing message accompanied by changing methods. This is why a growing gospel (rather than a gospel that shrinks to shorter and shorter formulae: four laws, four steps, five principles, whatever) is not necessarily a failure on the part of the gospel or its messengers; rather, it is a success. This is how it has always been; this is as it always must be.

Centered in Christ

THIS VIEW MEANS that those who stick by old methods and old formulations are not wrong; they may in fact be doing exactly what Jesus wants them to do, addressing the gospel to enclaves that need it exactly as they're expressing it. Or—perhaps more importantly—they may be preserving certain facets of the gospel that will be needed in a decade or century or two. Again, you never know when or how much you'll need something you almost threw away or cut down and burned.

For example, many of us who are seeking to live and communicate the gospel in these times are realizing how much we need to learn from our historic Catholic and Orthodox and Anabaptist brothers and sisters, who have managed to preserve forms of Christianity less influenced by modernity. We're finding that the antique furniture stacked in the basement is far better and will last longer than the modern pressed-muck junk with plastic "wood" veneer that we bought last year from Ikea and Wal-Mart. We're realizing that without oxygen-rich air from ancient rain forests, we'll all be wearing gas masks before long. Two hundred years from now, our Reformed brothers

and sisters may bring forth treasures that the church by then has forgotten and will desperately need again, and people will rise up and call blessed those who made sure those resources weren't lost forever. But what if, you might be asking, our gospel changes to the point that it stops being about Jesus at all? Then, of course, it has stopped being the gospel, and we have stopped communicating as Christians. {▷ *MICHAEL HORTON: But this is precisely what I see at risk in the suggestion that the content of the gospel is not only God's saving work in Christ for sinners but our achievements. While we should avoid simply repeating the words of past witnesses, Brian's own example should warn us against rewriting the gospel for each generation. Reconciliation with God through the perfect obedience, satisfaction, and victory of his Son is just the answer for those in every time and place who have been faced with the reality of God and their guilt.* } Branches that disconnect from the vine, Jesus said, will wither and die, as will we if we disconnect from our source of life and hope. Like Tarzan and Jane in the old black-and-white movies, if we let go of the vine, we'll crash—and fast.

Disconnecting from the vine is a risk we always face, but it is a risk that we will not avoid by seeking to repeat verbatim some unchanging articulation of the gospel from the past (recent or distant) or present. Because to memorize and repeat "word perfect" a past articulation of the gospel that fails to accomplish what the Spirit of Jesus wants to accomplish today is to be unfaithful to the gospel, which is always new wine, always bursting old wine-skins, always good news, always new, always the power of God to save. Perhaps those of us who think that we stay connected to the vine by repeating old formulations should think again and recall Jesus' words to those who said, "Lord! Lord!"

Sam's Frustration

THIS ALL BECAME POIGNANT to me a couple of years back when I was talking to Sam, an Irish gentleman with a charming accent who lives near my church. Sam had volunteered to water some freshly planted saplings on our church property until they were established. Seeing Sam standing with his hose tending our trees, I ran over one afternoon to say thanks.

"You've probably noticed I still haven't visited your church," Sam said, perky for his sixty-something age, his Irish accent lilting. "And I probably never will. You see, I'm Irish, but I'm a Jew. It's an odd combination, I know." He laughed but then grew serious.

"Let me tell you why I'm not interested in your religion," he said. "I was listening to one of your evangelical preachers on the television, and he said that if Hitler had said a little prayer so that he accepted Jesus into his heart or some such nonsense, then all the wrong he did wouldn't matter, and he'd go straight to Heaven."

I could imagine a TV preacher saying this sort of thing to emphasize the unfathomable range of God's grace, but I could also hear how, for Sam, as a Jew, this kind of talk didn't make God sound gracious. Instead, it made God sound capricious and unjust—careless about the suffering of the Jewish people, capricious about the horror of Hitler. It trivialized the Holocaust and reduced Christianity to a cheap ticket to Heaven, insensitive to the suffering of the oppressed on earth. I cringed.

But Sam wasn't finished. He kept talking as he watered another sapling. "Did I ever tell you about my son? Of course, I'm his father, and I'm bound to be proud of him. A few years back, he decided to go to Israel and volunteer for the Israeli army. He didn't have to; he wanted to do it. I tried to discourage him, but he's stubborn like his dad. He knew it was dangerous, but he felt he should do it for his people, you know? So he went. One night, he and his fellow soldiers were at a border crossing, and then a Palestinian chap came up."

Sam's eyes suddenly brimmed. "The other Israeli soldiers—not my son—started harassing the fellow, pushing him around, calling him names. Finally, they pushed him down and started kicking him. Then one of them pulled down the Palestinian guy's pants, and he took out a knife and said he was going to circumcise the fellow. You know, if he wanted to live in their land, he should be circumcised—the sort of stupid talk that soldiers might indulge in when they're under too much pressure and are going crazy. Well, at this, my son had enough. He pulled out his rifle and pointed it at his fellow soldiers. He told them they were doing wrong, that this man shouldn't be treated this way, that he was a human being, too. He told them not to move, and then he told the Palestinian to pull up his pants and get out of there. He told him he was sorry for the way his buddies acted.

"Well, they put my son in jail for pulling a gun on his fellow soldiers. He was in jail for a long time, but then they had a trial—it was in all the papers there—and in the end he was completely vindicated. In fact, he got a letter praising him for doing the right thing, the just thing. Now, Brian, here's my question: Would your God send my boy to hell because he never said, 'Jesus save me,' but he'd let Hitler go to Heaven for saying the magic words? Is that what you believe, like that TV preacher?"

What would you have said to Sam? I didn't answer his question; I didn't know how. So I said something like this: "Sam, I think your son acted a lot like Jesus would have acted. Jesus cared for the outsiders, just as your son did, and Jesus gave up his life to protect us all, just as your son risked his life for that guy. So I think your son was following Jesus' example, and I can see why you're so proud of him. Really, I think God feels about Jesus a lot like you feel about your son. And I know God must be proud of your son too. Anyway, thanks so much for watering our trees." { ▷ *MICHAEL HORTON: Since you asked...so what if there is a holy God and all people, Jew and Gentile alike, are under his condemnation—just as Scripture warns? This gentleman, fine in every respect as far as the rest of us sinners can determine, is nevertheless (with the rest of us) under God's judgment apart from Christ. Did Brian's words not simply confirm that good people go to Heaven and bad people (probably) go to Hell? The implication seems to be that Hitler is, after all, in Hell and not in Heaven. So some people go to Hell, but apparently only "others"—people who are not as good as I or my loved ones. To be sure, there are "fire insurance" distortions of the gospel that fail to affirm that God gives repentance along with faith and reduce even faith to saying some magical formula. But Brian once again presents us with a false choice, this time between justification by the sinner's prayer versus justification by loving one's neighbor. }*

Feeling Odd

I FELT ODD FOR THE REST OF THAT DAY and for a couple of days following, and I wasn't sure why. Sam was telling me something I needed to hear, something about how we've got our message muddled up, and we need to do something about it.

I felt the same way after the September 11 attacks in 2001. You'll remember how a number of news broadcasters brought well-known Christian spokespersons on the air to answer questions about the attacks and related matters. *These guys have been well coached,* I thought to myself as I listened to them respond to the inquiries of Larry King and others. *They know how to play the sound-bite game.*

Here's what they did: Like politicians who've been coached on how to stay "on message," they cleverly turned whatever question into an opportunity to squeeze in their sound-bite answers. Each of the interviews went something like this:

BROADCASTER: "Do you think that Islam is an evil and violent religion?"

SPOKESPERSON: "Well, [insert broadcaster's name here], I don't know much about Islam, but the real problem with all other religions is that they don't teach the gospel of Jesus Christ—that all men are sinners, and that good works are worthless before God, and unless people individually pray to receive Jesus Christ as their Savior, they'll never be forgiven for their sins."

BROADCASTER: "How do you think that Christians here in America should respond to Muslims here in America in the aftermath of these attacks?"

SPOKESPERSON: "Well, [insert broadcaster's name here], I think that Christians should tell Muslims that good works can never save anyone, but if they will admit they're sinners and receive Jesus Christ as their personal Savior, they'll go to Heaven after they die and experience eternal life with God forever."

BROADCASTER: "What I'm trying to ask you is whether you think there will be any reprisals against people of the Muslim religion, and if so, what should Christians do about it?"

SPOKESPERSON: "That's a difficult question, [insert broadcaster's name here].

But Muslims need to hear that there's only one way to be forgiven of our sins and inherit the free gift of eternal life: not by doing good works but by individually repenting of our sins and accepting Jesus Christ as personal Savior."

BROADCASTER: "I seem to remember Jesus Christ saying something about loving our neighbors. How do you think Christians should act toward their Muslim neighbors?"

SPOKESPERSON: "Well, [insert broadcaster's name here], one of the most important ways we Christians love our neighbors is by telling them they'll go straight to Hell after they die unless they accept Jesus Christ as their personal Savior. To do anything less would not be loving our neighbors."

These were good men, these spokespersons for the Christian faith. Better preachers than me, I'm sure; better Christians, too. But those days after the attacks, I felt ashamed. I felt that "our" message was not what Jesus would have said, and frankly, Sam's Jewish son may have been a better spokesperson that day than our respected Christian spokespersons.

Have we got the message right when we make it sound like God doesn't care about good works or justice or compassion or that all God cares about is whether we've said a little prayer? Doesn't our message need a change when we make it sound like God doesn't care about suffering and violence and injustice and anxiety here on earth, but rather that all God cares about is which people he will let into Heaven because of a concept that they need to affirm sometime before they die? "Live like Hitler or live like Sam's son, it doesn't matter; all that matters is if you've understood a certain theory of the atonement and affirmed it in a prayer." Does that message need a slight tweak? { ▷ *MICHAEL HORTON: Certainly not, but why again this false choice between a caricature and salvation by following Jesus' example? Our message does need to reflect God's concern for suffering and violence in the world, not because it needs to be changed in that direction but because the one gospel, in all of its mutifaceted brilliance, is broader than the salvation of individual souls. It is the announcement of Christ's victory over these forces and the recognition that sin and evil exist because we are ourselves sinners and not just victims. Brian forces a choice between mere assent ("understood a certain theory of the atonement and affirmed it in a prayer") and the justification of the righteous—or at least, those not as bad as Hitler—rather than that astonishing message that God justifies the wicked, even the wicked like Sam and his son, or any of the rest of us. ⊕ FREDERICA MATHEWES-GREEN: Yeah, that's messed up. Back to the drawing board! I know I'm supposed to be the person here most opposed to change, but if the topic is our current situation, I'm advocating radical change. ▽ ERWIN RAPHAEL McMANUS: It seems to me that you have chosen to make the story, the gospel, the message, and the articulation all the same. At times, like here, I agree with you 100 percent. At other times, I disagree with you on the very same point. There are other times I'm just not sure what you are advocating. It would help me so much if you would clarify your meaning of at least the gospel, the message, and the story. Are they really all the same thing? Or quite different but inseparable?* }

Trite Sound Bite

I DON'T CARE HOW SLICK and hip the methods are to package, produce, and promote a message like this. That message, constricted to the cramped dimensions of a shrink-wrapped, trite sound bite, is not the one I want to dedicate my life to. I don't think it's the unchanging message of Jesus or even about Jesus.

Here is where methods and message come together, because according to Jesus, it's easy to say the good and right words "Lord, Lord!" and according to James, it's easy to say you believe in God, which is good and right. But it's another thing entirely to do God's will. So the things we do—our actions, our forms, our art, our liturgy, our architecture, our practices, our good works, our community life, our infrastructures, the way we treat the least and last of our neighbors—are in fact an indispensable dimension of what we say; these methods are an essential dimension of our message. In fact, these methods are our message embodied in deeds and way of life, which must accompany our message articulated in words. And since neither our message nor our methods are currently perfect in their articulation, and since even if they were perfectly suited to address the questions and needs of our culture today (here), they will need to adjust to our new situation tomorrow (or somewhere else), I believe we are being most faithful when we are constantly open to change on both fronts.

Pray and Rejoice

I GUESS THE ONLY PEOPLE who never need to change their message and methods are those lucky ones who already understand and articulate God's message in word and deed perfectly and fully. {▷ *MICHAEL HORTON: But is this not to switch the terms of the argument? Thus far, Brian, it seems to me, has argued that the message changes, but here he accuses his critics of maintaining that their own interpretation or knowledge of that message is somehow unchanging. Again, perhaps there are some who think that this is the case, but they would have to reject the clear teaching of Scripture that believers "grow in the grace and knowledge of our Lord and Savior Jesus Christ" (2 Peter 3:18 NKJV). Once more, we must distinguish the message (textually embedded once and for all) from our interpretation (always attempting to better understand, to more faithfully hear and exposit the message). It is precisely in recognizing that there is a message that stands over against our interpretations that we are able to be corrected by the "other" and not force the "other" to reinforce our own prejudices.* }

I am certain that I am not one of those people. I still feel, when I contemplate the gospel, that I am a little child playing in the surf at the beach, confronted by a vastness I can't comprehend but that inspires me with awe, reverence, and a desire to explore and learn. So I, at least, need to keep growing in my understanding of the gospel message and my articulation of it, even as I continue to adapt and improve my methods. Those who feel they are in a different category should no doubt pray for me. And rejoice with me too about how wide and deep and long and high the love of God is, a love that surpasses all knowledge and leaves us humbled each time we try to convey its richness in word and deed.

One of my mentors often says, "Beware of theological success." Do you see what he means? If we feel successful—that we've captured the gospel just right, for example—we are in great danger. Maybe that's why I never liked that old bumper-sticker campaign, where Christians were supposed to proclaim to the guy stuck in traffic behind them, "I found it!" And maybe that's why I often feel slightly jealous of those we call "seekers," as distinguished from "believers." Because even though I believe, I am still seeking. Even though I've found something, I'm still finding more; my faith is still seeking more understanding. I'm not a fan of bumper stickers, but if I were, I guess mine would say, "Want to join me in my search?"

{ ⊗ *ANDY CROUCH: Brian, I'm with you in almost every way—see my comments on the polyphonous nature of Scripture in response to Michael. I would expand on those comments by noting that there is no way to resolve even a single line of melody, let alone a polyphonic composition, into a chord. Just because the first fugue in Bach's* Well-Tempered Clavier *is in the key of C major doesn't mean we can play a C major chord and be done with it. Indeed, we can't play just the main theme of the fugue through once and be done! The beauty, and the genius, of the piece is in the way the theme is developed, taken up, modified, echoed, inverted, and eventually brought to resolution at the end—a process inherently and profoundly time bound (see Jeremy Begbie's* Theology, Music and Time*). It seems to me that you are arguing against the various attempts, recent and ancient, to freeze the gospel into a single chord, or even a single theme, when in fact it is a story that must play itself out through all of history, from the first day until the last, in order to fully glorify its composer. ⊗ My only question is about this troublesome word* methods*. The very use of the term—as we both know—tends to drive us into a dichotomy between truth known and truth lived, as if one could figure out the "message" in one's head and then turn to the question of the methods that message requires for full expression. I would greatly prefer the term* practices*. To return to a musical metaphor, the Christian life can be sustained only through practice. As a pianist, the only way for me to "know" Bach's "Fugue in C Major" is to practice—to submit myself to disciplines, some of them maddeningly simple and repetitive, most of them humbling, that gradually develop in me the capacity to hear and perform a fugue. Without practice the fugue remains for me merely a collection of notes on a page, or at best a performance to which I am only a spectator. Conversely, the more I practice, the more I am able to understand and dwell within the fugue. (Similar observations could be made about a trumpet player improvising on a jazz standard or a sitar player elaborating on a raga.) ⊗ What is true for an individual musician is also true for a community. Our faith is sustained in no small part by practices that, in their repetitive and humbling way, gradually create in us the capacity to hear, know, and tell the gospel. To speak of changing methods as our understanding of the message changes is misleading—for only certain practices (the sacraments, prayer, fasting, and so on) can be expected to tune our hearts to the message in the first place. If the gospel is, as you say, performative, can our Christian practices be reduced to something as utilitarian and disposable as methods? ▽ ERWIN RAPHAEL McMANUS: I do want to join you, Brian. I am far more attracted to the essence of seeking than to believing. You confess here that you have found something. What is it that you have found, and what are we searching for? Are we searching for truth? For God? For clarity? For life? Together let's abandon the well-worn path of searching for truth in the midst of information and even reason. There is one who calls us both to follow him. The journey is filled with mystery, uncertainty, wonder, and adventure. To hear his voice and follow is to know him and find little need to know everything else. ⊕ FREDERICA MATHEWES-GREEN: Brian, anything that increases humility is indisputably good for the soul, so I do rejoice with you. I want to offer a few thoughts about searching, though. Seems to me that this process of searching to find a way to be in relationship with God is like searching for a spouse. If you have found the right guy or gal, you might well exclaim, "I found it!" Yet that doesn't mean you have exhausted that person's mystery; they will be a mystery to you, and even to themselves, all their lives. Yet when you set the* *wedding date, you have concluded your search: You are sure this is the right one and are ready to travel down the road with them, seeing what each day will bring. I sympathize with your desire to recall modern Christians from glibness that drains the encounter with God of mystery and turns it into mere transaction (get your sin debt paid by Jesus and you're set for life). Yet it's not quite right to say that we continue searching because we have found him whom we sought. We follow him and comprehend him better all the time, never exhausting his mystery yet able to say, "I know in whom I have trusted." ⊳ MICHAEL HORTON: Our old theologians distinguished between a theology of glory (which only the glorified saints in Heaven possess and is still at no point identical to God's knowledge) and a theology of the cross (which is available to believers). The latter, called "our theology" (nostra theologia), was nicknamed theologia viatorum, a "theology of pilgrims on the way." So I sympathize with the caution against triumphalistic, overrealized eschatologies. At the same time, a pilgrim is fixed on a destination in hope because he or she has already experienced liberation and has embraced the word of the liberator. It is this that separates a pilgrim from a wanderer. May we all aspire to be better pilgrims!* }

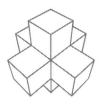

Brian D. McLaren's Rejoinder

THE RESPONSES TO MY CHAPTER WERE, for me, far more insightful than the chapter itself! As I reflect on what I wrote and how my friends responded, new questions arise in my mind, questions that I'll be thinking about for some time, I'm sure.

1. Most of us (not just those of us writing but "us Christians" in all our different forms) believe that "we've got it right" (or about right), so if someone says, "Do you need to change to adapt to culture?" we generally say, "No," or, "Maybe just a little." But when we're asked if "they" need to change (whoever "they" are—charismatics, Calvinists, Orthodox, TV evangelists, liberation theologians, feminist theologians, the religious right, liberals, moderns, hypermoderns, ultramoderns, postmoderns), we generally say, "Boy, do they ever!" So leaving the "we" out of it, I wonder: What do we wish "they" would change into, and why, and how, and what would happen if they did so?

2. Frederica emphasized a number of times her conviction that the gospel or the kingdom changes the world only by changing individuals. I used to believe this, and my life would be simpler, I think, if I fully agreed with Frederica. But I remain less than convinced because when I love individuals, I realize that they are powerfully influenced by social systems, regimes, cultures, philosophies, movements, countermovements, trends, economies, kingdoms, and the like. (Frederica probably used to have this emphasis, so we may be running on parallel tracks in our learning.) Many have suggested that when Paul used the phrase "principalities and powers," it was to these transpersonal realities that he was referring. When John's Apocalypse (11:15) says that "the kingdom of the world has become the kingdom of our Lord and of his Christ," (NASB) and when it repeatedly speaks of "peoples, multitudes, nations and languages," I can't help but think that there is something beyond (not more important than but in addition to) individuals being saved here.

When I think of the power of communism or consumerism or white supremacy or liberalism or conservatism over individuals, I keep thinking that one of the greatest things God could do for individuals is intervene and confront, redeem, subvert, convert, or save the principalities and powers that overpower them—for the benefit of all individuals involved. I also sometimes wonder if it is even possible to speak of isolated individuals ("monads," as Polanyi and Newbigin called them) apart from culture, since so much of what any of us is as an individual is actually something relationally shared with others in the transpersonal realities of family, congregation, friendship, nation, tribe, ethnicity, and so on. So I wonder: Is the work of the gospel (and the church) to be focused only on individuals, believing that only individuals can be saved (however we define that term!) and that any other kind of salvation is either needless or unrealistic, or is what we call culture itself a reality in God's creation, a reality that is part and parcel of "the kingdom of the world" that has or will or can become "the kingdom of our Lord and of his Christ"?

3. Erwin repeatedly emphasized the difference between the message about Jesus and the person of Jesus, and I agree with the thrust of his emphasis: It's not disembodied information

that counts, but rather a real and living encounter with "the person of Christ," the living God, Father, Son, and Spirit. Amen! But the question Erwin put to me (and that Michael raised as well) seems to come back around. Some Mormons may claim to have that living encounter, and so may some Buddhists, and some New Agers, and some white supremacists and Islamic fundamentalists too. Even among "orthodox Christians," people who claim to have had a living encounter with the person of Christ have burned witches and been burned as witches, have burned members of other denominations and been burned, have served the poor and oppressed the poor, have venerated icons and burned icons, have put American flags in their churches kept them out or burned them. So pretty soon we start wishing we could identify not just who has their message, story, doctrine, or theology straight but who has really had an encounter with the living person of Christ. How do we discern that? And as we engage people of the surrounding cultures (postmodern, modern, whatever) and invite them to encounter and follow the person of Christ, they naturally will ask, "Whose tribe do you recommend that I join in that journey? Eastern Orthodox? Reformed? Roman Catholic? Pentecostal? Anabaptist?" Depending on how we answer that question, they will have very different experiences and understandings of having an encounter with the person of Christ.

4. Andy and Michael both rightly point out that my dichotomization of method and message confuses and hides as much as it clarifies. I hope I made it clear in the chapter that ultimately I agree with them. I used that dichotomy not because I want to defend or spread it but because I hear it come up so often when we Christians discuss the church's relationship to culture.

Their insights will help readers think more deeply about the ways in which method and message are interwoven, which leads me to ask, not in general about everybody but about my own local church, which I love and where I serve: Where is our methodology undermining our message?

5. Michael rightly warns against sliding or overreacting from one polarity (gospel as slogan, formula, sales pitch) to its opposite (gospel as "radically indeterminate"). I keep wondering, How do we avoid swinging from one extreme to another? The answer I keep coming back to is mission. In other words, let's assume that we were at least somewhat clear on our mission (perhaps something like this: being and making disciples who do what Jesus commanded, immersed in the Father, Son, and Holy Spirit, so that God's kingdom comes and God's will is done on earth as in Heaven). What if our message and methods for this moment in history are simply to be the word of the Lord that our mission now requires? In other words, what if our mission is the horse, and our message and methods are the cart, and we've been trying to pull the horse by the cart for too long?

I must close by expressing deep gratitude for the conversation that has taken place among these friends in Christ through these pages. This methodology of conversing (respectfully, interactively) with one another (rather than merely about one another behind backs) is one that supports rather than undermines our message. "Speaking the truth in love" is a practice (to use Andy's term) that will help us better serve God and our neighbors in the years to come. May all who read and discuss these pages continue the conversation in a similar tone of respect and love.

❀   ❀   ❀   ❀   ❀

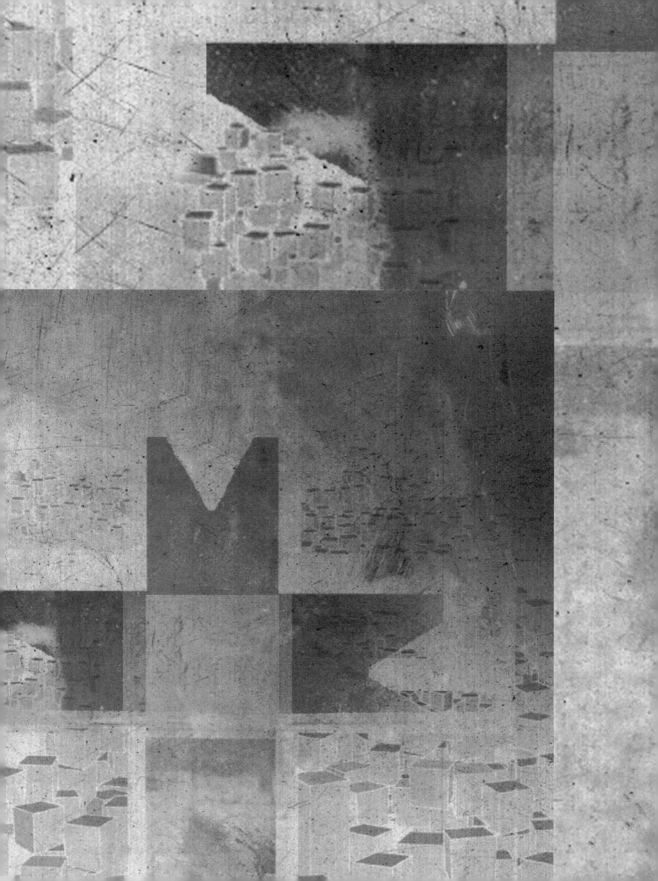

ERWIN
RAPHAEL
McMANUS

Erwin Raphael McManus

The Global Intersection

ONE OF MY FAVORITE PLACES to stand here in Los Angeles is on the rooftop of the nightclub where we have gathered for the past five years. Mosaic is the community of faith with which I serve and live. It has become a part of an unusual history that began with Prince's Grand Slam and was followed by the Shangri-La, the Downtown Soho, the Penthouse, Baby Doe's, and today the Los Angeles Entertainment Center (LAEC). In any given week the walls rumble from the sounds of rap, salsa, disco, and techno. Patrons of the LAEC vary widely, from Allen Iverson and Shaquille O'Neal to Ricky Martin and Austin Powers. Underneath my feet is a small reminder of the unique, eccentric, and diverse composition of the city in which I live. When the timing works out just right on those Sunday evenings when we've moved from downstairs to the rooftop for our service, we're greeted by the breathtaking sight of the freshly lit downtown as the sun disappears over the horizon. I will never grow tired of this image. I find myself continually inspired by what the cityscape of Los Angeles represents in relationship to the rest of the world. { ⊛ *BRIAN D. McLAREN: Erwin's introduction rings, for me, with a love for his city, a love for the world, which in turn resonates with God's love for the world. True, God judges the world; God sees its sin and ugliness. But I believe, with Erwin, God always sees the world with love in his eyes.* }

Our city's unique relationship to the rest of the planet constantly reminds me that Los Angeles inhales the world and has wonderful potential for exhaling the gospel. Living in Los Angeles is like standing on the corner of a busy intersection, except here the whole world is trying to cross to the other side. If you folded a sheet of paper in such a way that all the corners touch, you could call that intersection Los Angeles. The world meets here. And the future is born here. Whatever the world will be, Los Angeles already is—for better or worse. { ⊕ *FREDERICA MATHEWES-GREEN: This is so eloquent and so depressing! Los Angeles means entertainment and for better or worse, American entertainment is now the most powerful influence in the world.* }

L.A. is more than simply the new address of citizens relocated from as far away as China, Japan, the Middle East, and the Philippines and from as near as El Salvador, Mexico, and Michigan. It is more than the place where countless cultures intersect and coexist. It is a cultural biosphere. It is an active culture cultivating something more powerful and profound than microorganisms or bacteria. It is the context in which new strains of worldviews and belief systems are being formed. Los Angeles is a sociological and religious ecotonic state in which, when you put in the old, something new emerges. The relationship of the church to culture takes on new meaning in this context.

A River Runs Through It

CULTURE IS GENERALLY about how people socialize, how we group together, or more accurately, what holds us together. When we try to understand a culture, we often turn to beliefs, practices, and values. Cultures express themselves in as wide a range of things as view of the world to style of music. From this vantage point, religion and dance, philosophy and art are natural and illuminating expressions of culture. But similar to the way nature has been replaced by technology, culture has been replaced by change. To speak of culture we must move from talking about who we are to who we are becoming. { ⊗ *BRIAN D. McLAREN: Erwin's insight here is important. And historians would tell us that this has always been the case: No culture has ever been completely static. Yet it is true, as Erwin says, that modernity seems to have put cultural evolution (or devolution, or extinction in many cases) into hyperdrive.* }

The classice view of culture as more commonly understood is no longer an effective structure with which to consider the challenge the church faces. Certainly the view of culture as static, unchanging, or even permanent is inadequate and perhaps even invalid. Have you ever stood on a rock in the middle of a river, hearing, seeing, and feeling the power of water rushing all around you? Imagine deciding to take a bucket and dip it quickly into the river to fill it not with water but with the rapid itself. You would have an endless stream of rushing water from which to draw. Yet every time you would attempt to capture this amazing dynamic, no matter how quickly you dipped or how determined you were, when you looked inside your container, all you would find is still water. Your failure would be maddening, and all who observed your efforts would consider you mad.

Is it any different when we speak of ourselves outside of culture or of the church apart from culture? Is it possible that what we are attempting to capture is the river's movement but what we actually gather is just still water? In generations past the river moved slowly. What we saw in our bucket looked a lot like what we found in the river. But though they were similar, they were never really the same. The rapid pace of cultural change, the new fluidity in which we live, and the emergence of new strains and endless variations of human understanding make the distinction between the church and the culture difficult to ignore.

Our inability to distinguish between the water in the bucket and the rapids is perhaps one reason we are often so inept at impacting the culture we seek to engage. Whenever the church assumes the role of an institution committed to protecting its constituency from the emerging culture, we reduce our impact to a drop in the bucket. It is tragic enough when the church relinquishes its place at the dangerous edge of the rapids for the safety of the bucket. It is even more perplexing when the structures of the church actually become the buckets justifying isolation from the river. The church is not intended to be a bucket, saving the water from the rapids. Neither is the church intended to be the water settled in the bucket. The church is intended to always be an intricate part of the river and to be at her best in the midst of the white waters. The water will not drown regardless of how tumultuous the rapids become. { ❧ *BRIAN D. McLAREN: This is Erwin's powerful way of saying we should be in the world, not of it. Lesslie Newbigin said it this way: "We must start with the basic fact that there is no such thing as a pure gospel if by that is meant something which is not embodied in a culture...Every interpretation of the gospel is embodied in some cultural form" (Lesslie Newbigin,* The Gospel in a Pluralist Society, *144).* }

As safe as the still waters may appear to be, however, we must never forget that water left in the bucket will become stagnant, stale, and bitter. Church growth must go beyond filling up our buckets and then getting bigger buckets so we can save more water. The reality is that once we leave the river, what we gain in stability we lose in movement. Separation intended for our sanctification secures our isolation. We must resist becoming the buckets and instead remain in the river. { ⊕ *FREDERICA MATHEWES-GREEN: Very helpful analogy, Erwin, and I agree with your point. Christians are never out of the river; any separation between church and culture is illusory. Dipping buckets in and then trying to reformat the church to match is futile (for example, changing musical styles to make it more up to date; as they say, if you can see a bandwagon, it's too late to get on it). Our challenge is to remain uniquely our uncompromised selves, flowing with the river and using discernment to reach those caught in the torrent, knowing that this is always our Father's river and that we are uniquely gifted to understand it.* ⬡ *ANDY CROUCH: Erwin, I so want to go along with you here, and you're saying something vitally important. But I hesitate. Is contemporary culture really a fast-moving river—with the freshness and dynamism that implies—or is it a jacuzzi, a frothy bath of aimless activity designed to simultaneously coddle and stimulate enervated postmoderns? In some ways our world is more static than ever. In your opening paragraphs you talk about the Los Angeles Entertainment Center's "varied" clientele—from Allen Iverson to Austin Powers. But all of these celebrities are part of a seamless entertainment industry—in fact, one of them doesn't even exist outside of that industry. (The task of determining which one is left as an exercise for the reader, and it may be harder than it appears.) They are employed by a handful of indistinguishable media conglomerates, which control an impressive percentage of this country's—and the world's—production of "culture." The sounds of "rap, salsa, disco, and techno" increasingly borrow from and interpenetrate one another, and all of them answer to the same bottom line. Now if you had said, "from a janitor at Universal Studios to an entertainment lawyer to a permanently disabled Vietnam vet to a Special Olympics participant," I'd be more impressed. If the musical genres on offer ranged from Tuvan throat-singing to Brahms, to Eminem, I'd take notice. But what if postmodernity (a.k.a., consumer culture) is ever more homogenous, not less, for all its frothy chaos and aspirations to novelty? If so, the church risks becoming bacteria-ridden precisely because of its attempts to participate in culture, and the cultural diversity and pace of change that we find so exhilarating is actually superficial in the worst way.* }

Past the Expiration Date

THOUGH WE USE LANGUAGE to articulate our core values, we recognize that language is limited. Mosaic's fourth core value is simply "Relevance to culture is not optional." We found this emphatic statement to be necessary to our congregational health in that people often long to live in an experience already lived. We seem determined to time-date the sacred. We are the religious version of Bono's "Stuck in a Moment." As if that were not strange enough, most of us live in time-place confusion—or should I say delusion? Contemporary churches are usually reflections of the 1970s and '80s, reminding us that most of us confuse the past for the present. { ▷ *MICHAEL HORTON: But doesn't this just illustrate how tough it is to take our cues from pop culture? Is relevance a matter of hearing your pastor quote Chris Rock (which, of course, would be relevant only to a very narrow segment of God's people anyway)? Or is it a matter of hearing something that you've never really heard before, even if it has been said by Christian sages before you time and time again? What's more, what could be more relevant than the Lord's people being personally assembled and addressed by him? The sheep hearing their Master's voice and not their own echo is the desire I hear expressed among many young Christians and seekers today.* }

Like manna from Heaven, our expressions of faith need to be fresh and life-giving. Even the bread of Heaven came with an expiration date. Many of our faith expressions are out of touch not because they're ancient but because they're antiquated. { ▷ *MICHAEL HORTON: But antiquated by what? By no longer being taken seriously by the world—a world that, Jesus assured us in advance, would despise us for his sake and would, as Paul reminds us, regard the gospel as 'foolishness'? Perhaps "antiquated" here refers to the style of music or the stuck-in-the-fifties ambience, vocabulary, and "feel" of so many conservative churches. If it's the latter, "I feel your pain."* }

In my work as a futurist, I have discovered that the present is as much of the future as most people care to handle. When a church starts working toward relevance, it admits that somehow it was left behind. { ⊕ *FREDERICA MATHEWES-GREEN: I found myself confused by this whole section on relevance. It sounds like a meeting of two institutions—I picture them at the negotiating table, the culture huge and complex and self-absorbed, and the smaller, anxious church studying it and trying to figure out how to get in. This image is wrong on both sides. All this world—this river, to stick to the metaphor—is God's; the church is those people who know him and bear his light, scattered all through the river. The culture, the ever-shifting river, is not our concern. We want to reach the millions of individuals bobbing along in the rushing water, who are trying to make sense of their lives with limited resources and in little solidarity with each other (except, Erwin, as you imply, the unhappy solidarity of being formed by the same entertainment). They are sheep without a shepherd, harassed and helpless. Analyzing the river is pointless. People are affected by it in too many different individual ways, and it keeps changing all the time anyway. The seductive illusion is that we can come up with some big "socko" message, put it on a billboard, and snag whole nets full of fish at one time. This isn't how true conversion happens. It's one to one, friend to friend, and our more modest goal should be loving, listening to, praying for, and bearing witness to the individuals around us. Forget the dreams of glory. Think small. Instead of a few huge churches that house thousands, let's have thousands of small churches, where people can form close, lasting connections, can mix naturally in a family of generations and backgrounds, and where a spiritual father and mother can disciple them personally and in depth. Transformed Christians are made carefully, slowly, one at a time; anxiously monitoring the rushing river has nothing to do with this process. }* To become relevant is to catch up with the time in history you were intended to serve. Relevance is not about conformity; it is about clarity and connectedness.

Relevance is not about having everyone agree with you. It is about speaking the truth of Christ honestly and credibly into a person's life. When we speak relevantly to the world we live in, there is a resonance of reality and authenticity. It is a tragedy that when people reject our approach or attitude, we conclude that they're rejecting Christ and his message. In regard to culture it has never been our intent at Mosaic to simply relate effectively. Again, in Los Angeles, culture is fluid and fast moving. If you're going to hit a moving target, you need to aim ahead of it. If you shoot where it is, you are certain to miss it. This alone is motivation enough to think in new ways about engaging culture. Our intention is not simply to relate to culture but to create culture.

{ ⊛ BRIAN D. McLAREN: Erwin's stated intention of creating culture resonates with my understanding of what it means to be human. Creating culture is what humans made in God's image do, and culture is the "world" that humans create in God's world. This is a vision of the church far different from an isolated and elite few "just passing through" on our way to Heaven; rather, we are called to be a spring of pure water gushing into the world, believing that even though it is a trickle compared with the many streams that are swollen with trash and smelly with pollution, "the knowledge of the Lord will cover the earth as the waters cover the sea." An impossible dream? Dare we use impossible? }

When we work from this framework, relevance can never be equated with pragmatism. Relevance isn't about what works best or gets the job done fastest. The focus on methods borne out of the church-growth movement has at times made us look more like the disciples of John Stuart Mill than of Jesus the Christ. Relevance is instead about embracing the principle that we are to value the one lost sheep even more than the 99 that are found. It is waking up to the realization that the church isn't here for we who believe, but rather that we in fact are the church, and we are here for a world drowning in disbelief. { ▷ *MICHAEL HORTON: But let's not do away so quickly with the church being here for us who believe. After all, the church is God's ordained institution through which he promises to save the lost and continue to save the found by means of preaching and sacrament. The church is not just the sum of God's evangelizing force but a family of sinners who are in constant need of nourishment and divine blessing "from generation to generation."* } Relevant engagement of culture, when borne out of the heart of God, is less about marketing and more about passion. It is Paul offering up his own damnation if only Israel could be saved. It is fleshed out in the willingness to become all things to all men that we might somehow save some. { ✦ *BRIAN D. McLAREN: The passion of the preceding paragraph explains so much of why I'm in ministry, in spite of all its discouragements and difficulties.* }

Simply Timeless

RELEVANCE IS ABOUT accepting the conclusion of the Jerusalem Council, which dealt with this issue of Christianity in culture. The issue was whether every believer would have to become a Jew. Was there one culture that was inherently sacred and required preservation? Would the church be forever bound to one time and cultural expression? The conclusion, stated by James, was simply this: "It is my judgment, therefore, that we should not make it difficult for the Gentiles who are turning to God" (ACTS 15:19). { ⊕ *FREDERICA MATHEWES-GREEN: Yet the Acts 15 council still named certain observances that Gentile converts were required to observe. Their "judgment for simplicity" continued to include specific moral, sacramental, and disciplinary practices, as evidenced in Paul's letters to Gentile churches. We have to rely on Scripture, and not our own understanding, in determining what is "nonessential."* } The council's judgment was for simplicity; its commitment was to remove every nonessential barrier between God and man. We seem to love complicated religions and philosophies, but the Scriptures remind us that simplicity is timeless.

Relevance is also about the realization that we tend to sacramentalize methodology, practices, and traditions. We tend to find more comfort in superstitions created out of our own imaginations than in the simplicity of faith to which God calls us. { ⊕ *FREDERICA MATHEWES-GREEN: I join you in categorically condemning "superstitions created out of our own imaginations." However, "superstition" is a classic Enlightenment insult to throw at any religion that claims to have a supernatural dimension. Christianity has been cowed by this prejudice for two hundred years and has responded by claiming to be merely useful (socially, personally) and avoiding implications that God is real, immediate, and intervenes in our lives. Scripture, however, has no such hesitation, and it is time we recaptured that boldness.* } Jesus chastised the religious leaders of his time when they rebuked him for not observing their rituals. He replied with a cutting and condemning question: "And why do you break the command of God for the sake of your tradition?" He follows this question with a quote from Isaiah the prophet: "These people honor me with their lips, but their hearts are far from me. They worship me in vain; their teachings are but rules taught by men" (MATTHEW 15:3, 8-9).

We must never allow ourselves to be deluded by our own sense of accuracy or rightness. Whatever the culture, era, or generation, it is essential that we examine our practices, rituals, dogmas, and traditions and measure them against God's intent as communicated through the Scriptures. { ▷ *MICHAEL HORTON: This, I believe, is one of the fundamental points to be made in this whole debate. But while evangelicals tend to be pretty good at finding splinters of humanly crafted methods or traditions in the eyes of those who lived a long time ago, they are less critical of their own, more recent innovations. In some churches a service without an altar call of some form would be considered incomplete, even though the practice itself is a century and a half old. If we as younger believers are to honor our fathers and mothers, we must patiently hear their reasons and listen to the logic of their exegesis of Scripture. It is a measure of our lack of wisdom that instead of at least listening to the elders (dead or alive), we tear down the house they left to us and build our own in its place. I call this generational narcissism, and it is a temptation for all of us these days.* } It is critical that every generation struggles to reclaim the essence of the Christian faith. { ⊕ *FREDERICA MATHEWES-GREEN: Or better yet, encounter Christ. It's not about ideas but about the living presence of God.* } We must hear what God is saying above what we're saying about what God is saying. One way we articulate this at Mosaic is "ancient text, present context, future textures." This framework has led us to such expressions of faith as using five elemental metaphors—wind, water, earth, fire, and wood—

to express our critical environments for discipleship and to such experiences as having, during our Lord's Supper, a pretext experience in which participants must share or learn the story before partaking of the elements. We use art, sculpture, and dance not as entertainment but as primal expressions of our faith. { ▷ *MICHAEL HORTON: I'm not sure what "primal" means here. And since it has been argued that we must return to Scripture for our cues, I'm wondering how a use of art, sculpture, and dance can be justified on the basis of New Testament principles of worship. I'm all for art, sculpture, and dance, but are these divinely ordained means of grace and therefore elements of worship?* }

It is not our intent to find a better place in the past for the future church. It is our intent to find a better place in the future for the ancient church. The emerging demands of a pluralistic society informed by Eastern and not Western culture challenges us to create dramatically different expressions of our faith. This can be done only if we are willing to detoxify the church not only from its modern but also from its Western wrappings. { ▷ *MICHAEL HORTON: Not to be a pain here, but earlier the argument was that the church should not be seen as distinct from the world, but here we read that the church needs to be detoxed from its modern wrappings. Does it also need detoxing from its postmodern (or future-church) wrappings? Or are we protecting our own tense (in this case, the future) from criticism while relativizing every other one?* } The premodern journey leads us not to a European church and its sacramental essence but to a primal church with an elemental essence. { ⊕ *FREDERICA MATHEWES-GREEN: I don't know what "elemental essence" means, but the primal church was sacramental. ▷ MICHAEL HORTON: I'm not sure yet what's involved with the "sacramental essence" versus the "elemental essence," but I have to admit I'm nervous.* } The church is in the truest sense a biblical community when we incarnate the presence of Christ, reflect the character of God, and open the eyes of the world to the reality of God evident in all of creation. Like creation, the church is here to reflect God's glory, and like Christ, we are here to bring the world to its Creator. At our best, we express his personhood and represent him well in a world proceeding without him.

A Generative Culture

FOR THE LAST SEVERAL YEARS I have been asked, "What do you think is coming after the postmodern era?" For the longest time my answer was simply, "I have no idea." But if September 11th has reminded me of anything, it is that the future is shaped by the decisions of men under the sovereignty of God. My answer today is quite different. Now I answer, "Whatever we choose."

I think this answer is important when we consider the theological passivity of contemporary Christianity. Without realizing it we have slipped into the view that the world creates culture and that the church reacts to it. In our most innovative moments we analyze cultural trends and project historical movements. Then like a twig determined to stop a tsunami, we brace ourselves for the future. But is it possible that the church was intended to be the cultural epicenter from which a new community emerges, astonishing and transforming cultures through the power of forgiveness, freedom, and creativity? { ◈ANDY CROUCH: *Amen, amen. This beautifully expands on your earlier observation that we are part of the river (or the jacuzzi, as it may be). We are not at the mercy of culture but indeed are cultural agents. Unless—the all-important unless—we lose the ability to bring another and better story to bear on our own moment in history. In a sense this whole book is a conversation about the meaning of that unless. But thank you for articulating so beautifully the importance of cultural creativity, which is ultimately much more powerful than any cultural critique, let alone cultural consumption or capitulation.* } Have we overestimated the effectiveness of methods, programs, and structures and underestimated the transforming essence of faith, love, and hope?

The mandate that Jesus gave to his disciples was far from passive or even reactionary. It was proactive and revolutionary. He entrusted a handful of men and women with a commission to make disciples of all nations. With this broad stroke he sent them out to change the contour of human history and left the details for them to work out. Ironically, perhaps the first cultural reorganization was the creation of the weekend. The Jews worshiped on the Sabbath. The newly formed Christian community now worshiped on Resurrection day, which was Sunday. Little did they know they were introducing for all the Western societies to come two days in which to ignore their spiritual condition but have plenty of time to mow the lawn and watch football. Of course, this brings us to one of the few potentially positive influences of Islam on American culture. Since Muslims hold Friday as sacred, the emerging culture gives us the potential for a three-day weekend. All this is to say that values shape beliefs, which shape practices, which shape culture.

Cultures are not born in a vacuum. The fuel of a culture is what is referred to as ethos (see my book *An Unstoppable Force*). The fuel of ethos are values, which I am convinced are deeper and more primal than beliefs. It is far more important to change a person's passions than their beliefs. You can believe many things without being passionate about them, but you cannot be passionate about something without believing in it. The revolution Jesus began 2,000 years ago does not simply change our theology, but more powerfully it transforms our pathos. The dynamic tension between the message and the culture is not about what Jesus once said but about what Jesus is saying. The intersection is not simply between an ancient message and a contemporary context but between an eternal God and this moment in history.

The real issue facing the church is not essentially about methodology or even the preserving of the message; the real issue is why the church is so unaffected by the transforming presence of the living God. { ⊕ *FREDERICA MATHEWES-GREEN: Amen!* } Jesus lives in every time and place in human history. He both makes himself known and manifests himself through the body of Christ. We should give up our role as preservationists—the church was never intended to be the Jewish version of the mummification of God. God is not lost in the past; he is active in the present. Our mandate is to continue the revolution Jesus Christ began 2,000 years ago. The Scriptures are more than our textbook; they are our portal into the presence of God, where we not only come to know his mind and heart but also are transformed to become like him. { ⊕ *FREDERICA MATHEWES-GREEN: Amen! Preach it!* }

Beyond the Message to the Person of Christ

THOUGH CULTURE IS RAPIDLY CHANGING, we must not conclude that God is desperately trying to catch up. Christ is present in our context. He spoke and history was created, and his voice will resonate beyond the end of time. Our efforts to relate the message to the culture in which we are speaking have often been framed in terms of what doctrines must be known and believed. In more recent times, the conversation about the message and about truth itself has been deconstructed and reduced to a more critical question, What can be known? I am convinced both approaches address this issue from the wrong end. As a follower of Jesus Christ, my focus is, What is Jesus' intent? What is it that he does not want us to miss? What are his nonnegotiables? In John 17:1-3, Jesus unwraps the core of his mission through his prayer. "Father, the time has come. Glorify your Son, that your Son may glorify you. For you granted him authority over all people that he might give eternal life to all those you have given him. Now this is eternal life: that they may know you, the only true God, and Jesus Christ, whom you have sent."

Whatever the range of views may be, if we are defined by the person of Jesus Christ, then our mission must be to bring to humanity life that is borne out of an intimate relationship to God through Jesus Christ. The knowing that Jesus speaks of is best described as intimacy. The power of this relationship changes our relationship to everything else. The power of the gospel is the result of a person—Jesus Christ—not a message. The gospel is an event to be proclaimed, not a doctrine to be preserved. { ▷ *MICHAEL HORTON: I'm amazed at the number of false choices I've been asked to make in this, as in Brian's essay. "A person...not a message"; "an event to be proclaimed, not a doctrine to be preserved." The only way we have any access to this person is through the message. Whether we like it or not (I don't know why we would not), gospel means "good news, a message." It is by definition a message. But of course Jesus is himself the good news incarnate, so it's both. As far as the antithesis between "an event to be proclaimed" and "a doctrine to be preserved," what would we make of the exhortation to "contend earnestly for the faith which was once for all delivered to the saints" (Jude 3, NKJV), or to hold fast to sound doctrine at a time when "they will not endure sound doctrine..." (2 Timothy 4:3, NKJV)? To guard the doctrine and teach it faithfully, says Paul, is "the work of an evangelist," not a distraction from it (v. 5). I detect in this essay a pervasive contemporary expression of what some have called the "orphaned self." Paul reminds Timothy, "But you must continue in the things which you have learned and been assured of, knowing from whom you have learned them, and that from childhood you have known the Holy Scriptures, which are able to make you wise for salvation through faith which is in Christ Jesus" (2 Timothy 3:14-15, NKJV). But I wonder if modern evangelicalism has taught us all for too long to uproot ourselves from this faith we have received and act as though we were ourselves the first to discover it. Surely there is an option that avoids either dead orthodoxy or dynamic heterodoxy.* } The revolution brings people to the person of Christ through the declaration of an event in history. The proof of the message is the transformation of individuals who have met God at the cross. { ❋ *BRIAN D. McLAREN: I know I'm being repetitious, but it's hard to contain my enthusiasm for what Erwin is saying.* }

Jesus makes clear that the ultimate end of his mission for humanity is that we may know God in Christ. Paul describes in euphoric language the transforming result of knowing Christ. In Philippians 3:8-11, Paul declares, "I consider everything a loss compared to the surpassing greatness of knowing Christ Jesus my Lord, for whose sake I have lost all things. I consider them rubbish, that I may gain Christ and be found in him...I want to know Christ and the power of his resurrection and the fellowship of sharing in his sufferings, becoming like him in his death, and so, somehow, to attain to the resurrection from the dead."

Do You Hear What I Hear?

IF CHRISTIAN PHILOSOPHICAL thought is genuinely grappling with the question of what can be known, we must conclude without ambiguity that God can be known. { ❋ *BRIAN D. McLAREN: Of course, the crux of the matter is that the word* known *is used in two ways in this sentence, one way referring to an abstract, rational, impersonal certitude, and the other referring to personal knowledge. That difference makes all the difference.* } When Jesus asked his disciples, "Who do you say I am?" Simon Peter answered, "You are the Christ, the Son of the living God." Jesus replied, "Blessed are you, Simon son of Jonah, for this was not revealed to you by man, but by my Father in heaven" (MATTHEW 16:15-17).

God can be known because he makes himself known. He is the initiator of every transforming relationship, revealing himself and bringing us into a knowing that comes only through his presence. It is this encounter with God through Jesus Christ that separates Christianity from world religions. Peter's declaration of Jesus' identity is not incidental in this process. Whether the declaration precedes the revelation or the revelation precedes the declaration may remain a mystery to us. But this we can know: When revelation and declaration intersect, there is transformation—and this intersection happens only in and through the person of Jesus Christ.

Every follower of Jesus Christ can also know something else—that God speaks. And we know that God speaks that which is beyond natural under-standing yet not beyond human comprehension. God is both mysterious and clear. Both Judaism and Christianity emerged out of a conviction that God speaks and can be heard, understood, and obeyed. The act of God speaking is the basis of faith. { ▷ *MICHAEL HORTON: A fantastic point, often overlooked but enormously suggestive for our understanding of preaching and its significance (see Romans 10:17).* } If God does not speak, then we believe in vain. True religion is not our desperate search to make God intelligible. It is a response to what God has spoken. And the words of God are far more than divine information—they are life to the listener. Creation begins with the act of God speaking. The recurring theme of Genesis 1 is simply, "And God said..." The end of all created things will come as a result of God speaking again.

The writer of Hebrews warns us to "see to it that you do not refuse him who speaks. If they did not escape when they refused him who warned them on earth, how much less will we, if we turn away from him who warns us from heaven? At that time his voice shook the earth, but now he has promised, 'Once more I will shake not only the earth but also the heavens'" (HEBREWS 12:25-26).

We can know that God speaks, that his words can both create and destroy, that hearing his voice and obeying it is the path to life. To ignore his voice places us in great peril.

Life-Giving Words

WE CAN ALSO KNOW not only that God has spoken but also that he has written his words as a treasure for us. The idea of God using written text is not a modern construct. Long before the modern world, God not only spoke to Moses but also etched by his own finger his commandments to his people. In fact he did it twice, since Moses destroyed the first copy in a fit of anger. It is also clear that God shaped his people through the truth and power of his words in the text. To Joshua he commanded, "Do not let this Book of the Law depart from your mouth; meditate on it day and night, so that you may be careful to do everything written in it. Then you will be prosperous and successful" (JOSHUA 1:8).

The writings of David illustrate that Israel engaged with the Scriptures as a living text and not simply as a source of biblical history or merely a theological document. What we find in them is a dynamic relationship to the Scripture. In Psalm 119:105, David declares, "Your word is a lamp to my feet and a light for my path." Rather than seeing the Scriptures as an instrument of legalism or a book of regulations, they are described as a pathway to life and freedom. In verse 32 of the same Psalm, David writes, "I run in the path of your commands, for you have set my heart free." Jesus reinforces a living relationship to God's written word. When driven by the Spirit into the wilderness to be tempted by the Devil, Jesus not only uses the Scriptures as both his weapon and guide but illuminates the very reason for this relationship. In response to being tempted to turn stones into bread to alleviate his hunger, Jesus says, "Man does not live on bread alone, but on every word that comes from the mouth of God" (MATTHEW 4:4).

Jesus' quoting Deuteronomy 8:3 points to God's reminder to his people that he allowed them to wander for 40 years to test them and know what was in their hearts, that he fed them manna from heaven and did not allow their clothes to wear out nor their feet to swell, all to teach them one transforming truth—that man does not live on bread alone but on every word that comes from the mouth of God. This was not a spiritualized truth. It was God revealing to them the essence of reality. Life comes not from the created but from the Creator. Bread nourishes us only because God has declared it to be so. If God were silent, death would reign. When God speaks, whoever has the ears to hear experiences life.

In modern times the Scriptures have been demeaned into God's comprehensive encyclopedia. We have developed the discipline of theology to study God and his ideas. We have moved from a missiological hermeneutic to a theological hermeneutic and have lost the power of the Scriptures in the transition. Jesus warns us that the written word brings death and the Spirit brings life. In other words, to know the Bible is not necessarily to

know God. The information neither saves you nor transforms you.

Divine Cryogenics

IN THE SAME WAY THAT JESUS simplifies God's purpose when he declares, "The work of God is this: to believe in the one he has sent" (JOHN 6:29), so the ultimate end of the Scriptures is for us to encounter God, be transformed in his presence, and join him in his mission. The Scriptures are more than a record of God's activity. They are a portal into God's presence and activity. Jesus reminds those who inquire of his ways that "it is written in the Prophets: 'They will all be taught by God.' Everyone who listens to the Father and learns from him comes to me" (JOHN 6:45). The greatest evidence for the authority of the Scriptures is that God speaks through them, and we are translated into his presence and transformed by his power.

The Scriptures are not God's Word frozen in time, conveniently available for us to defrost whenever we need them. They are the living words of God inviting us into the presence of the God who is a consuming fire. Jeremiah described his encounter like this: "But if I say, 'I will not mention him or speak any more in his name,' his word is in my heart like a fire, a fire shut up in my bones. I am weary of holding it in; indeed, I cannot" (JEREMIAH 20:9).

The writer of Hebrews expresses this dynamic when he explains, "For the word of God is living and active. Sharper than any double-edged sword, it penetrates even to dividing soul and spirit, joints and marrow; it judges the thoughts and attitudes of the heart. Nothing in all creation is hidden from God's sight. Everything is uncovered and laid bare before the eyes of him to whom we must give account" (4:12-13).

To see the Scriptures as God's definitive book of knowledge is to demean them. The Scriptures are so much more than that. When engaged with humility, they translate us into the very presence of God. To have a high view of Scripture is not to conclude that the message never changes. For it is not simply that God has spoken but that God is speaking. To have a high view of Scripture is to engage the Word of God with the heart of the psalmist: "Do good to your servant, and I will live; I will obey your word. Open my eyes that I may see wonderful things in your law" (PSALM 119:17-18).

God is always speaking to those who would listen, revealing himself and his ways to those who would see. His message is always timeless and timely. The issues of our time matter to God. He does not walk blindly through human suffering, injustice, or evil. His word never loses its edge. It is always sharp, precise, and relevant.

Shaped by the Voice

WITH BOTH the nation of Israel and the church of Jesus Christ, God was forming a people shaped by his voice. A people to whom he would speak and who would distinguish themselves by their obedience to his word. The great irony we find in the gospels is that the people, who had been entrusted with the words of God, did not recognize the Word of God. To have the Scriptures, even to know the Scriptures, is not the way to life. To hear God speak, to heed his voice, and to respond with passionate commitment to the path he calls us on is the journey to life. When God speaks, those who hear and obey live. This is the defining characteristic of God's people.

Hebrews 1:1-3a describes God's intentionality in this process: "In the past God spoke to our forefathers through the prophets at many times and in various ways, but in these last days he has spoken to us by his Son, whom he appointed heir of all things, and through whom he made the universe. The Son is the radiance of God's glory and the exact representation of his being, sustaining all things by his powerful word."

His point is simple: God has spoken through many people, in a variety of ways, and in many different times, all for the purpose of preparing us to hear the voice of the Son of God. Again, this is the chief end of all that God speaks, that we would know the one who has spoken. It is not enough for us to know or even believe all that is true. It is essential that we know the one who is true. In this sense, the nature of truth is critical. Contemporary philosophy would propose that all truth is subjective. This position embraces relativism and makes the individual the center of reality. Science and modern Christianity would advocate that truth is objective, standing outside of the individual and empirically or rationally provable. The Scriptures give us a different position. Truth is neither relative nor objective. The biblical view is that truth is personal, relational, and subjective. The critical difference, of course, is that we are not the subject. God is. {✵*BRIAN D. McLAREN: I can think of a dozen radio preachers who I wish would read the preceding paragraph. I think Erwin does a masterful job, in simple language, of getting to the real issue behind words like* relative and objective. *The subjectivity that really counts, as Erwin says, is what the Ultimate Subject feels and knows and says!* ✵*ANDY CROUCH: Of course, it goes further—just as postmoderns have rediscovered the "intersubjective" nature of truth, Christians are no mere monotheists but have come to know a God whose very being is "intersubjective."*} Jesus states emphatically that he is the truth. He is not simply the definer of truth, the teacher of truth, or the great advocate of truth. He is the source of all truth. Truth exists because God is trustworthy. The biblical understanding of truth is that all truth comes from God. Our experience of an objective reality is the result of the very character and nature of God. The integrity of the cosmos is an extension of the personhood of its creator. Everything and everyone that moves away from God drifts from truth. Outside of love, perhaps no characteristic is more significant in defining a follower of Jesus Christ than a relentless pursuit of truth and personal trustworthiness. This is no small distinction in that for many followers of Jesus Christ, it is clearly the Scriptures that led us to Jesus. But in the emerging pluralistic environment, it is Jesus who leads us to the Scriptures.

God Still Speaks

SUE CHO WAS A FIRST-TIME GUEST at Mosaic. She had come with her sister, who, unlike her, was a follower of Jesus Christ. When she was growing up in China, she was both an accomplished athlete and intellectual. After the close of the Sunday worship experience, she expressed appreciation for the teaching and asked if there was an Internet dialogue she could engage in. She added that she had many questions about the existence of God and would like very much to pursue them. In the midst of our conversation, I ventured into the mystical. I suggested to her that I knew something about her though we had never met. And she asked me what that was. I stated that during the worship experience that night God had revealed himself to her and that this disturbed her, since she had no intellectual validation for his existence. And I told her it was my sense that beyond revealing himself, God had spoken to her and told her that Jesus was his name.

There was no small awkward silence after that moment. Her lack of eye contact let me know she was considering her response carefully. I simply invited her to consider that it was okay to acknowledge whether or not this was her experience. She quietly looked up and said yes, that was exactly right. And I asked her if what she needed through the Internet dialogue was the intellectual validation to support what her spirit already knew to be true. She gave me a resounding yes. I assured her we would be more than happy to help her brain catch up with her heart or her mind with her soul. It was hardly days after this encounter when her emails began to read like the female version of the apostle Paul, expressing a vibrant, dynamic, and passionate relationship to Jesus Christ. { ⊕ *FREDERICA MATHEWES-GREEN: What a terrific story. This expectation that God can move supernaturally in our lives is what I was talking about earlier.* }

The modern Christian era places far too much confidence in the power of knowledge to transform. Legalism and dogmatism result when we lack confidence in the power of transformation to move us toward truth. If God does not reveal himself, then all of our words are empty and will fall silent in the end. If God does reveal himself, and this I know to be true, then the message of Christ is a treasure we must not neglect to share with those so desperately in need of the love and life that come only in relationship to the living God. In the end, there is no greater demonstration of what the inter-section of the people of God and culture is to look like than the person of Jesus Christ. His conversation with the masses was not simply an abstract intended to gather dust on the shelf of some seminary library. Jesus was a man of his times. He resonated with his culture and spoke in a language that was easily understood. He was a Jew among Jews. Ministry that expresses this same texture is still possible today. It is equally important to be in the world as it is to be not of the world.

It is this tension that God calls us to—an intersection of culture and communication. Incarnational ministry of this magnitude can be done, done well and in a way that both honors and glorifies God. Jesus pulled it off— the Word of God made flesh walked among us. The God of creation became a Jewish carpenter. He was in culture, a part of culture, transforming culture, creating culture. Through the church he continues this journey today.

{ ✢ *BRIAN D. McLAREN: Although in this volume I am supposed to represent a position different from Erwin's, I resonate with enthusiasm with all that Erwin has written here. (Of course, he may violently disagree with what I've written!) His reference to Hebrews (God has spoken in a variety of ways at different times) expresses what I mean by "a changing message" in my chapter. The message changes because God spoke, and still speaks, in a variety of ways—forever, and most decisively, of course, in his Son! ✢ To me the most important sentence in Erwin's piece is this: "When I'm asked what will follow the present cultural movement, I answer, 'Whatever we choose.'" Some of my colleagues may toss a rock at Erwin for this overstatement (although I think we all live in glass houses in this regard!), but his overstatement does exactly what hyperbole should do: it focuses our attention on something important. "Whatever we choose" may be an overstatement, but it reminds us that we can engage with our culture in constructive and transformative ways—ways conveyed by Jesus when he spoke of our being salt and light in the world, or when he sent us into the world as the Father had sent him. ✢ In my view, paradigm shifts have two phases. In the first phase, the tone is primarily negative: Looking back and critiquing (deconstructing) the reigning paradigm. Eventually, though, innovators must move to a more constructive mode in which they begin designing the emerging paradigm. (By the way, when Erwin says he is asked what will happen after postmodernity, in these terms he is really being asked what will happen after the early critical stage of postmodernity.) ✢ As I've often said, I think we're still in the earliest transition phase into postmodernity, as we may still be decades from now. Although some groups are further along in the transition than others, nobody is very far along; a few are just beginning to enter the more constructive phase. This explains (a) why so many of what Andy calls "postmodern prophets" seem strident at times, making overstatements that seem ridiculous and foolish to those who prefer the old paradigm, and (b) why defenders of the old paradigm seem to lash out in response in sometimes indiscriminate ways: they can't put their fingers on what postmodernity really is because whatever it will be can't be defined while it is still barely emerging and forming—and that's frustrating! ✢ This is why Erwin's tone makes my heart sing. He realizes that if we become paralyzed in either critique or defense, we become passive and miss our moment to help the emerging culture become something it wouldn't become without our influence! (If my exclamatory punctuation didn't make you give the previous sentence a second look, perhaps this parenthetical remark will.) If Erwin is right—that we are entering a moment when we can, even in some small way, shine our light as agents of Jesus Christ and help the emerging culture become something other than it would have become—then we must surely do three things:* ✤ *1. We must stop attacking our troops who are advancing into new territory. Or for a less militaristic metaphor, we must stop labeling as betrayers and abandoners those who head west to colonize the frontier; rather we must see them as pioneers on a risky but necessary trek.* ✤ *2. We must, as Erwin said, be transformed from our "passive or even reactionary" attitude to a "proactive and revolutionary" one. I am naive about many things, but not about this: I know this won't be an easy transformation. Modernity (if you agree there has been such a thing) was a tough adversary; it put us on the defensive for a long time. Can we recover from our well-practiced defensiveness quickly enough to follow Paul's admonition: "Do not be overcome by evil, but overcome evil with good" (Romans 12:21)?* ✤ *3. We must engage in serious, thoughtful, and respectful dialogue—as we're doing in this volume—to reexamine what our relationship to culture should be, but not in the abstract, thinking about culture as a disembodied, timeless entity. Instead we need to challenge one another to think (again, as I hope this volume will do) in fresh ways about what our relationship should be to this culture, in the midst of these changes, however we describe them. And this dialogue must be conducted in ways that "normal people"—not just scholars or intellectual heavyweights—can understand. Erwin's chapter is a shining example of that kind of dialogue, and I'm glad he wrote it for such a time as this.* }

Erwin Raphael McManus' Rejoinder

MY FIRST INTENSE CONVERSATION WITH GOD happened when I was about 10 years old. I tried to run away from home and got caught in the process. Finding myself in solitary confinement in my bedroom, I screamed to the ceiling, "God, you're so stupid!" I was desperately hoping to provoke some kind of response from Heaven, but nothing came. I concluded God was indifferent.

Years later I saw a beautiful building that evoked in me a sense of worship. I thought perhaps God might be inside, available for conversation. I was familiar with priests and altars and was drawn to the symbols, rituals, and sacraments. On that particular day, with a heightened sense of need, I quietly walked to the doors and hoped to slip inside without notice. The doors were locked. I couldn't get in. I walked away wondering if God was real. And if he lived in cathedrals, shouldn't he be available 24/7?

A decade had passed, and I was home for the weekend during my freshman year in college when my parents sat me down and explained that their marriage had come to an end. The news of their divorce felt seismic. My emotions ranged from confusion to rage to pain to disappointment. I found myself running through the open woods not far from our home for what seemed like hours. I wept until I had no tears left, and I ran until exhaustion slowed me down.

There was a clearing in the forest, and I saw a small church, simple and nondescript yet with a warmth that drew me to it. In my weariness I stumbled to a door that appeared to lead to a chapel. It was locked. As quickly as I turned away, someone was behind me. Speaking in a warm tone that was comforting but not intrusive, a woman opened the door and invited me inside. I was a stranger to her, but in her graciousness, she allowed me the privilege of being there alone.

After a time of kneeling at the altar, I realized a father and son were to the side of me, praying in silence. When I was ready, they asked if they could help. I don't really remember all that happened. My recollection of our conversation is vague and spotty at best. They did not lead me in any kind of prayer, but somehow I knew that they had prayed for me. God met me there that day—through people, through strangers.

It would be nearly two more years before I would identify myself as a follower of Jesus Christ. And for me there is a precise moment when I yielded my life to him as my Lord and God. Yet I look back and wonder where the journey began. I have almost no memory of life absent of a desperate search for God. As a child my faith was naive but genuine. I had no idea who God was, but I knew I desired him. Rather than drawing me to God, religion seemed to expand the gap between us. And then of course there was the whole issue of my sinfulness. It seemed that my guilt and shame were the church's best leverage to keep me in line. In the end I gave up on both religion and, tragically, God.

Then came Jesus. He offered me forgiveness of my sin and freedom from all my guilt and shame. He would not use guilt and shame as leverage but had absolute confidence in the power of his love to keep me near to him. Because he became my friend, he ruined his reputation and was slandered as the friend of sinners. Though I experienced compassion through the acts of others, I knew it was his compassion. Though I heard his words from the lips of those who would witness on his behalf, it was clearly his voice. This movement wasn't just about Jesus, it wasn't just on Jesus' behalf, nor was it just in his power—it was Jesus. He had come to seek and save that which was lost, and that was me.

All this is to say one simple thing: The issue of the relationship of the church to culture must not remain in the realm of theory. Our condition is too desperate for that. The church can make life in the world work. We are not too holy to live in this place, though perhaps we are not holy enough. Jesus lived here. He pulled it off. Though he ascended to Heaven, he has returned to us in his Spirit. He leaves us here not to struggle through the discomfort of being misplaced but to astonish the world with the beauty and wonder of God. We can thrive in this context, and we can enjoy the experience. I feel almost embarrassed to say that I love my life. I am so grateful to live in this time. I am not overwhelmed by the despairing problems we face. It's just so good to be alive and to know that it is possible to pass this life on to others.

At the time I was writing this I heard that Len Sweet, in his introduction, had chosen a naturalist metaphor for each of us and that he had dubbed my position "the park." I shared with Len my great disdain for this metaphor. Don't give me a park. Give me a jungle instead. My position is all about thriving on the dangerous edge. The Scriptures provide us the tools with which we can thrive as we brave the harsh elements. Culture is neither our enemy nor our friend—it's simply our context. We are naturalists who know how to extract the good from the poison. We discard all that is not essential for our journey and hold on to that which is primal. We reject the park for the jungle—and the deepest jungle we can find.

The deepest jungle I could find is Los Angeles. I choose to live in L.A. I choose to live here with my wife, Kim, and to raise our children here. While it seems others would describe this place as a cultural cesspool, I see it as a place where Jesus would choose to be. There was a man who was born blind, and all Jesus' disciples could do was begin a theological discussion about the nature of sin. Jesus, after declaring it was all about bringing God glory, took dirt and spit, made mud, and placed it on the man's eyes. Then he told him to go to the pool and wash, and when the man did, he left seeing.

I love this passage of Scripture. Jesus could have just spoken and cured the man's blindness. Yet here Jesus crudely reminds us that God is willing to play in the mud, that God can use the basest of materials to accomplish amazing things. What we are incapable of accomplishing with all of our pomp and ritual Jesus can pull off with just a little dirt and spit. We seem prone to creating rituals and sacraments that stand between us and God. It seems to me that it's just simpler than that. God has come into the world in the person of Jesus Christ. When we hear his voice, all we need to do is follow.

☗   ☗   ☗   ☗   ☗

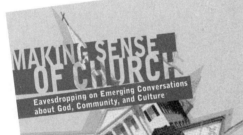